Nelson and Kay:
Great meeting you
in your beautiful home
and trophy room!
Ken Wilson
2-17-12

Sport Hunting on Six Continents

*Hunting around the world...
from Alaska to Australia...
from the Americas to Africa, Asia, and Europe*

By Ken Wilson

Copyright © MCMXCIX by Ken Wilson. All rights reserved.

Published by: Sportsmen on Film, Inc.
P.O. Box 1818
Kerrville, Texas 78029

No part of this book may be reproduced or transmitted in any form or by any means, electronic or mechanical, including photocopying, recording, or by any information storage or retrieval system, without written permission from the publisher, except for inclusion of brief quotations in a review.

ISBN 0-9666040-0-8

Library of Congress Catalog Number 98-96390

Photos of the Kerrville, Texas trophy room (Epilogue #1, pages 319-324) by Jody Rhoden.
All photographs from the collection of Ken Wilson.

 Printed in the United States of America
Burke Publishing Company
San Antonio, Texas

*This book is dedicated to the following people
who were there when I left and, more importantly,
were still there when I returned:
My wife, Lorraine
My daughter, Summer
My son, Ryan
My father, Giles
My mother, Beverly*

TABLE OF CONTENTS

Prologue 1

NORTH AMERICA

Sheep
(1) Alaska 5
(2) Mexico 16
(3) Alberta, British Columbia, Montana 26

Deer
(4) Luck in Mexico (Both Kinds) 35
(5) North America's Third Favorite Deer 42
(6) A Lad Shunneson Adventure 48
(7) Thank You Deer (Thank You, Dear) 55

Cats and Dogs
(8) Cats Can Be Tough On Dogs 64
(9) Beating the California Deadline 68

NORTH AMERICA, *continued*

Mixed Bag

(10) Elk and Pronghorn 72

(11) Boating for Black Bears 81

(12) Tatanka 89

(13) Oomingmak 96

Exotics

(14) The Super Slam 102

(15) The Blue Bull 111

(16) Super Exotics 117

AFRICA

(17) Kenya 125

(18) Tanzania 129

(19) Zambia 141

(20) C.A.R. (Bingo on Bongo) 151

(21) Zimbabwe (Leopard Charge) 165

RSA

(22) Zululand Safari 169

(23) Kudus and Caracals 177

(24) Three of a Kind – Twice 185

(25) South African Mountain Game 190

(26) Bucks and Boks 194

AFRICA, *continued*

The Unforgettable Peter Hathaway Capstick

(27) First Meeting/Lasting Impression 199
(28) Capstick/Botswana 203
(29) Capstick/Namibia and South Africa 215
(30) Capstick/Small Safari 222
(31) Peter Capstick's Last Safari 229
(32) Capstick Retrospective 237

THE SOUTH PACIFIC

(33) First Safari Into Eastern Arnhem Land 243
(34) From Cobourg to Caledonia 252
(35) From the North Island to the Southern Alps 258

EUROPE

(36) Racing Through Spain 267
(37) The Eastern European 6 275

SOUTH AMERICA

(38) Argentine Safari 285

ASIA

(39) Saiga Saga 297
(40) Hunting the Land of Genghis Khan 304

EPILOGUES

(1) The Evolutionary Trophy Room 314
(2) Sportsmen on Film: The First 15 Years 325

SPORT HUNTING ON SIX CONTINENTS

x

PROLOGUE

First, the philosophical question: Why the word "sport" in the title to this book? Is hunting a sport? My answer is "no," but I have lots of reasons for liking the word "sport" in the title:

(1) Hunting is not a sport in the athletic/competitive sense. It is a recreational activity; yet the hunter does compete with weather and terrain and flora and fauna.

(2) Hunters are sporting; that is, they match their preparation, skills, and experience with their quarry and with Lady Luck.

(3) Hunters are sportsmen inasmuch as they operate within the rules of game management as promulgated by governments, agencies, landowners, and their own organizations.

(4) Many of the early hunter-explorers of Africa and Asia used "sport" in the titles to their books such as *Sport in the Highlands of Kashmir* (Darrah), *Sport and Folklore in the Himalayas* (Haughton), and *Sport and Travel East and West* (Selous).

When I formed the video production company Sportsmen on Film in 1984, I chose the word "sportsmen" because the word can mean "ethical hunters" or "ethical athletes." As a matter of fact, none other than Mr. Webster says that a "sportsman" is "one who engages in sports and esp. in hunting and fishing" and also is "a person who is fair, generous . . . and a graceful winner."

As for the word "film" in Sportsmen on Film, I have shot on video from the inception, but "video" is three syllables so "film" is simply more succinct.

The "six continents" in the title to this book was easy to select. The world is full of hunting opportunities virtually everywhere except Antarctica. For the price of a North American caribou hunt, you can hunt one or more species on any of the six hunting continents, and you can hunt during prime time somewhere in the world every day of the year.

I know that some hunters hunt whitetail out of the same camp year after year, and there is nothing wrong with tradition and repetition, but think of the new adventures and challenges and rewards that those hunters would experience if they spent the same amount of time and money hunting a different continent each year!

The hunts described in this book took place from 1983 to 1998; my first 15 years of big game hunting. My very first big game hunt took place in 1983 at the age of 40. I'm not one of the majority of hunters, like my son, Ryan, who started hunting with his dad before his teens. I played football and baseball with my dad and uncles and didn't fire my first rifle until I went into the Army in 1967. I won an expert badge for marksmanship during Advanced Infantry Training, but I didn't hear the call of the wild after my discharge because I didn't shoot a rifle again until preparing for that 1983 hunting trip.

It was early in 1983 that my wife, Lorraine, and I bought a house with a large rock fireplace and I told my friend, Dave Harshbarger, who is an avid hunter, that I would like to hunt a moose to hang over the fireplace. Dave thought for awhile and then said, "If you want me to go with you, we'll have to go on a 'real hunt.'"

Now that I look back, I believe Dave felt that, with my athletic background (having played rugby and baseball internationally) and my choice of business (as a real estate developer), he needed to hook me with a challenging adventure or chance losing me as a continuing hunting partner. So, in September 1983, Dave accompanied me to Farewell, Alaska to hunt Dall sheep, grizzly bear, and Alaska-Yukon moose with John Latham for 14 days. What a hunt! My very first big game trophy was a hard-earned Dall ram. I was hooked!

Two months after Alaska, I took my wife, two-year-old son, Ryan, and six-year-old daughter, Summer, to Texas (where we eventually moved in 1992) to hunt whitetail. Two months later I hunted desert bighorn in Northern Baja. Six months after that I hunted Tanzania with Dave. And I've gone on two or three hunting adventures a year since then. Dave, you owe me a lot of time and money. But I owe you a lot of unforgettable experiences.

In planning that Tanzania safari into the Selous with Luke Samaras as our professional hunter, I couldn't find any films or videos to see what it was like to hunt in Tanzania or anywhere else for that matter. So I bought a video camera and, on our safari, Dave videotaped me hunting and I videotaped him. When I returned to Los Angeles, I took eight hours of rambling footage to Dave Goldson, a news editor for NBC, and we collaborated to edit "Elephant Hunting in Tanzania" and "Cat Hunting in Tanzania." Sportsmen on Film was born, but it took two more years for me to gain the expertise and gather the equipment to advance to broadcast quality.

From the beginning, I was enthralled with the travel and adventure that hunting offered as well as the challenges of the actual hunt. Thus, the title sequence for every Sportsmen on Film video, even during the early years when I had only hunted

PROLOGUE

North America and Africa, starts with: "Hunting around the world, from Alaska to Australia, from the Americas to Africa, Asia, and Europe, Sportsmen on Film presents . . . ." It took me 15 years, but I finally fulfilled those words by having hunted and produced hunting videos on all six hunting continents.

Ken Wilson
P.O. Box 1818
Kerrville, Texas 78029
1998

1

ALASKA

Background

I first met Dave Harshbarger in Mammoth Lakes which is the top ski resort in California, about 280 miles north of Los Angeles on the eastern side of the Sierras. At the time, we were both in our early 30s and Dave was the life of the party on and off the ski slopes. He skied well, was a successful building contractor, and he owned the Mammoth Tavern. That, my friends, is a combination that most only dream about!

I lived and worked in Los Angeles and vacationed in Mammoth where my parents lived because they loved skiing. "Vacation" usually meant driving to Mammoth Friday nights and driving back to L.A. Sunday nights. I was usually fully recovered by Wednesday morning.

I knew Dave was a big game hunter. His office and condominium had several nice mounts from both North America and Africa and he hunted mule deer near Mammoth every season. Many of the locals hunted before and after work and, on weekends, some hunted before and after the Mammoth Tavern.

I remember being at the Tavern for lunch one opening day of deer season when Carl Preston, a local plumbing contractor, pulled into the parking lot in his pick-up and soon had a crowd from the Tavern looking in the bed of his truck at a great opening morning buck. It was lying on its side and Carl had pulled a tarp back so everyone could see the head and antlers. Carl was about 15 minutes into the story about his hunt when someone put down his beer and touched one of the deer's eyes. It was glass! Soon the tarp was off the shoulder mount of last year's buck and the hay that had looked like the body. All offers to buy Carl a drink were retracted. That was Mammoth!

I had hunted ducks and doves with Dave on several occasions, but I had never hunted a big game animal in my life or, come to think of it, anything except ducks and doves. When, in 1983, I decided that a moose would look good over the fireplace of the home Lorraine and I had just bought, I thought Dave might be able to advise me where to go and who to go with to shoot one. Dave not only advised me, but he booked a mixed bag hunt with John Latham in Alaska and decided to accompany me. He also loaned me his rifle and spent some time at the range to make sure I could shoot it.

My First Big Game Hunt at Age 40

I met Dave Harshbarger at his parents' condominium in Santa Monica, about 15 miles from Los Angeles International Airport. In their garage, Dave emptied my duffel bag and then started putting things back in . . . underwear, long underwear, wool socks, Levis, boots, gloves, ammunition for his .300 WM semi-auto, etc. Some of my stuff went into my carry-on bag like my still camera, film, binoculars, flashlight, and batteries. But a shocking amount of perfectly good ski wear didn't make the cut such as my orange and tan parka, a vertically striped sweater, and a multi-colored knit cap.

In Anchorage, we went to a sporting goods store and I bought a camouflage jacket and a pair of ankle fit hip boots that would be a necessity where we would be hunting.

We checked into the Captain Cook Hotel and met John Kemhadjian who would be hunting with me 2 x 2 with Dave along as my observer and advisor. I also remember going to a place called The Alaskan Bush Company, but I don't remember returning to the hotel. If you have hunted Alaska, maybe you have had a similar experience.

The next morning we flew westerly in some kind of old transport plane to the Alaska

Farewell, Alaska was not exactly a boom town. One family moved out and reduced the population to three!

Alaska

Range and landed at Farewell which was a rather small town. In fact, the town sign announced a population of "7" crossed out and replaced by the number "3."

John Latham met us in his Jeep and we loaded up, piled in, and headed directly to sheep camp since there wasn't much going on in Farewell. Sheep camp consisted of a clients' tent, a guides' tent, and a cooks' tent that also served as the kitchen, dining room, and home for the cooks (a couple who loved taking a long working vacation in Alaska each year). It was 15 miles of bumps and switchbacks from Farewell to camp. About halfway, I couldn't stand being cooped up in the Jeep any longer, so I got out and walked the rest of the way to camp which felt good. But I was soon to find out that walking for sheep is more vertical than horizontal!

John Kemhadjian had hunted all over North America and was trying to collect the North America 29. This consisted of four species of sheep, three species of moose, five species of caribou, etc. I was on my first hunt and could not fathom why anyone would want to hunt more than one sheep or one moose or one caribou. Little did I realize that, four months later, I would go on my second sheep hunt.

The next morning, we got in the Jeep and rode across some rocks about a half mile to the first creek where we got out and started to hike. At the time, I wondered why John bothered to drive that piddling little distance but, at the end of the day when I kissed the hood of the Jeep, I understood.

John Latham with dog. Standing L to R: John Kemhadjian, Joe Piscotty, Carol Mulhardt, Dan Demers, Herb O'Haver, Dave Harshbarger, and me.

Each day, John K. and his guide, Dan Demers, would hike into one drainage and John L., Dave, and I would hike into another. We saw sheep each day and even tried to get close to one group of rams, but lost them in the fog.

By day four, I was somewhat educated. In the mornings, the wind blew generally down so we stayed in the drainages and glassed up. Glassing was a lengthy process, but it also allowed welcome rests. If we saw rams, out would come the spotting scope. If they were good (say 36 inches or better), a stalk would be planned. In the afternoons, the wind would generally blow up, so we would climb and climb and climb in order to get on top and glass down. Bedded rams looked like patches of snow but, on closer inspection, the rams looked a little yellow . . . and they have horns!

The old Jeep deserved a kiss, because it meant the long hike was over.

John Latham spotted a group of five rams feeding the morning of my fourth hunting day. I couldn't see them until he showed them to me through the spotting scope. He said three were good. The route of the stalk would take us up an adjacent mountain, over to a ridge, across a shale slide, and down to a point overlooking the rams. By then the wind would be blowing from the rams to us.

Up we went and up some more. John would stop occasionally, Dave and I would catch up, and as soon as our breathing returned to normal, we'd climb some more. When we finally crossed over to the ridge, John said we'd have to wait there because the sheep had bedded down and one or two might see us if we moved. We were only a thousand yards from them at that point.

Making a climb for a group of rams that we eventually lost in the fog.

That ridge on that mountain in the Alaska Range was the coldest place I had ever been including several ski resorts in the western U.S. The wind pushed the cold air right through to our bones as the hours passed . . . two and then three. Dave and I were passing the time by discussing other hunting opportunities; all of them tropical in nature. We had just decided on parrot hunting in Tahiti when John said, "Let's go! They're all up and walking away from us."

Since the sheep were, by then, out of sight, we raced across a shale slide to a cut with a small ridge which John very carefully looked over. "It's clear. Let's go!"

At the next ridge, John made sure my breathing was under control and then we looked over together. He whispered, "Still nothing. And it flattens out here so we better spread out about 50 yards apart and slowly walk forward together. If either of you sees a sheep, sit down fast and I'll come over and take a look."

We were near the end of a huge basin, at least a thousand feet higher than the mouth, but it was another thousand feet to the top of the bowl. The ground was slightly undulating and all broken rocks, each bigger than a bread basket. We slowly walked toward the closed end of the basin with John in the middle, me 50 yards to his left, and Dave 50 yards to his right. After walking step by slow step for about a minute, I could see the head and horns of a Dall ram at about 30 yards. He was staring away from me and looking slightly left. I remember my shock at being so close to this magnificent creature. His horns were rugged and yellow-tan in contrast to the coarse, white hair covering his head and thick neck.

I looked at John and sat down just as the rams started to run. While sitting, I couldn't see them for a few seconds, but when one came into view at about 75 yards, I raised my rifle and aimed. John yelled, "No! Don't shoot. Come over here . . . and run!" He didn't want me to shoot any ram, he wanted me to shoot the biggest one in the band.

After about 50 yards, John reached a drop-off, put my pack down at the edge, grabbed my rifle from me and placed it on the pack and said, "Shoot the one in the lead!"

At the end of the basin, the flat area we were on dipped down about 50 feet and then, after about 100 feet, rose abruptly 1,000 feet. All five rams had sprinted down and then across the depression and were already 250 feet up the other side. I pressed into the stock of Dave's rifle, found the lead ram in the four power scope and fired, apparently missing. John said, "Make sure you're shooting at the lead ram!" I fired again and the ram turned left as the other four thundered past him. Then I dropped him with my third shot.

John and Dave were shouting and laughing as I turned to face them in jubilation. They stopped laughing for a second and then started up again twice as loud. The right lens of my eyeglasses was shattered and blood covered my face from my eyebrow to my jaw. In the excitement of shooting, I didn't realize how close I placed my eye to the scope so that the recoil from at least one of the shots smashed the scope into my face.

At the ram, we took lots of photos. It was the most magnificent animal I had ever seen. I was fascinated at how John field dressed it, caped it, and boned it. Then we divided the meat and John tied the head, cape, and horns to the top of his pack

SPORT HUNTING ON SIX CONTINENTS

My first shot at big game resulted in broken glasses and a cut eyebrow, which John Latham thought was hilarious.

With my first big game trophy. Dave is in the middle and John is on the right.

Alaska

and led the way back down the mountain. I had wanted to carry the head out, but John had insisted. It didn't take me long to appreciate his carrying the head because, whenever I felt like it, I could look up and see those magnificent horns in front of me (not to mention that my load was half as heavy as his!).

When we finally reached the Jeep, I kissed the hood again and happily fell into the passenger seat for the short, bumpy, and very pleasurable ride back to the best party a hunter ever had . . . beer, wild sheep ribs (still the best meat I have ever eaten), and lots of stories.

On day five, I slept in and fished in the afternoon. On day six, John Kemhadjian shot his sheep, and on day seven, we moved to a camp in the foothills to hunt Alaska-Yukon moose, the biggest sub-species. What a different kind of hunt from sheep hunting! There was spongy tundra instead of shale and rock; little hills instead of big mountains; big, brown animals instead of little white ones; and huge antlers instead of horns.

"Is that a Jeep out there by the second clump of trees?" I asked on day nine. Dan was with me instead of John Latham. He said, "I don't see a Jeep, but I see a bull moose in that spot!" I looked through my binoculars again and saw big, gray antlers on top of the Jeep. Wait a second, Dan was right; it was a moose!

"Let's go for it," I suggested.

"No, we'll wait awhile and see what it does," Dan said. "He's with some cows, and the cover is thick down there."

After about 15 minutes, it was apparent that the bull moose and his cows were going to keep feeding in the same area, so we left Dave on the hill and walked down, got the wind right, and started our stalk. The bull was still about 200 yards off, with no clear shot, when the first cow saw us and let out a meow. They all stopped feeding and started looking. The bull melted into the trees; then the cows took off and our stalk was over.

The next day I was sitting on a hill that formed a perfect half sphere about 100 feet high when John Latham casually said, "This is your lucky day."

"Moose?" I asked and started glassing in the direction John was looking.

"No," John said. "Today is September 10. Do you know what that means?"

"I have four more days to hunt after this one?"

"No. September 10 is the opening of brown bear season and I'm looking at a grizzly right now!"

"Wow," I thought. I'd seen three black bears eating blueberries while I was hunting sheep, but when I found this one in my binoculars, it was the first grizzly bear I had ever seen!

"He's not a monster," John said. "But mountain grizzlies don't get big. This one's a boar . . . a male, and he's not rubbed. Do you want him?"

"I do."

"Then let's go."

Hand signals were worked out with Dave. Then John and I climbed down and hiked out into the bush where visibility was 25 to 50 yards. I was trying to walk quietly but John kept turning around and signaling me to put my feet down softly on something other than dry sticks.

About the third time he looked up at Dave with his binoculars, he whispered, "Well, Dave says the bear left, so we'll walk back, but let's still be quiet."

Now that was disappointing! We had probably been within 200 yards of the bear, but had not seen him after climbing down from the hill. Then Dave started waving, so we trained our binoculars on him. Apparently we had not worked out a signal for "the bear moved left and then back right and is now feeding again about 100 yards to your left at 10 o'clock." But after a few steps more, we could see the bear and figured that's what Dave was signaling.

John whispered, "Shoot him behind the right shoulder so your bullet exits on the left shoulder. As soon as you shoot, I'm going to shoot, so make your first shot count."

So I shot, John shot, then I shot twice more. "You got him," John said. "Now let's make sure he's dead."

After a little shouting and stick throwing, John touched the bear's eye with his rifle barrel. He was dead. On inspection, we found three entry holes; two in the right place and one in the hip. "You made three good shots," John said. "I guess I missed mine." At the time I believed him but, when I told Dave the story, he seemed to think that John was a good shot and also knew how to be a good guide.

The bear squared $6\,^{1}/_{2}$ feet after John skinned it out. Only then did I realize how thirsty I was and how excited I still was.

Dave holds up the paw of my mountain grizzly, shot on the opening day of the brown bear season.

So I emptied my canteen and then I put the contents of John's pack in mine so he could carry out the bear skin and skull. When we reached an area accessible by Jeep, we dropped our packs and John walked to camp, got the Jeep, and brought it back to Dave, me, and the bear.

Back at camp, we found that John K. had shot a nice black bear the same day, so we posed for pictures and then had a great feast complete with fresh apple pie, compliments of our cooks, who lost their tans when we told them where we had shot the grizzly. It seems they had jogged right by that area, for exercise, about the same time John L. and I were in the middle of our stalk. That may have explained why the bear went one way and then the other, causing Dave to improvise his hand signals.

The next morning, I awoke with the realization that I only had four days left and I had not shot a moose which was the primary reason I was living in a tent in the middle of the Alaska Range in September.

John Latham decided we needed to hunt farther from camp, so he unwrapped his "tundra buggy," kind of a topless tank moving on belts or tracks which allowed him to drive over the thick, spongy tundra. This allowed us to cover more miles than we could on foot and, just as importantly, would eliminate the physically draining chore of packing out a moose on our backs.

In the middle of day twelve, after not seeing any moose from various observation points, we took a break and I shot some ptarmigan and a Wilson's snipe (no relation). The next afternoon at about 3:00 PM, I caught a glimpse of a bull moose from the buggy and pointed to where it disappeared. John turned to Dave and John K. and said, "If we're not back in an hour, drive the buggy back to camp." As it turned out, we didn't see Dave and John K. until the next morning.

John and I searched over an hour for the moose that I had seen, but never found him. We did see several groups of cows, so John decided we were finally in moose country and shouldn't leave. At that time of the year in the Alaska Range, darkness doesn't fall... it slowly fades so that, by 9:00 PM, shooting light

Down at "moose camp," John K. and I hold our sheep horns and pose with our bear skins.

has about gone, but you can still see well enough to walk without a flashlight until 11:00 PM.

At 7:00 PM, John spotted a good moose; a big, old bull with lots of points, long and wide paddles, good fronts, and okay spread. He was in a meadow about 400 yards off, so we planned a stalk to get within 200 yards. But the bull filtered through some trees so, when we next saw him, he was still at 400 yards. After we did this once more, John said, "We're losing light and he's getting suspicious. You're going to have to try a shot from here. Hold about six inches above his back. . . not much. . . and squeeze the trigger. But wait until I stop him."

With that, John let out a grunt that made the bull stop and think, "What the heck was that?" Then I shot and missed. Again the bull thought, "What the heck was that?"

John later told me that he was about to tell me not to shoot again, because we couldn't track a wounded animal in that light, when my gun went *blam!* and the moose dropped like a Jeep falling off a bridge. The crack of his body sounded louder than my gunshot. John looked at me with the same look that moose had when last standing and finally said, "Nice spine shot!"

The day after I killed my moose, Dave and I returned in the "tundra buggy" to retrieve the meat, hide, and antlers.

When we reached the moose, he couldn't move, but he was still alive so I shot him again... and then again as John instructed me where to aim from 20 feet. This was not the most thrilling part of the hunt. Actually, the moose would have died from the first shot, but neither John nor I wanted to see the animal suffer, even though he probably never felt a thing.

"I'll field dress him and then we'll have to leave him here and hike back to camp," John announced, handing me a flashlight. There were aspects of this procedure that I can still remember as if they are happening right now. This moose probably weighed 1,600 pounds. It took some doing just to get it on its side and then John started cutting while I held the flashlight and a leg (of the moose). John pulled out the stomach and reached in to cut the windpipe. At that point he was literally in the body cavity up to his waist (John's and the moose's). Try that at midnight with a flashlight and you won't forget it.

Most of our walk out was over thick tundra so we had to step high, sink in, lean forward, and step high again. Our flashlights gave us only a vague idea of what we were walking over and toward. And the entire three hours I was thinking scary thoughts like we were probably being followed by a pack of hungry wolves at that very moment.

The middle of the next day, Dave and Dan and I returned to my moose in the tundra buggy and spent the afternoon skinning, cutting, and loading. Fortunately, the moose had not been fed upon and he had thawed enough to aid the cutting process. Most fortunately, we had the tundra buggy to lug the meat and hide and antlers 12 miles back to camp.

At the Captain Cook Hotel in Anchorage, I checked in with a duffel bag, rifle, horns, antlers, capes and skins which was treated as business as usual in the lobby. Then, that most wonderful of post-hunt experiences; a long, warm shower and fresh clothes. Simultaneously, I was thinking about where to hunt next.

MEXICO

My Alaskan hunting experience absolutely knocked me over. When I returned home, I subscribed to several hunting magazines, joined Safari Club International, and planned my next hunt (for whitetail deer in November at the YO Ranch in Mountain Home, Texas just a few miles from Hunt and Kerrville, all of which I had never heard of before).

I quickly learned that most North American hunting takes place August-December, so I asked Dave Harshbarger what I could hunt after my November deer hunt. The year before he had shot a Boone & Crockett desert bighorn sheep in Mexico, so he said, "You can hunt desert bighorn, but it's difficult to get a permit. You might be able to pull it off for 1985, but 1984 is only a couple months off and most of those hunts take place in January and February."

Dave gave me the phone number of Mike Valencia, a U.S. citizen who speaks fluent Spanish and who handles the permit processing for desert bighorn on a fee basis. Mike said he'd try for a 1984 permit but I shouldn't plan on it. A month later he called and said, "I might be able to get you a permit because it looks like a hunter who is already booked can't make it. You need to send me a cashier's check for the full price by Federal Express today and, if yours is the first check that the government receives, you'll get the tag."

Most hunts have increased in price during the period this book covers (1983-1998), but few have increased like the price of a desert bighorn hunt in Mexico (priced at $65,000 at this writing). For 1984, the price was $12,000 which was twice the cost of my Alaskan hunt that included sheep, bear, and moose.

I would not encourage a novice hunter, as I was at the time, to go on an expensive sheep hunt. Too many things can go wrong that only experience can resolve. But I was old and naive, so I sent in my money and, not too long later, Mike Valencia called, "Congratulations! You'll be hunting on your birthday [January 4]."

When I finished my hunt, I met Craig Boddington of *Petersen's Hunting Magazine* at an SCI-Los Angeles Chapter meeting and he asked me a couple questions about my hunt. I answered and then said, "I wrote a report on it. Would you like me to send it to you?" Craig said, "Yes," so I sent him a copy.

No, I didn't get discovered as a writer because of that report. In fact Craig never said anything about it to me which probably makes you wonder why you are going to read it now:

Desert Bighorn Sheep Hunt
Baja Norte, Mexico

This report was prepared by Ken Wilson at the request of Jorge Mendoza (Biologist, Direccion General De Flora Y Fauna Silvestres), Ramon Aguilar (Director of Guides, Direccion General de Flora Y Fauna Silvestres), and Lloyd Zeman (Foundation for North American Wild Sheep) in order to contribute to the body of information being developed by each.

Day One (January 2, 1984)

I flew from Los Angeles to Tucson to Hermosillo. On the flight from Tucson to Hermosillo, I met Paul Jensen, an attorney from Houston, who would also be sheep hunting. I struck up a conversation because I noticed he was wearing a FNAWS hat.

We were met at the airport in Hermosillo by Jorge Mendoza, a biologist and authority on desert bighorn, whose findings are quoted in the book titled *The Desert Bighorn* (copyright 1980, The University of Arizona Press). Meeting Jorge was a big relief because I had talked to hunters on previous hunts who were not met by anyone and had spent up to a day locating someone connected with the hunt.

Day Two (January 3, 1984)

We were informed that the hunting permits had not arrived in Hermosillo for any of the hunters!

I met Juan and Josecho, two hunters from a suburb of Mexico City (they said the cost of the hunt for Mexican residents was $2,000), and Hans, a hunter from Austria, and his wife Elfie. [1998 note: I didn't realize it at the time, but Hans' last name was Buchsbaum, and he was one of the world's most famous hunters.]

Jorge, who speaks very good English, spent a half day helping Paul obtain his military gun permit. I obtained mine while in Los Angeles because I didn't want to chance a problem.

Day Three (January 4, 1984)

The hunting permits arrived by being hand-carried from Mexico City by Antonio, the sixth and last hunter. It was on this day that we learned that:

(1) Four groups of hunters were originally scheduled to hunt between November 1 and December 15, 1983 but, because of bureaucratic problems, that was changed to only one group, so we were only the second group for the 1983-84 season.

(2) The first group had to wait seven days in Hermosillo for their hunting permits to arrive.

Juan and Josecho flew to Bahia De Los Angeles in their own private plane. Hans, Elfie, and Paul took an air taxi. Antonio, Jorge and I waited for the same air taxi to return to Hermosillo to pick us up.

We arrived in Bahia De Los Angeles at mid-day. As the hours drifted by it became obvious that we would be spending the night at the Hotel Villa Vitta. I must admit that we made the best of it and I had a good 41st birthday celebration in the bar-restaurant.

My 41st birthday celebration at the Hotel Villa Vitta. In front, Paul Jensen. Back, L to R: Josecho, me, Juan, and Hans.

Day Four (January 5, 1984)

At 10:00 AM Alfredo finally arrived by pick-up truck. Paul and I loaded our gear. We were the first hunters to depart Bahia De Los Angeles.

Alfredo drove us to Punta Prieta (about one hour) where it took another two hours to load two trucks with water, gas, food, equipment and people.

Paul and I got in separate trucks. In my truck, I met my guide, Francisco Martinez. Because of the poor roads, we managed to reach only San Luis Gonzaga Bay by nightfall. We camped out there.

Day Five (January 6, 1984)

At daybreak, we loaded up and took off again. I found out that I would not be hunting the Punta Final area as I had been informed by officials in Mexico City. Instead, we headed up a canyon at Miramar and Paul and his crew headed up a nearby canyon. We stopped at about 10:30 AM and the hunt finally began 2 ½ days later than scheduled.

In the early afternoon we heard two rifle shots, one after another, and then a third shot a half-hour later. It appeared that Paul had a very quick hunt.

Guide Francisco Martinez with white hat. I guess we did eat some hot food.

At about 4:00 PM, Pancho spotted borregos and I saw my first desert bighorn through my binoculars. There were six rams feeding on a mountainside about three miles away. Through my spotting scope, we determined that two of the rams would achieve my goal of 170 points or better. Since darkness would fall at about 5:15 PM, it was too late to make a stalk. Needless to say, I spent a partly sleepless night in my tent (which I'm glad I brought because none were supplied).

Day Six (January 7, 1984)

With spotting scope at full 45 power, we could see the same six sheep feeding at daybreak straight up the canyon about four miles. Inexplicably, Francisco had us pack up camp and move up the canyon by truck about one mile. We then climbed a hill to again observe the sheep, but they had apparently moved into a lateral canyon.

We commenced our stalk. During our climb, I asked Francisco to tell me which sheep was the biggest one from the left. He even picked up five small stones and one larger one so he could lay them out when we spotted the sheep. If I didn't have much time for a decision, I wanted to assure myself the best opportunity of taking the biggest sheep despite the language barrier. This was planted in my mind because Jorge had told me that the hunter with Francisco in December had shot the smallest of four rams running up a bowl.

We ended up climbing over ridge after ridge, and I had a bullet chambered and my rifle ready for over two hours, but we never again saw those sheep. When we didn't see any other sheep, we changed our camp that night to the canyon Paul had been in.

SPORT HUNTING ON SIX CONTINENTS

Glassing for sheep. Francisco wore his white hat morning, noon, and night. I should have burned it.

I will always wonder if the six sheep heard our truck when we moved up the canyon that morning or if they moved for other reasons. At the time, I wondered why we were moving by truck, but because it was only the second day and because I speak very little Spanish, I did not question the move.

Day Seven (January 8, 1984)
We saw footprints from Paul's hunt, but when we had seen no sheep by midmorning, Francisco decided to move camp. On the way out the canyon, we had a flat tire and put on a spare. But with no patching equipment for the flat, we drove back to San Luis Gonzaga Bay. There we happened into Roger Lundberg, an oil worker and elk hunter from Wyoming who winters in a waterfront bungalow for $30 per month. Roger had patching equipment, but by the time the job was finished, it was too late to hunt again. We ate dinner at a small roadside house-restaurant and then drove to our third campsite.

MEXICO

Day Eight (January 9, 1984)
Late in the morning, Jose spotted four sheep grazing on a hillside about four miles out from our observation point. Through the spotting scope, Francisco thought one of the four had a low likelihood of being a decent trophy. I agreed to climb for a better look even though the terrain and wind dictated a circuitous route that would take about three hours.

When we climbed out about a half-mile from the sheep, we took a good look through the spotting scope. Unfortunately, the biggest ram was only about six years old, so we decided to return to camp.

About half way back, we encountered a steep drop. Jose started his climb down, and I waited to see if he would be successful before starting my descent. In the meantime, Francisco and the others had walked about 25 yards away to explore another route down. As I was watching Jose, I heard some yelling and turned to see Francisco and Jesercho waving me to come to them. Looking beyond them about 50 yards, I saw the horns of a ram running left and the left horn looked good as it disappeared in a ravine.

I knew enough about wild sheep to know he would probably try to escape uphill, so I took off on a parallel path and ran about 200 yards through rocks and cacti before seeing the ram emerge about 450 yards in front of me. I dropped before a large rock and, using it as a rest, got off two quick shots that missed. The ram then topped the ridge at about 500 yards and I got a clear view of his backside and horns. I knew that my 150-grain bullet would drop 35" at that distance, so I raised my crosshairs about that height above the head and squeezed off my final round before the ram disappeared over the ridge. I missed. And to confirm my miss, the ram topped out of the mountain about five minutes later (at a point from which it had taken us almost an hour to climb down).

Later Francisco said that he estimated the distance of my final shot at 400 meters (about 440 yards) and that my last shot just missed the ram's head by a couple inches. At 440 yards my bullet drop would only have been about 20 inches. In retrospect I should have aimed lower (maybe even to the top of the horns) and used the ram's whole body to absorb the bullet drop. That night, we moved camp again and, as I went to sleep, I pictured the left horn and rated the ram at 170 points.

Day Nine (January 10, 1984)
We climbed to an observation point with a magnificent view of miles and miles of good sheep country. Unfortunately, it remained very windy the entire day and any sheep that may have been in the area stayed out of the wind and out of sight.

Jose spotted two ewes and a small ram at quite a distance in the late afternoon, but we saw nothing else. We hiked back to our truck and it took five hours of driving up a rocky wash, mostly after dark, to change camp to San Augustan. I crawled into my tent about 10:00 PM and went to sleep. Usually I was in my tent by 6:30 PM and would read by flashlight until 8:00 PM. With sunrise at 6:15 AM and sunset at 5:15 PM, we all got plenty of sleep.

The saguaro and sagueso cacti were record book quality.

Day Ten (January 11, 1984)

I arose to learn that the plan was to carry full packs with all sleeping gear and take two to three days to hike from San Augustan to Miramar. We climbed to our first observation point and glassed for about an hour. Finally, Pancho spotted sheep. As he tried to describe where, I kept looking but I couldn't find them. Francisco set up the spotting scope and cranked it up to 45 power. I took a look through and couldn't believe that I was looking at the farthest table top ridge about seven miles away. We could see the upward and backward sweep of horn on one of the sheep but, at our distance, we couldn't determine the length of horn.

The decision was now mine. Did I want to wait out the day by glassing from where we were or did I want to hike seven miles with full packs in hopes of relocating the sheep that had been on the ridge? I chose to hike because we had glassed for several hours the day before without success.

As we climbed down to the valley below, Jesercho said, "Borrega." We turned and saw two ewes behind us not more than 75 yards up the canyon. We had them boxed in because of a vertical ledge behind them so they remained motionless. We then saw a ram reclining in the shade at the base of the ledge. I was surprised to see him there because of the lack of an upward escape route. Unfortunately, he was only about five years old. I looked through my rifle scope to see what a motionless desert bighorn ram looked like at 100 yards, and then we moved on.

At about 4:00 PM, we arrived near the base of the mountain on which Pancho had spotted the sheep four hours earlier. The climb out to the top would take an hour, so it was too late to try it. Instead we climbed to a nearby hill and glassed without success. We climbed down at dusk and made camp. Our dinner was like every meal: canned food. But we had plenty of fruit juice and "V- Ocho" and I had no problems with lack of energy.

Day Eleven (January 12, 1984)
This was the seventh day of the hunt, but because of the delay in the start combined with Mexican logic, it would be my next-to-last day. As I looked up the rocky slopes of the high table top mountain at daybreak, I knew that this would be my last chance to hunt a desert bighorn.

Three-quarters through our climb, we stopped to glass and Pancho spotted four ewes. Francisco instructed Jose, Jesercho and Francisquito to stay put on the mountainside. Francisco, Pancho and I then climbed out to the table top taking care not to spook the ewes. We then slowly moved along the slightly rolling, one mile long table top looking for sheep or sign.

At one point, Francisco received a signal from Jose that a ram was below us. I chambered a round and removed my scope cover and we slowly climbed down the steep ledge, but saw nothing. Jose finally climbed up and over to us to orally confirm he had seen a ram moving below the ledge.

We ended up searching for an hour before Francisco spotted three rams at our level about a half-mile away. He said they were good. I didn't see the rams because I was above Francisco and we didn't take the time for me to climb down. Instead we climbed up to the table top and walked around to relocate the three rams from above. We never found them.

In the course of glassing, I spotted two ewes and a ram of about six years in one group and two ewes or young rams at quite a distance. Since we were exhausted from the tension of the closeness to the sheep and had not eaten for seven hours, we signaled up Jesercho and Francisquito to eat our usual lunch of cold tortillas, cold tuna, cold beans, and cold juice while Francisco set up the spotting scope. I anxiously awaited the word. The word was *chiquito* (small). But then Francisco saw a second ram in the scope and thought it might go 160.

The decision was mine and my decision was to go for it. My decision would have been different earlier in the hunt. Both rams were grazing on a ridge slightly lower than we were. Francisco, Pancho and I shed our packs, left them with Jose, Jesercho and Francisquito, and climbed down to the valley floor. We then quickly walked along the wash and, when we came in view of the ridge that the rams were on, we glassed and found they had gone over the top.

The set-up was now perfect as we climbed the ridge with the wind in our face. Just before we reached the top, we paused so my breathing wouldn't interfere with my shooting. Francisco said in English, "Your sheep there," and he pointed over the ridge.

The blood in front of the hip was where my first shot exited.

We cleared the top, but neither ram was there. So we climbed down and up the next ridge and, again, neither ram was there. We were out of ridges and faced with a long slope. Francisco then spotted the larger ram running at ³/₄ speed about 350 yards away and he pointed and yelled in English, "Shoot, shoot."

As I kneeled and looked through my rifle scope, I heard Pancho say, *"Muy lejos"* (very far). I rested the rifle on my left knee and found the ram in my variable power scope which was set at four power in expectation of a short shot at a grazing target. Remembering that my lead was too long three days before, I moved the crosshairs to the front of the ram's neck as he ran quartering left. I squeezed off the round and saw the ram immediately take two quick jumps and disappear over the lateral ridge to my left.

Francisco and Pancho both ran to where the ram was when I shot at it. I questioned their move (silently) and ran uphill hoping to get another shot if the ram appeared. After I had run about 200 yards, I saw horns and then the entire ram emerge from an adjacent arroyo. I knew it was the bigger of the two rams and I immediately dropped to the prone position since there were few obstructions.

The ram was running at about half speed directly away from me and apparently unaware of my presence. My only target was his white rear-end at about 150 yards, but he had another 100 yards to go to clear the next ridge, so I took my time and squeezed off the shot. It connected and the ram's haunches sagged almost to the ground, but he quickly recovered and turned obliquely to my left which gave me a good target, and I dropped him with a shot that passed through the heart.

About two minutes later, Francisco and Pancho arrived on the scene to congratulate me. When I realized that I had to connect with the ram running at 400 yards and then guess his escape route and connect twice more in order to get him the day before the end of my hunt, I thanked my good fortune in avoiding a shutout.

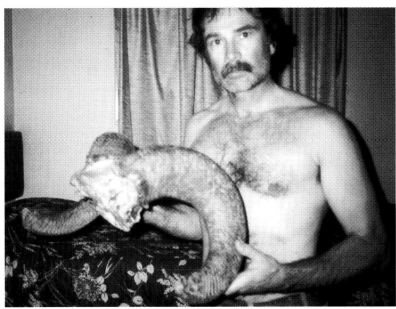
Displaying the horns back at the Hotel Villa Vitta.

After the picture taking, the cape and horns were removed and the meat divided among the packs. Francisco did not field dress the ram. Instead he employed an interesting method of simply cutting around the entrails and leaving them intact. It then took us three hours to hike out to Alfredo's waiting truck and make camp.

Day Twelve (January 13, 1984)
We got another flat tire on the way out so we stopped to see Roger Lundberg again at San Luis Gonzaga Bay and asked him to fix it. Roger and I had a good laugh when we counted 11 patches on the innertube!

[1998 note: Craig Boddington sponsored me for membership in the Outdoor Writers Association of America in 1984 and I've been an Active Member ever since.]

ALBERTA, BRITISH COLUMBIA, MONTANA

My next sheep hunt was for Rocky Mountain bighorn with Randy Babala. My number one cameraman, Rick Morgan, and I flew into Edmonton and then drove to Cadomin. Then Randy packed us into his tent camp by horseback.

This was going to be a tough 21-day hunt . . . tough because we would live in tents surrounded by snow, ride horses four hours each day, climb four hours each day, and glass for sheep four hours each day. We would be hunting next to Jasper National Park and hoping that sheep would move out as winter moved in.

Randy had two tags for my September 1-21 hunt and two more for the three weeks after that. Sharing camp, but hunting with one of Randy's guides, was an Austrian who spoke limited English. The only time I really understood him was on the morning of day 11 when he said, "Ten days too much. I quit."

The afternoon of the 11th day, we saw our first ram standing on the ridge separating the park from the hunting area. Randy walked in the open toward the park and the ram ran into a big bowl in the hunting area. When it was out of sight, we climbed to a ridge overlooking the bowl and peered over. The ram was about a thousand yards off, but coming our way. When he got to about 400 yards, Rick raised up just a few inches in order to videotape and the ram turned and ran back toward the ridge.

Randy said, "Shoot in front of him and maybe he'll turn." So I made a 600-

yard shot that hit about 20 yards in front of the ram and, sure enough, he turned and came toward us again. When he got to 400 yards, I followed him with my crosshairs only to see him turn and bolt back up the mountain. I looked behind me, but Rick was well-hidden. Then Randy pointed down the mountain and we saw a park ranger with a packstring of 12 horses heading our way through the hunting area to the park.

We didn't see another ram over the next 10 days. The Austrian had made the right decision!

Randy offered me the chance to come back for the last few days of the second hunt and I was able to free up three days plus travel; a long shot at best. One of Randy's guides escorted me that first morning. In the middle of the day, we saw five rams from horseback. The rams immediately trotted out of sight, so we tied our horses and climbed to the pass between two peaks where the rams had disappeared. We found them in a big bowl, standing and looking around but not at us. The distance was about 400 yards, so we crawled to about 300 and my guide whispered that I better shoot from there.

I lay prone and looked over the rams through my scope. "I'm going to shoot the one on the left," I whispered. "No," my guide whispered back. "He still has his lamb tips. Shoot the heavily broomed one; second from the right." The one I wanted had the longest horns, but the one my guide wanted me to shoot was no doubt the oldest and would score the best, so I moved my scope slightly right, placed the crosshairs on the ram's shoulder, held my breath, and fired my Sako .300 WM.

"You hit the rocks in front of you," my guide gasped. "Shoot again!" The sheep had run in a little circle and were looking around trying to figure out which way to escape. I moved forward a few feet, put my pack on top of the rocks, put my left hand on the pack and laid my rifle across my hand, found "my guide's ram," and shot again. At the shot, the sheep exited the bowl into some trees, never to be seen again. My guide sadly said, "You hit the rocks again."

The basin was convex, and even though my crosshairs had been unimpeded for both shots, my rifle barrel was a couple inches lower than my scope and I never got high enough for the barrel to clear the rocks. When Randy Babala, one of the best sheep hunters in North America, heard the story a few days later, he said, "*&!#+! sheep! I don't know why anybody hunts them!" And he was serious.

A year later, I traveled to British Columbia to hunt Stone sheep with Ed and Dave Wiens' Stone Mountain Safaris. For this hunt, I picked the end of the season instead of the beginning. My guide was Marty Kjos.

Ed Wiens helped us load all our food and camping gear into panniers and we set off, with a string of horses, on a 10-hour ride into beautiful country. We spent the first few days in a log cabin and climbed the adjacent mountains in search of sheep. We found one on day three but Marty dismissed it as having "donut horns" (full curls but so tight they would barely make 30 inches).

On the fifth day, we were on horseback traveling to make a climb when Marty

Marty Kjos cooking breakfast toward the end of the season.

saw a bull moose... a real good bull moose. These were the western Canada sub-species, the second largest behind the Alaska-Yukon variety and much bigger than the eastern Canada and Shiras types. We had seen several cows and calves near our cabin, but this was our first bull. He was climbing a hill below us and moving into shooting range. So we dismounted and I jacked a round into my .300 and moved forward to get a clear shot.

When the moose turned broadside, wandering uphill to my right, I shot and missed, shot and missed, and shot and hit. Marty was calling my shots. "You missed him [surprise]! You missed again [shock]! You hit him; he's down."

The moose was down about 250 yards away, but he raised his head, so I shot him in the neck and that was that. When I later reviewed the video footage, I found that the cameraman missed me missing my first two shots or I would have shown them in the video. Instead, you will see my third and fourth shots as if they were my first and second, which just goes to show that you don't need to be a good shot; you just need to be a good editor.

In lieu of a tundra buggy to haul out the moose, we had our two horses. Marty removed the cape and skinned the head while I quartered the carcass. We decided to take two quarters and the trophy with us and return for the rest of the meat the next day, but after a couple miles, we encountered dense forest and the horse carrying the antlers kept getting hung-up. With only about an hour of daylight left, Marty decided to hang the antlers high in a tree, hopefully to discourage porcupines from chewing them. Then we finished our ride back to camp.

The next day we returned; first for the antlers and then for the rest of the meat stashed farther along the trail. All those trees looked alike to me, but Marty found the antlers without a problem and, to my relief (since I had been thinking about them all night), they were uneaten. This time we brought a couple pack horses in addition to our riding horses, and Marty brought an ax in order to hack a path for the antler-laden horse.

We spent the entire sixth day on the front porch of the log cabin fleshing the cape and storing the meat and horns (okay, antlers) for later retrieval. Then, on the seventh day, we packed up and headed off to a series of fly camps, moving each day that we didn't see sheep.

ALBERTA, BRITISH COLUMBIA, MONTANA

My western Canada moose shot in B.C. with Marty Kjos.

On the 11th morning of my 16-day hunt, we awoke to a sagging tent and three feet of snow. Marty said, "We need to get out of here. As it is, the horses won't be able to make it, but we should." So we turned the horses loose, which is normally how they spend the winters anyway. Then we stashed our camping gear and supplies, and walked out with Marty breaking trail all day. We were two tired puppies when we reached the trailhead and Marty was able to radio for Dave Wiens to pick us up and return us to the ranch. Three days later, the highways were cleared enough that I could be driven to the airport and escape to sunny southern California.

The following year, I returned to British Columbia, but this time with Charlie Stricker as my outfitter and guide. This was the hunt where I flew to Charlie's base camp by float plane. Charlie walked out onto the dock to greet me and help offload my gear. As I stepped off the right pontoon and reached to shake his

Before leaving for fly camp, we hung the moose antlers as high as we could in the log cabin.

hand, my foot hit the slippery moss at the end of the dock and down I went, hitting nothing but wood and water. Charlie laughed so hard I thought he would fall down with me. This scene was on video because my cameraman, Mike Rogers, had gotten out first and stood onshore in order to record the momentous occasion of hunter meeting outfitter.

I was going to hunt Stone sheep (again) and Rocky Mountain goat. On the video, I hunt goat first, but in actuality, I hunted sheep first since that was the more important animal.

After I sighted in at base camp, we rode horses for five hours where Charlie's crew set up "sheep camp." Transportation was by foot from then on. When we climbed on top of the first mountain the next day, we could see dozens of peaks and ridges for miles and miles. This place would require a lot of looking, and look we did. After three days, Mike and I nicknamed Charlie "One More Mountain Charlie" because, at the end of each day, we would always climb "one more mountain."

On the fourth day, we stalked close to a band of rams, but they spooked and ran left to right below us. Charlie shouted for me to shoot the lead ram, so I dropped prone on the rocks and was just about to put the crosshairs on the leading ram when my gun went off. The rams were gone in an instant. Charlie walked up to me and said, "You shot the stone instead of the Stone sheep."

I was a little bewildered at my gun shooting before I wanted to, but I figured I must have had my finger on the trigger when I pushed the safety off. Six days

Mike Rogers videotaping Charlie Stricker saying something intelligent.

later, I would find out what really happened. On that day, we had made a long stalk to within 300 yards of a pair of bedded rams. One was full curl and symmetrical. The other had one good horn and one stunted one. "Symmetrical" was 25 yards closer to me than "Unsymmetrical."

Charlie said, "Put your scope on the closest ram and really squeeze that trigger." So I put my rifle in position, slid a round in the chamber, and firmly closed the bolt. As I did so, the rifle went off! Both sheep jumped up and started running up the mountain directly away from us. Later, Charlie's assistant guide, Rod, said he wondered how anyone could miss that badly since my bullet hit about 20 yards low at 300 yards.

Fortunately, I instantly realized that my rifle had developed a propensity for firing when the bolt was shut without waiting for the trigger to be pulled. So I very, very gently closed the bolt on a new round and it didn't shoot. That solved that problem, but the other problem was that both sheep had been running away for several seconds and were at least 600 yards off. I knew I was facing a heckuva bullet drop, so I put my crosshairs on the head of the lead ram (Mr. Unsymmetrical) and, when Mr. Symmetrical lined up behind him, I finished my trigger squeeze.

As soon as my rifle went *bang!* I started the process of slowly reloading when Charlie said, in a somewhat amazed voice, "He's down and you shot the right one!" Apparently Mr. Symmetrical ran under my bullet and died from the impact, just like I had diagrammed in my mind.

When we reached my ram, it seemed like we were on the roof of the world. After photos and skinning, we divided the meat, hide, and horns among our backpacks and hiked out for a couple hours past sunset, but with a clear sky and full

SPORT HUNTING ON SIX CONTINENTS

With Charlie Stricker and my dark-caped Stone sheep.

moon assisting our movement. Then we set up tents, Rod made a fire, and when the wood burnt down to coals, we each roasted a section of sheep ribs to perfection. Ribs and water... one of the greatest meals I ever ate.

Three days later, Charlie got me above a nine-inch Rocky Mountain goat. I slid forward on my stomach and then slowly closed the bolt on a cartridge, grimacing to make sure that it didn't fire. Then I carefully put my crosshairs on the back of the billy.

We had actually first seen this goat and a younger one from about two miles, and Charlie studied them a long time before determining they were billies and not a nanny and kid. Then he said, "If we try for him this late, we'll have to 'jungle out' because we won't be able to hike back to fly camp tonight [where Rod had our tents, sleeping bags, and food]."

ALBERTA, BRITISH COLUMBIA, MONTANA

"What's 'jungle out'?" I asked.

"Sleepin' out with no tent, no bag, no food, no nothin'."

I thought about this for a few seconds. Then I looked at the billy goat through the spotting scope and cavalierly said, "Let's jungle out."

With the goat finally filling my scope, I pulled the trigger. *Bang!* The billy stood up, but couldn't move. It took a few seconds for me to carefully close the bolt on another round so I could shoot again. At the shot, my goat rolled down the mountain a couple hundred yards and we hiked down to retrieve him.

We were just able to drag ourselves and the goat down to a roaring creek by dark. And there we jungled out. To keep from rolling into the creek, we each slept on the uphill side of a fallen log. Personally, I prefer a king-size bed with a comforter and down pillow. On the bright side, we had plenty of drinking water and more old goat than we cared to eat.

Still needing a bighorn sheep to complete my slam, I booked to hunt Montana's unlimited area with Jack Atcheson, Jr. Everyone entering the drawing for an unlimited license gets a license. The problem, besides lots of hunters and limited sheep, is

I don't know why Charlie and I were laughing, because it would soon be dark and we had to "jungle out."

that when the quota is reached in a district, the season closes. The hunter is responsible for checking sign locations daily in order to find out whether or not he can keep hunting. Plus, this hunt is strictly macho-style . . . completely on foot, with backpacks. All these challenges make this a great hunt. Of course, it doesn't hurt to have one of the world's greatest sheep hunters as your guide.

Jack hunts the unlimited area by stashing food and supplies at various locations before the start of the season so you can carry a reasonable load up the mountain the day before opening day and then remain mobile while hunting. After the initial climb to the first stash, the rest is glassing, climbing, glassing, climbing, and more glassing.

Unfortunately, during my 10-day hunt we never saw a single sheep! We worked hard from dawn to dusk daily, but finally had to climb down empty-handed. But so did everyone else that year. You never know in the unlimited area. Some years the quota is reached the first day. One year, a poacher shot two immature sheep before the season started and that ended the hunting in that district because the quota that year was two.

Maybe Randy Babala is right: "!&*#! sheep! I don't know why anybody hunts them." But as this book goes to press, I'm booked to hunt bighorn again.

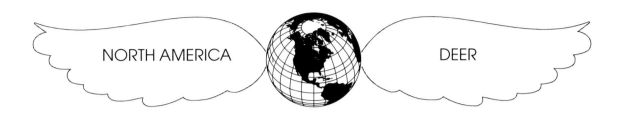

4

LUCK IN MEXICO (BOTH KINDS)

The Coues deer camp had been erected in a beautiful setting surrounded by hills covered with cacti including saguaro, sahueso, pitaya, ocotillo, tasajo, cholla, and barrel, along with scattered palo verde, palo fierro, and mesquite. I had arrived well after dark, so I didn't realize how beautiful the area was until the next morning as we departed *el campo* 15 minutes after first light. As in Africa, the game surrounds the camp, so you don't need to leave in darkness to improve your chances.

The camp itself reminded me of a traditional African safari camp . . . a first class one. There were five double tents for clients in order to accommodate both single hunters and those with hunting companions or spouses. Inside each tent were one or two cots, a night stand, and a couple unique features: red shag carpet and an overhead light bulb hooked to the camp generator. The staff had their own row of tents where I could see dozens of strips of jerky drying on a line. The dining tent was *muy grande* and featured propane heat lamps in addition to lots of good food and drink. Food preparation was generally conducted outdoors with the pots, pans, and utensils hanging from a large palo fierro tree. Even the toilet facilities were first class with "his and her" enclosures and an African-style tent shower accessed by a rock-lined path known as *el camino real*.

Around the campfire the first night, I met Richard Manley from Augusta, Georgia and Dennis and Kay Finfrock from Las Vegas, Nevada. Richard had already taken a nice eight-point deer and a javelina, but he had enjoyed the hunting so much that he received permission from the Finfrocks to accompany them on the balance of Kay's hunt. She had bought the hunt at a Sables auction at the Safari Club International Convention in Reno and then talked her husband into joining her as an observer. Kay filled her tag the next day with a good nine-pointer and that night there was a celebration that continued from the campfire to the dining tent.

The ranch in which the camp was located is known as El Tule and had been in the family of Felipe Hoyos for several generations. It is about 12,000 hectares, which is about 30,000 acres, but the hunting area included four surrounding ranches for a total area of 110,000 hectares, which is over 400 square miles.

My outfitter was Carlos Gonzalez Hermosillo, whose specialties are the little but beautiful Coues deer of the hills and the big mule deer of the desert.

By the time I arrived in Hermosillo (the capital of Sonora, which was named after Carlos' great-great grandfather, a general in the Revolution of 1910-1914), I was starting to think that a life-sized Coues deer mount would be a good gift for my wife. With me, to operate the BetaCam, was professional cameraman Pedro Bonilla, known as Peter Bonilla in the States. I selected him because he is bilingual. Carlos had told me that I didn't need to know Spanish in order to enjoy the hunt or to be successful, but I was worried about communications among me, Pedro, and my guide. As it turned out, Carlos, who speaks perfect English, was able to accompany us on this last hunt of the season because the other hunters had filled out.

The Coues deer is one of the smallest whitetails, with mature bucks averaging 100-110 pounds. Interestingly, its ears are quite large for its body size. In the erect position, the tip-to-tip ear spread is about 13 inches but, when held straight out, 18 inches is typical. Whether the pronunciation is "cooz" or "cowz" always makes for a lively discussion, but everyone agrees that the deer is named after a former U.S. Army doctor, Elliott Coues.

We were going to be looking for a mature buck of at least eight points and a spread at least as wide as the ears in the erect position. The hunting method was to drive out of camp in one of the Dodge or Toyota trucks to a promising area and then hike two to three miles over a couple hills with vertical rises of 500 to 1,000 feet, glassing all the way. With extra personnel available, I had the luxury of two guides, Armando and Benjamin, and a driver, Alejandro, in addition to Carlos and Pedro. The number of people didn't help but, with Alejandro driving around to meet us after each excursion, we were able to continually cover new territory.

The Coues deer season in Mexico, at the time, was mid-November to the last Sunday in December, but Carlos didn't start his hunts until after Thanksgiving. He said there is no difference in the success rate as to when you hunt (always close to 100%). Prior to my hunt, 15 of 18 hunters took trophies and the other three each missed several deer.

Before the rut, which begins about mid-December, the bucks are by themselves

Luck in Mexico (Both Kinds)

Coues deer habitat in Sonora.

or in small groups. During the rut, the mature bucks are generally with the does. I was hunting during the rut, so each time a deer was spotted, I immediately chambered a round, found a rest or shooting lane, and prepared to shoot even if all we saw were does.

Though speaking Español *no es necesario*, it's a good idea to be aware of a few important words that your guides might use. I was looking for a *buro*, a male deer, also known as a *buro macho*, not an *hembra* or a *bura* which is a female. *Cola blanca* means whitetail, but I never heard it used in the field, although I did hear the slang word *toro* in describing a buck. The most important words to know are the names of the various cacti and trees because the diminutive deer are very difficult to see and knowing that one is standing next to the pitaya, 20 yards down from the two 15-foot high saguaros and about 60 yards to the left of the 30-foot high sahueso, is invaluable.

We ate lunch under a few palo verde, the bushy trees with the green trunks and branches, and then started up the next little mountain at about 1:30 PM. In less than an hour we were on top and glassing when Carlos spotted two *hembras*. As usual, I chambered a 180-grain round in my .300 WM and looked for a rest. Finding a rock, I put my pack down, my rifle on top, and turned the scope up to six power. Behind me, Pedro still couldn't find the two does which he badly wanted to get footage of after having hauled the 25-pound camera around for seven hours. As I looked through the scope, I could hear Carlos telling Pedro about the two does and the next canyon and the ridgeline and the ocotillo cactus.

Suddenly I saw a buck through my scope. "Carlos, there are three now and the last one has horns."

"*Si, si*, he must have just stood up. He's at least 13 inches wide and has high tines. He looks good. Do you see him, Pedro?"

The buck was facing straight at us just below the ridgeline and about 300 yards away, according to Carlos. Pedro couldn't see the deer, let alone put the camera on him. I turned my scope up to nine and waited. In fairness, the *cola blanca* is grey and blends well with much of the flora, and is especially difficult to see in a black and white viewfinder when it's not moving.

My crosshairs were rock-steady on the chest of the buck who could not make us out because we were below the opposite ridgeline and not moving. Then I heard Pedro say, "Oh yeah." Carlos confirmed, "He's on him." Suddenly it was back to me and, just as suddenly, my calmness was gone and I started shaking in the middle of my trigger squeeze. So I let off and started over. At the sound of the shot, I saw the buck drop just before the recoil jumped the scope off track. And the smiles on the faces of the guides confirmed what I had seen.

A few minutes later, when Carlos and I reached the eight-point buck, it was my turn to smile because the tines were much longer than I had thought and the main beams were much heavier and the symmetry was nearly perfect.

After gutting the deer and tying its legs, Armando and Benjamin cut a pole, hung the buck from it, and carried the deer about a mile down to the two waiting trucks. The second truck belonged to Felipe Hoyos, who was in the middle of an afternoon of rabbit hunting with some friends (using pellet guns) when he had heard my shot. Felipe congratulated Carlos and me and then brought out a bottle of tequila in order to offer me a drink. I declined, but I could tell by the look on the faces of Carlos and Felipe that I had given the wrong answer, so I quickly changed my mind and took a swig. Then the congratulations continued.

Around the campfire that night, I was presented with an interesting choice made possible by my early success. I had licenses for both desert mule deer and Coues deer, but my mule deer hunt had been canceled because of flooding from the same storms that had dumped 11 inches of rain in two days in parts of Texas. Carlos had to cancel several hunts on his 250,000-hectare concession in the north desert because you literally couldn't walk the hunting areas, and the classic method of hunting the

Carlos Gonzalez Hermosillo posing with my eight-point Coues deer. Its ears measured 18 inches, tip-to-tip.

big desert dweller is by tracking. But there was one ranch, about two hours away, that was located on higher ground and had a large section of rolling hills. Tracking would be very difficult due to the rocky soil in the hills but, unlike the flatlands, we could gain some altitude and glass for bucks instead of jumping them.

Of course I agreed, and the next afternoon found myself on a little hill glassing a harem of does and a mighty desert mule deer buck. With the band feeding in and out of palo verde and ocotillo, it was decided that I should shoot from one hill to the other, a distance of about 300 yards, rather than risk a stalk. After all, the distance was the same as for my Coues deer, but this buck was now standing broadside and he was over twice the body size of the little Coues.

Carlos was matter-of-factly telling me that the antler spread was over three feet! That little bit of information didn't hit home immediately because Pedro announced that he still couldn't see the deer and, furthermore, he was now out of tape and needed another cassette. Carlos urged me to shoot, but I dug another cassette out of my pack and told Pedro to forget the color bars and just roll tape. Now the buck had moved another 25 yards away and was facing obliquely to the left and was behind a big ocotillo cactus with its many branches fanning out toward the blue sky. When Pedro said he thought he was taping the buck, I shot through the ocotillo. The buck disappeared but, a few seconds later, Carlos told me that I must have hit the left hip as the buck was facing away because he caught a glimpse of it limping over the top of the hill. Then he told me about the buck; he was big and old and his antlers were very heavy and wide and high. He was a truly great deer.

We waited about 15 minutes and then started on the blood trail, tracking until dark. Many times the drops would disappear for 20 to 30 feet and our trackers, Timy and Armando, would split up until one found a drop and then they would continue. At Carlos' instruction, I walked immediately behind Timy with my eyes scanning ahead and with my rifle held in front of me with a cartridge in the chamber and my thumb on the safety.

Near dark, with Timy and Armando split up again, I saw Armando stop. Then the buck bolted at about 25 yards. He was visible for less than two seconds and Timy was between me and the deer so I couldn't shoot. *El buro grande* had moved much quicker than we thought he would, so we decided to leave him for the night.

At first light the next day, we started from the ocotillo that we had broken when we stopped tracking the night before. At about 10:00 AM, we came across two blood trails but quickly determined that our buck had been attacked by another and had repelled it, drawing blood in the process. We tracked from drop to drop without stopping until we reached a large pitaya cactus at 2:00 PM and determined that that was where the buck spent the night.

At the pitaya, Antonio, a third tracker that Carlos had added, felt the buck had recently left his bed, so we climbed to the top of the hill in hopes of spotting him. Suddenly, Carlos motioned me forward and pointed.

My son, Ryan, had good luck on his javelina hunt in Sonora.

Down on the valley floor, I could see movement between the palo verde. Carlos said, "That's him." I asked, "How far?" "500 meters." I looked for a rest and could find none, so I moved to a shooting lane, mounted my rifle, and waited for the buck to appear. When he did, he was an estimated 600 meters out and 100 meters down. I didn't shoot, but I got a good look at his great antlers for the first time ... at least eight inches outside the ears on both sides, at least $2\,^1/_2$ feet high, and very heavy. I couldn't tell if he had brow tines, but the trackers assured me he did. What struck me most was the way he walked, like a brown bear with heavy shoulders and his head held low to the ground. I asked Carlos if he held his head low because of his wound. "No," Carlos replied, "the big, old ones hold their heads low because of the weight of their antlers."

We descended and tracked the rest of the day without stopping for lunch, but the going was very slow in the rocky soil. Carlos said we would have had several chances at the buck in the northern desert because the trackers can look five steps ahead in the sand, but now Antonio and Armando and Timy had to search for evidence of each step as the smart old deer continually changed direction.

The next day was the last of the season. With tracking out of the question, we climbed hills and glassed all day, but to no avail. *El buro grande* is still out there.

NORTH AMERICA'S THIRD FAVORITE DEER

"He's a 'toad,'" Steven Smith whispered to his brother, Christopher. "You've got to change that expression for a 'buster,'" I said. "How about he's a 'load?'"

Our guide and outfitter, Jim Schaafsma of Arrow Five Outfitters, took one more look through his spotting scope and said, "We're looking at a B&C buck."

Christopher nodded back to his older brother, "He *is* a 'toad.'"

The blacktail that Jim had spotted was pursuing a doe in an open meadow over a mile away. It was the last half of November and the rut had been going strong for two weeks. The big bucks were starting to wander over a much larger range in search of the ever-diminishing supply of unbred does, so we would have to get this toad in a hurry to have a chance.

Jim Schaafsma has been Mr. Blacktail for 15 years. He lives on the Stewart Ranch in Trinity County, California and guides hunters for big Columbia blacktails throughout the long California season that culminates with the Private Land Management tags allotted the Stewart Ranch during the November rut. Trinity County, located in northwestern California, is so rural that there isn't a stoplight in the entire county!

Columbia blacktails are distributed along the western coast of Canada and the U.S. from Bella Bella, British Columbia in the north, down through Washington and Oregon, to Monterey County, California. The SCI and B&C record books designate

Jim Schaafsma glassing for big bucks. The habitat is surprisingly open for Columbia blacktail.

exact boundaries for Columbia blacktails outside of which deer are considered Rocky Mountain mule deer to the east.

Pure Columbia blacktails are considerably different than mule deer. The blacktail has smaller ears, a smaller metatarsal gland that is located lower on the leg, and a solid black tail on top (although the upper part of older bucks' tails turn brownish during the rut), whereas a mule deer's tail is white or brown with a black tip, and blacktails generally weigh less than mulies.

Jim estimates that only 5% of blacktail bucks are 4 x 4s. The rest are spikes, forks, 3 x 3s, or 4 x 3s with or without brow tines. When you're hunting in the west, you need to do as the westerners do and use the "western count." A three-pointer, for example, has three points on at least one side, with or without brow tines. Personally, I don't care for either the western or the eastern count (all points added). I think it's helpful to know if a buck is a 4 x 3 with one brow tine, for example.

You might ask, "Why do hunters travel to California, Oregon, Washington, and British Columbia to hunt 'small mule deer?'" Now that I've completed my first hunt for Columbia blacktail (named for the Columbia River that separates western Washington and Oregon), I can tell you that the main reasons are the thrill and challenge of the hunt due to the different habitat and hunting techniques employed.

Jim advises: "Add 12 inches to a blacktail's spread to equate to a mule deer's spread, so a 20-inch wide blacktail is about the same as a 32-inch mule deer." But Jim is quick to point out that spread is empty air. He much prefers to look for deepness of forks, weight of antlers, and length of main beams. "Shoot them between the eyes if you want spread; then your taxidermist can make them as wide as you want," he likes to say.

One night Calvin Stewart, Jim's old high school buddy, stopped in to hear the latest jokes going around hunting camp. Calvin said his ranch is 11,000 acres with an elevation from 400 to 4,000 feet above sea level and is located about 30 miles from the Pacific Ocean. It is certainly a beautiful ranch and is home to lots of cattle, deer, wild boar, a few bears, and an occasional mountain lion. The rolling hills are covered with oaks (white, black, tan, live, and pin), the constantly peeling madron trees, pines, and lots of grass flats, meadows, and hillsides. Therein lies the fun of hunting blacktails in this area. You can often spot deer at great distances, plan long stalks, and sometimes get close to a buck that you saw from one to two miles away.

Such was the case at hand when Jim packed up his spotting scope and said to Christopher Smith, "We'll go down this ridge, cross the drainage, parallel those hills, climb up the left side of that line of oaks, and crawl out on that little knob above those pines. It'll take us 30 minutes and that buck could still be with that doe or he could breed her and be a mile away."

Steven (30) turned to younger brother, Christopher (20), and asked, "Do you still want first shot?" Christopher replied, "Of course." Steven said, "He's only a three-point." Christopher smiled at big brother and said, "Yeah, but Jim said he's 24 inches wide with high tines and good eye guards." "Just don't miss," Steven said, "or he'll be on my wall instead of yours."

With that, we took off. Down and over and up we went. Jim checked the wind a couple times and, finally, we started our crawl out to the knob that he had picked out from the other side of the valley. It had been a half hour since we had last seen the buck, but we were still disappointed when we peered over the top of the knob and could only see a distant doe. The buck was gone. Jim said, "Stay here and I'll climb down and get a different angle." He then backed up, hiked down about 50 yards, and crawled out on the little hill below us. No sooner had he reached his vantage point than he backed up and hustled to where we were laying.

Christopher had his 7mm Weatherby resting on the ground with a 165-grain bullet chambered and the safety on. Steven was to Christopher's right with his 7mm ready as back-up. I had my Sony VX-1000 digital video camera on standby with my thumb on the red button. Jim crawled out to us and urgently whispered, "He's straight down below us!" With that, we all crawled forward in unison.

A doe came into sight and stomped her foot. Then the buck became visible, almost straight down and slightly to our left. He was looking up in our direction.

Christopher Smith's huge 3 x 3 plus fish-hook eyeguards.

Simultaneously, two safeties clicked off and one record button clicked on. Jim whispered, "Just look at the shoulder; don't look at the horns." *Bang!* The buck sprang straight up and fell backwards.

It takes 135 to make B&C, all-time. Christopher's buck netted 145, one of the highest scoring three-pointers (3 x 3 plus brow tines) ever taken. As Jim pointed out, a 145 three-pointer is a lot more impressive than a 145 four-pointer and this buck was impressive down to his twin fish-hook eye guards. He was about the equivalent of a three-point whitetail (3 x 3 plus eye guards) that nets 185 B&C.

Jim designates his hunts as "gold medal" (shoot the biggest one you can), "silver medal" (shoot anything except four-pointers and the rare monster three-pointer like Christopher's), and "bronze medal" (cull bucks; primarily large, old forkies). I was on a silver medal hunt which reminded me of hunting in Europe where trophies are priced according to their CIC score so, depending on your budget, you often pass on both larger and smaller animals to find the category you are looking for. There are no snap shots with this kind of hunting. Rather, trophy evaluation precedes each decision to make a stalk.

I certainly had my chances, and I guess it was the number of chances that made my hunt enjoyable rather than the size of my trophy. On the first day, I turned down shots at two 120 class bucks. One was a high and narrow three-pointer with brow tines and one was about 20 inches wide with one weak G4 (using the B&C method of counting tines). The second day we spotted a very wide three-pointer that Jim estimated at 24 inches, making it the equivalent of a 36-inch mule deer. We made a climb for him but he disappeared on us. Then Jim spotted a three-pointer with brow tines that guide Dale Williams and I made a 30-minute climb for. I could have shot three bucks I didn't want on that jaunt, but the big one got away.

The third morning, in a typical northern California November rain, Jim spotted a 20-inch wide three-pointer working a doe. We moved downhill into the fog as fast as we could. The doe trotted off, but the buck stopped under an oak tree. Visibility was poor as I placed my .300 WM on my favorite Tripod Systems shooting sticks and waited for Dale to get on the buck with the video camera. As soon as Dale said, "I'm on him," I rolled the buck over at 70 yards.

I shot my 3 x 3 in a rainstorm. Jim scouts constantly, but had never seen this buck before.

After pictures, we dragged the field-dressed buck up to a dirt road where we could bring in a truck. Then, on the ride back to camp, I videotaped a three-pointer with brow tines lying not 50 yards from the dirt road. "He'll score in the 120s," Jim said. What he could have said was, "He's 5 to 8 points better than yours, Ken." But it's pretty hard to find fault with a hunt where you see lots of trophy-size animals every day; especially those of a species that are as challenging as North America's third favorite deer (based on number of deer and the hunters who hunt them).

A LAD SHUNNESON ADVENTURE

Background

I've hunted with Lad Shunneson literally all over the world . . . on six continents. Most of the hunts were outfitted by others and we hunted 2 x 1 with Lad serving as a co-cameraman for Sportsmen on Film. But a few hunts were outfitted and guided by Lad, including Rocky Mountain mule deer, which is the subject of this story.

When *The Hunting Report* asked me to comment on Lad as a guide and a person, I said, "He guides, accompanies clients, and hunts half the year (literally) but still finds time to be a circuit judge, a divorce attorney (representing men only) and to add to his collection of over 450 mounted big game animals. When you hunt with Lad, you know you are going on a hunt that you will never forget with a Colorado character that you will never forget. Seventy percent love him and the other 30% don't know how to have fun."

The Adventure

First off, you have to realize that Lad Shunneson is a hunting fanatic, born and bred. There is a picture of him in his company brochure as a three-year old-carrying a shotgun and a pheasant accompanied by his dog, also carrying a pheasant. There is also a picture of his mom and dad in 1940 with what looks like about 100 recently

A LAD SHUNNESON ADVENTURE

deceased ducks and pheasants in their hands, on their car, and in front of their car. Lad started hunting for the family table when he was seven, earning his way as a trapper when he was 13, and operating his mule deer hunts east of Boulder when he was 23 and in need of money to finish his education.

My hunt took place during the third Colorado mule deer season in early November 1997. The third season generally starts the first Saturday of November and many hunters like it because it is closer to the rut and there is a better chance for cold weather. The first Saturday can be as late as November 7. For my hunt, it occurred a few days sooner, but the earlier start and the unseasonably warm weather didn't seem to matter, which is why Lad's hunters who hunt the full five days have been 100% successful on this hunt for 31 years!

Because two hunters couldn't make it until the fourth day, my hunt started out "only" 4 x 1, instead of the usual 6 x 1 (since the ranch owner requires that Lad be the only guide). On most hunts even 2 x 1 is a detriment, but on this hunt more hunters can be fun if you like hunting action because you get to experience your hunt and observe everyone else's.

Day one opened, as usual, with a 4:00 AM wake-up call, 4:45 AM departure from Lad and

Lad Shunneson, three years old, with his trusty dog, Rusty.

Lad's parents in 1940 with their food supply for the winter.

SPORT HUNTING ON SIX CONTINENTS

Lad and Lenka Shunneson's "Lodge Above Boulder;" a combination hunting lodge, wildlife museum, and bed & breakfast.

A typical scene at the end of the morning hunt on Lad's deer lease... lots of hunters and two deer loaded for the trip to the meat processor.

Lenka Shunneson's Lodge above Boulder, 5:30 AM arrival at the ranch, and 5:45 AM start of hunt at the glimmer of first light. The deer, of course, can be anywhere on and off the ranch, but there are five main observation points (Beech, Honey Hole, Arena, Poles, and Valley Side), so the routine is to drive to each and glass. Bucks are only stalked after being seen. There are no exploratory stalks because Lad has found that they generally result in deer being run off the ranch. Also, hunting takes place only in the mornings and evenings in order to reduce pressure on the deer when they lay up in the middle of the day.

The first morning we saw 11 bucks and dozens of does, but only one "shooter buck," and he was seen at Poles. Bill Paulin was first up when we saw the shooter... a 4 x 4 plus brow tines intent on a particularly lovely doe. When Bill confirmed he wanted the buck, Lad said, "We'll wait until that doe seduces him over the first hill. Then we'll walk straight to the top of the hill, find the buck, and shoot it." And that's exactly what they did. And we all got to see the shot because when Lad and Bill reached the top of the first hill, the buck ran up the mountain, into our view, and stopped long enough for Bill to pole-ax it with his .30-.378 Weatherby (serial #1).

Next up were a father-son muzzleloading team. The father, Mitch Strew, was originally from Grass Lake, Illinois where he was a high school classmate of Lad's (and, after listening to several post hunt conversations, it was a wonder they both graduated). The son, Roger, was a recent Texas A&M grad. Both were decked out in authentic 1840s garb made by their own hands. Mitch was shooting a .54 caliber caplock and Roger a .58 caliber flintlock long rifle. I was shooting my usual Sako .300 WM using 180-grain Federal Nosler partition bullets. And I was decked out in an authentic 1997 outfit with two to four times the required 400 inches of hunter's orange, depending on whether my down jacket was on over my down vest.

The Strews were kind enough to give me first right of refusal since I could Yellow Page a buck ("reach out and touch someone") faster and farther than their equipment would allow. We couldn't find a shooter that first afternoon, but we did the second morning on the Valley Side. It was a nice buck; wider than his 23- to 24-inch ear spread and with all the typical points (4 x 4 plus brows), but I decided to wait. So the stalk was planned for both Roger and Mitch with Roger to have the first shot,

L to R: Mitch and Roger Strew, Bill Paulin, Lenka, me, and Lad. In the background are a pair of elephant tusks. Lad's second wife kept one tusk after their divorce, so I constantly reminded Lad that he had "the Big 3 ½." When Lad finally procured the second tusk, he could once again claim "the Big 4."

Lad and me reviewing his photo albums in the living room of the lodge.

Lad, with his son, Drake, and the buck for whom "Buck" was named.

Mitch to shoot if there was a miss or wounding, and both to reload as fast as possible. As events unfolded, it was a good thing that this buck was pitifully in love with several unready females and that he was deaf to boot.

Roger got to where he could see the buck walking away at 100 yards (the end of his confident shooting range with an open-sighted flintlock). He poured powder in the flashpan, rested his long rifle on shooting sticks, checked to make sure his dad was ready, and missed! As planned, Mitch fired immediately upon seeing the miss and he missed also! Then it was a race to see who could reload the fastest. Meanwhile the buck ran a few steps, looked left and right at his does, and started eating! In retrospect, Lad believes that the lower percussion of the muzzleloaders, as compared to a centerfire rifle, resulted in the buck's lack of alarm. Mitch won the reloading race and killed the deer with his next shot. Why wait for your son when you're paying for the hunt?

Two deer in two days resulted in some lively conversation around the dinner table (which no one wants to leave early when Lenka Shunneson is cooking). One of the best stories was Lad's answer to the question of how his fourth son came to be named "Buck."

"'Buck' was born before

first light on the opening day of whitetail season. With mother and baby doing well, I departed for a deer blind along the river bottom where I hunted a particular buck for the previous two seasons without getting a shot. On this blessed morning, the buck walked by my blind at 40 yards. I shot him and returned to the hospital with the good news that my deer had gotten even bigger... a 7 x 7 with an 11 $^{3}/_{4}$-inch drop tine and a 25-inch inside spread. I thought that 'Buck' was therefore an appropriate name for our baby boy. My wife disagreed and insisted on the name 'Wesley.' I didn't want to argue with the new mother, so I agreed and then went downstairs and signed the birth certificate 'Buck Wesley Shunneson.'"

Day three dawned slightly overcast. At 5:45 AM, we started the circuit. A buck and 12 does were off the ranch at Beech, so we departed that point right away hoping that they might work their way over. We spotted a decent buck at the Honey Hole but I passed and it was in a location that would present Roger with too long of a shot after a stalk. At Arena there was yet another buck that I passed, so we decided to wait and see if it would move over to Valley Side where Roger might be able to get a shot. While we were waiting, I saw some movement up the mountain. It was a

Mitch, Roger and Lad with Roger's flintlock buck.

Lad and me with my old buck. He was 27½ inches wide, but only 18 inches between the main beams.

buck... a good buck... and, for the first time, I wasn't the cameraman and I wasn't going to wait for a bigger one! There was no cover for a surreptitious stalk and not enough time for a circuitous one, so Lad said, "He wants to get down to those does. Whenever he isn't looking at us, let's walk straight towards him... nice and slow with you right behind me. When we get to that gully, we'll be out of sight and we can climb to that tree and you can shoot from there."

At the tree, the buck still hadn't moved, so I was only 90 yards from him. He was facing me and looking from the does to where Lad and I had disappeared and then back to the does. I aimed for the right side of his brisket. *Bang!* The partition bullet exited behind his left shoulder and he dropped instantly. I started to walk up, but Lad said, "First, let's get that other buck for Roger." As it turned out, Roger didn't shoot that buck, but he did shoot one in the Honey Hole (a perfectly symmetrical, tall 4 x 4 with brow tines and good antler weight).

Returning to my buck, Lad and I puffed our way uphill, through a slick-wired horse fence, and to the buck. The closer I got, the more kickers I could see. When I picked up his antlers, he was a 12-pointer eastern count, six-pointer western count, 6 x 4 with brow tines proper count, with a nice 27½-inch outside spread. He could have been taller and heavier, but so could I!

7

THANK YOU DEER (THANK YOU, DEAR)

If I were a whitetail fanatic, I'd have a wall full of whitetails and not much else. Lots of hunters are whitetail fanatics. I'm not one of them, but I've still managed to shoot six whitetails, which is double that of any other species I've hunted. I even wrote a song rhapsodizing whitetails that, I've been told, is the deer hunters' anthem. It goes like this:

> *I love the way you look at me*
> *When we are both so near*
> *And for that, I thank you deer*
> *Thank you deer*
> *Thank you . . . whitetail deer*
>
> *And to you, my dear back home*
> *Who lets me hike the hills and roam*
> *You mean much more to me*
> *Than any big-antlered trophy*
>
> *I've watched you in the season*
> *And I've tracked you in the snow*

*I've suffered in a tree stand
And I've marveled at a doe
But to get my heart a pumpin'
I just need a little luck
There ain't nothin' like huntin'
A big, big whitetail buck*

*I've grown to love your flag
I admire your use of fear
And for that, I thank you deer
Thank you deer
Thank you . . . whitetail deer*

*Now darlin', you're my first love
And by far my greatest find
But when I see a big, big rack
You're not always on my mind*

*I've watched you in the season
And I've tracked you in the snow
I've suffered in a tree stand
And I've marveled at a doe
But to get my heart a pumpin'
I just need a little luck
There ain't nothin' like huntin'
A big, big whitetail buck*

*For weeks I've hunted with the hope
Of seein' your horns through my scope
And for that, I thank you deer
Thank you deer
And thank you . . . dear!*

That song is at the start of "Blind Hunting for Big, Big Bucks." With a good singer (not me) and good deer on-camera, it will make you want to go hunting whitetail. I wrote "Thank You Deer (Thank You, Dear)" by dictation on Texas Highway 281 when I lived in California. I had just finished videotaping some huge whitetail bucks on the Grimland Whitetail Ranch near Waco for a "how to" video on whitetail deer management and was so excited about the deer I had seen, combined with missing my wife and family for the last several days, that I drove back to San Antonio Airport with my left hand on the steering wheel and my right hand on a tape recorder.

Thank You Deer (Thank You, Dear)

The YO Ranch

My second ever big game hunt was on the YO Ranch near Mountain Home, Texas. Now I live 35 miles from the YO. But in November 1983, I lived in California with my wife, six-year-old daughter, and almost-two-year-old son. I don't remember when I heard about the YO, but it must have been just after my first big game hunt to Alaska that September. I was desperate to go hunting before the end of the year and someone said "whitetail" which led to Texas, which led to the YO.

Today I'm friends with Louie and Walter Schreiner, the men in charge of the hunting and

My first YO whitetail. They have bigger ones, but I didn't know it at the time.

cattle operations, respectively, and visit the YO at least three times a year. Once a year my wife and I go to the YO Social which is touted as the greatest annual party in Texas. Ticket sales (at $125 a whack) are limited to 2,000. Arrive hungry and thirsty after 6:00 PM and leave the next morning before 6:00 AM with a designated driver. Eat, drink, dance, and gawk at the denim, diamonds, and cleavage. Recent singers have included George Jones, Tanya Tucker, and George Strait.

The other two times my wife and I don't miss visiting the YO are for their April and October exotic game auctions. They are the two best parties in Texas for the money ($20) . . . if you don't buy anything at the auction. Free food, booze, and after the auction, a first class dance band in the pavilion.

In the 1880s, Captain Charles Schreiner (who joined the Texas Rangers when he was 16) owned 550,000 acres and the YO brand. Deaths and divorces have knocked the acreage down to about 40,000, but that's still 60-some square miles, which is a lot of country.

On this, my first deer hunt, I shot prematurely, as most out-of-state hunters do when they see the quantity of deer for which the Hill Country of Texas is famous. Actually, I shot two deer.

My first buck was a spindly 10-pointer of which I was proud. We loaded it in the truck and started to drive back to the lodge when a buck ran past our front bumper with his left leg hanging. My guide said, "We need to kill that buck because he's hurt pretty bad." I volunteered. But it's surprising how well a four-legged animal can run on three legs, and this buck was no exception. I was finally able to shoot him about an hour later. He was a spindly nine-pointer.

When I met Louie Schreiner for the first time that evening, I asked if I could keep both bucks for the price of one. My guide explained the circumstances and Louie said, "No problem. You have two tags." I had the bucks shoulder-mounted with their antlers locked in fighting position.

Pennsylvania

Three years later, I was wearing orange on the opening day of the Pennsylvania deer season. I was not alone. The game department later announced that over 1,000,000 hunters were in the field on the opening day of 1986. It was probably the most dangerous place in the world. Scattered among the trees were splotches of orange vests, jackets, hats, pants, and gloves . . . all within rifle range of each other.

I was producing a video with Wayne Pocius on hunting whitetails "north and south." The south portion had already been completed in Texas with Wayne shooting a nice nine-pointer during the archery season. When he added a good 10-pointer with his rifle in PA, it was my turn to hunt.

At that time I had spread disease. All I wanted was a buck with spread and, since 20 inches is the grail for whitetails, that's what I was looking for. For 2½ days, I still-hunted (hopeless with the dry leaves), stand-hunted at the base of trees (almost hopeless because of limited visibility), and participated in drives (probably my best chance, but drives take manpower and lots of real estate), all without success. After that third morning, Wayne suggested that I try one of the permanently constructed elevated stands. I was ready.

I was directed to a hilly area with lots of high brush and 40- to 60-foot tall deciduous trees that had, of course, dropped their leaves by December. My stand was a four foot by four foot platform built across two trees growing next to each other, about 30 feet off the ground, and accessed by a ladder of two-by-fours nailed up the two trees. Once on the platform, I could see a couple hundred yards in each direction and occasionally saw deer appearing and disappearing in the brush.

My PA whitetail. . . decent spread, but no height or weight.

Thank You Deer (Thank You, Dear)

In the middle of the afternoon, I spotted a whitish-horned buck and immediately judged his spread at the magic 20 inches. Fortunately, I waited for him to give me a side view and was disappointed that he only had six points. I didn't shoot, so I guess spread wasn't everything after all. Still later, I thought I saw the same buck again, but when I got an angle on his antlers, I could see 10 points so I quickly raised my rifle and shot him in the right shoulder. He was right at 20 inches outside, but the tines off the main beams were short and the antlers were thin. That's when I realized that tine length and antler mass were more important than the empty air between the main beams.

East Texas

Thompson Temple had leased the hunting rights to a ranch in the Piney Woods of East Texas that had not been hunted in five years, so everyone who was booked was excited and, as it turned out, the excitement was justified and the resulting video was named "The Greatest Whitetail Hunt." Peter Radke killed a buck with 25-inch main beams; current SCI Vice President Mike Rogers, Sr. shot his first whitetail; and that famous hunting couple, Stan and Pam Atwood, each killed nice bucks (and that was when Pam's last name was Sanders).

This was the hunt in which Dr. Paul Broun got into a lengthy conversation with his guide, Thompson Temple, as to whether or not a certain buck feeding in a meadow had a 20-inch spread.

Paul: "I don't want to take a deer just to be taking a deer. I'm going to be disappointed if it is not 20 inches."

Thompson: "You'll be pleased."

Paul: "You're sure?"

Thompson: "He's a nice buck."

Paul: "I want a big 20-incher."

Thompson (after Paul hesitates for several seconds): "If I've ever seen a 20-incher, he's a 20-incher."

Etc., etc., etc.

Amazingly the buck stayed in the open until Thompson convinced Paul to shoot. Paul got his 20-incher and hunters still tell me that is one of their favorite video scenes.

When everyone had shot their deer and departed, it was my turn. Thompson and I decided to hunt a heavily-treed area that no one had yet searched. I told my cameraman, Rick Morgan, to just turn on the camera and let it run. Then we started still-hunting very, very slowly. As good luck would have it, after we reloaded the camera several times, a very heavy-antlered 12-pointer casually walked in front of me and I shot it on-camera. No one had even seen that buck in the previous five days of hunting.

SPORT HUNTING ON SIX CONTINENTS

My east TX whitetail, guided by Thompson Temple . . . terrific antler weight with a back-facing sticker on each side. Are they points?

Washington and Texas

With four whitetails on the wall (actually, three on the wall and "my good one" full-mounted), and after having videotaped over a dozen other whitetail hunts, I didn't really have a burning desire to hunt another whitetail, but three opportunities caused me to make an exception. They were the chance to hunt whitetail in the Pacific Northwest with a muzzleloader guided by Lad Shunneson . . . all major handicaps. Just kidding. The muzzleloader wasn't a handicap out to 100 yards. Just kidding again. Lad guided me to a "smokepole nine-pointer."

Whitetail number six was a result of my producing "Blind Hunting for Big, Big Bucks" the year after I moved to Texas. For my on-camera segment, I hunted near

THANK YOU DEER (THANK YOU, DEAR)

Brackettville on Frank Schobel's ranch. The hunting there is primarily from ground blinds and, since I can't stand the monotony of blind hunting (except when a big buck walks out, of course), I hunted only two days at a time, drove home for a few days, and then drove back. I did this four times during the two-month season before shooting a buck.

Sitting in a blind causes me to daydream. One of my dreams had a nice buck walk into an opening as I turned my back to it, placed the rifle over my shoulder, pulled out a mirror, and shot the buck behind me. The dream was so real that I duplicated it on the video and still have people comment on it with a few wondering if I really did it.

My east WA whitetail taken with a caplock muzzleloader and guided by Lad Shunneson.

My Most Enjoyable Whitetail Hunt

Having videotaped Don Myers shoot a 213-point buck and David McGinnis a 190-pointer, and having shot six whitetail bucks myself, I still can't pick any of those as being my most enjoyable. That honor goes to my son's first whitetail. When he was 11, he attended the YO Adventure Camp that included a hunter's certification course (which he had to take again when he turned 14 and which I took with him at that time). So, for his 12th birthday, I took him on a South Texas whitetail hunt on a large, unfenced ranch that Thompson Temple was hunting. Trophy management was just starting there and the trophy fees were $3,000 for a 10-pointer or better or $1,000 for less than 10 points. I told Ryan that we were going to look for a good eight-pointer, and would pass any 10-pointers. He agreed.

In the video, little (at that time) Ryan is hunting by himself, but of course the cameraman (me) was with him. Thompson lets Ryan off at an elevated blind, Ryan climbs into it with his unloaded rifle, and once inside he loads up his .243 with four 100-grain bullets, puts the safety on, lays the rifle down, and starts glassing. What really happened was Thompson let us off when it was still pitch black, we both climbed into the blind, and I put the camera on tripod. Ryan then lay down on the floor of the blind and, using his rifle as a pillow, went to sleep.

As the sun slowly rose, Ryan was sleeping so soundly that I decided not to

L to R: me with BetaCam, guide Larry Grimland, and hunter Don Myers with buck that green-scored 213 B&C gross.

wake him unless I saw a shootable buck. About 7:00 AM a good buck walked onto a *sendero* (really a dirt road) and I put my binoculars on him. As I suspected, he had five points on the right side, but when I got a good look at the left side of his rack, I wasn't sure if I saw four points or five. Not wanting to make a $2,000 mistake, I waited a few more minutes for better light as the buck continued to feed on the edge of the *sendero* at about 150 yards. Finally, I decided that the left beam hooked up at the tip like a 10th point, but that it was a nine-pointer, so I woke up Ryan. Naturally, he was excited and groggy. He wiped away the cobwebs, put his rifle through the opening in the blind, and pushed off the safety. To his credit, he said, "I can't shoot. My crosshairs are bouncing all over." I told him to look away for a few seconds, take a deep breath, put his crosshairs back on the shoulder, and slowly squeeze. And he did.

At the shot, the buck kicked his hind legs, sprinted for the brush, and disappeared. Ryan was concerned, but I calmed him down and told him that we'd wait 20 minutes before even opening the door to the blind and climbing down. After the full 20 minutes, we walked up the *sendero* and then followed the blood trail. When we found the buck, I could see that I had made the correct decision because the shot had

THANK YOU DEER (THANK YOU, DEAR)

only clipped the brisket and the buck had run 75 yards and then lay down, no doubt alert until he died from blood loss. If he had been spooked, he could have run several hundred yards and, in that thick brush, we might not have found him before the vultures.

Ryan was ecstatic because it was a good buck with an acorn on his left rear tine. Dad was also happy, and not just because the buck was, in fact, a nine-pointer.

Ryan Wilson's buck. One more point would have cost another $2,000. The acorn was free.

CATS CAN BE TOUGH ON DOGS

After my last fall, I struggled back to my feet and just let my glasses hang from their cord around my neck and flop around on my chest as I waded through the knee-deep snow. The glasses weren't doing me much good anyway. They were completely frosted over on both sides and it would have taken several minutes to return them to prescription-performance levels. I didn't have several minutes because I was a quarter mile behind.

It was now 10:30 AM, and we had been following the dogs for over three hours since we had found the two sets of bobcat tracks in the snow on top of the river ice. If I had known at that moment that I had three more hours before I would get a shot, I might have given up. But as I trudged forward with my gaiters frozen solid around my lower legs as a result of my having broken through the river ice a couple miles back, I could hear my guide, Keith Huff, as he used his forearm to batter through the brush ahead of me.

Then I heard the dogs barking and, once again, the adrenaline returned and the tiredness faded away.

My hunt had been planned three weeks earlier when I received a letter from Len Barnes of the Michigan Outdoor Writers Association advising me that my company, Sportsmen on Film, was the winner of the 1990-91 Teddy Award for the Best Hunting Video of the Year for our production titled "Hunting in Spain." The MOWA

Cats Can Be Tough On Dogs

Outdoor-Travel Film Festival is conducted annually for video and film productions in various outdoor, travel, and adventure categories, including hunting and fishing. The 1991 festival was held in Grayling.

Two years prior, when retired Detroit News outdoor editor James A.O. Crowe presented me with the Teddy for "Hunting Sheep, Goat, and Moose in B.C." at the 26th Annual Awards, I had participated in an exciting goose hunt with several MOWA members. This time, the packet of information accompanying the notification of the award included a variety of programs lined up by Charlie Guenther, including hunting for rabbits, coyotes, and bobcats. Sitting at my desk in Los Angeles with the sun shining through the office windows, I thought that a bobcat hunt might be good exercise, so I notified Charlie of my plans and I sent away for my nonresident furharvester's license in Zone 2 (northern Lower Peninsula) which would be good for one bobcat.

When I reached Keith, he was standing motionless at a bend in the river and he nodded for me to do the same. Since this was the second day of our hunt, I knew the drill and the reasons for it.

After we first found the tracks of the male bobcat with a big female, we coldtrailed them until one of the dogs jumped one of the cats, and then the chase was on as the dogs were released and the hunters tried to keep up. When a bobcat is chased, it tends to run in a circle or a loop and, when it performs enough loops, the dogs can get confused on the hot trail and end up losing the cat. Keith had heard the dogs getting closer and hoped that one of the cats was going to complete a loop in front of us so I could get a shot as it raced by.

The previous day I brought my bow, but it was so difficult dragging it through the heavy cover that I opted to use Charlie Guenther's turkey gun with #2 shot. Charlie had admonished me that his shotgun was one-for-one on turkeys and he didn't want to teach it any bad habits.

As the vapor from my heavy breathing subsided, we could hear the dogs moving away instead of toward us, so we took up the chase again . . . the dogs chasing the cats and me chasing Keith.

Keith lives near Gaylord. He trains his stable of treein' Walkers in his big back yard which also provides good winter range for elk (we had seen 13 the previous morning). In addition to his duties as an animal control officer, Keith stays in good shape by hunting bear and elk in the fall, and bear again in the spring, and bobcat in between. In addition, he logs several hundred miles on foot each year, adding to his extensive collection of dropped elk antlers. But he needs all that exercise because his wife, Sherry, is such a good cook.

"It sounds like the cat may be treed," Keith yelled at me. With the sound of the dogs only about a half mile away, I struggled forward and upward away from the river, where the trees were spread out and the going was a little easier. But, after a short while, we no longer heard the dogs, and Keith remarked that he felt something unusual may have happened.

As we listened, I reflected on the team effort involved in this hunt. Keith's brother, Richard, had driven us at first light in search of tracks. When we found some big ones, Keith unloaded two of his dogs, Barbie and Daisy. From another truck, John Cryderman, down from the Upper Peninsula, took out two of his treein' Walkers, Goose and Magnum. Eventually, as the hours passed, Kim Gainsforth, Frank Krapsey, and Dwayne and Joey Robinson with their dog, Gyp, all joined the chase.

At that moment we heard the dogs again, but seemingly well over another mile away. And then Barbie trotted up to us out of the trees, her face and neck scratched and bleeding. Two hours later, when all of us reconvened at the trucks, we were able to piece together what had happened.

The two bobcats had split up, with Barbie and Goose staying with the tom, and Magnum, Daisy and Gyp after the female. I eventually reached a very large cedar tree growing with two smaller ones. The female bobcat was high in the tallest tree, with the three dogs continuously barking while looking up at the cat looking down. A couple of the dogs had been scratched before driving the cat up the tree.

The 20-pound female was a fine trophy, but I decided not to shoot until Keith was able to determine the possibility of my still getting the bigger tom. What we later found out made shooting the female anticlimactic.

We had been following the cats in a three-mile loop along the frozen river. The lighter bobcats had the advantage as the dogs chased them along the surface. On the banks the snow was two feet deep, and running in the deep stuff would be more difficult for the cats than the dogs.

While the tom followed the river, John's dog, Goose, came from behind by cutting across a land area at a turn in the river and caught the cat. As is typical, the 30-pound cat grabbed onto the head of the 60-pound dog and they fought briefly on the ice until it give way and they plunged into the water at a bend where the current carried them under the frozen surface. And that is where they both died.

John had temporarily lost dogs before, but thanks to their tracking collars, had been able to locate them within a few hours. This time the collar was located in the river and that is where Keith's son, Troy, chopped a hole in the ice and waded into waist-deep water to retrieve the lifeless dog from its icy grave.

Keith and his friends mostly hunt bobcats for fun and to train their brave dogs to track and tree the equally smart and brave cats. Then they leash their dogs and hike back to the trucks, letting the bobcat go.

This time the hunt wasn't as much fun as it usually is, but John was philosophical. He said that only one dog in a hundred would make a good bobcat dog, but he still had Goose's mother and father and, with a little luck and a lot of work, he might end up with another good one.

CATS CAN BE TOUGH ON DOGS

Three pictures with Keith Huff and his eyes are closed in each one.

NORTH AMERICA   CATS AND DOGS

9

BEATING THE CALIFORNIA DEADLINE

My bobcat hunt had been booked just three weeks in advance, and I had participated without much planning or preparation. When that hunt was over, I had written about it immediately because the challenge of the hunt surprised me, the loss of the dog was tragic, and it was one of my few hunts not videotaped.

My mountain lion was another story. I booked the hunt almost a year in advance with Red Creek Outfitters (Val Robb and sons). I planned on hunting with a bow, so I bought one and practiced, practiced, practiced. The hunt would be videotaped. And since I lived in California at the time, without having yet thought about moving to Texas, I needed to succeed during the winter of 1989-90 or risk not ever being able to display a mountain lion in my trophy room.

As it turned out, shortly after my hunt California voters did, in fact, elect to discontinue mountain lion hunting and, the way the law is written, you cannot even legally hunt a mountain lion elsewhere (such as in Utah, where I hunted mine) and bring it into California.

In January, I met Val, one of his sons, Chris, and his son-in-law, Bart Bertrum, in Paragonah, bought my license and off we went, driving logging roads in southwest Utah looking for track. On the second day, we found an old deer kill and, later, mountain lion tracks. The dogs were released and off we went. As the dogs sniffed along, it was great to be in beautiful country, walking at a leisurely pace, and breathing that clean, fresh air.

Then the dogs hit hot track, the cat started running, and it was suddenly an endurance contest just keeping up! The cat was trying to lose the dogs and it seemed the Robbs were trying to lose me and my cameraman, Steve Anderson. Every step was either up, down, or over. And the barking was getting farther away. Eventually all the dogs started barking at once and the barking started getting closer. The cat was treed!

I huffed and puffed up to a big pine and saw the mountain lion crouching on a limb, glowering down. It was a big cat with a long, fluffy tail. I was trying to figure out how to stick an arrow into its chest when Val said, "That's a big one. They don't get much longer, but its head is smaller than a tom's. It's an old female with no kittens. The choice [to shoot or not] is yours." I chose not, and three days later I doubted my choice.

We treed a tom on the fourth day, but it was smaller than the old female we had let go. On the fifth day, we awoke to two feet of snow. We tried to get around to look

L to R: Three Robbs (Shawn, Val, and Chris), one Wilson, and one cat.

My first animal shot using a bow. Would it be my last?

for track, but our truck got stuck and the snow pack was too soft to travel by snowmobile. So I headed back to California and did what I could to promote a "no" vote against banning mountain lion hunting in the Golden State.

Adult pumas reportedly kill a deer a week, say 50 a year per cat. Sometimes they kill sheep and other stock by the score in one night just for fun. And, when they aren't hunted, they lose their fear of humans. But California voters are 90% urban, so the vote wouldn't be determined by ranchers and game managers. Therefore, I was glad to hear Val's voice on the phone in March: "The conditions for tracking are good again. Do you still want a cat?"

So I returned to Utah, but without a cameraman. I couldn't find one in good physical condition on short notice, but Val said he could run the camera with no problem if I brought a small one instead of a big one.

I shot about 40 arrows in my backyard that afternoon and flew to Utah the next day. This time Val had Chris and another son, Shawn, with him and they went all-out to get me a big cat. The first step, of course, was to find some prints. With us split up in two trucks and with lots of sharp eyes, we found some big tracks but, after a short walk, Val determined that they were made two days earlier. His dogs could follow the tracks, but we might have a heckuva long hike because a male mountain lion can cover a lot of ground in two days.

"A track in hand" as they say, so I chose to follow and follow and follow. This time the cat in the tree was a big tom and he was high up . . . about 30 yards up. He was facing us directly but, from every angle, his chest was protected by branches, so my only shot was straight-on. Val put the camera on him, then I looked to make sure

BEATING THE CALIFORNIA DEADLINE

it was recording (I've been on the wrong end of that surprise before), and then I drew, put the 30-yard pin in the middle of the cat's chest, and stuck him where I had aimed. He turned sideways, but didn't fall. Being primarily a rifle hunter, I wanted to end it quickly, so I put two more arrows in him and he crashed down 30 yards plus another 20 because the tree was on an embankment. The dogs were all over the dead cat, then the Robbs were all over the dogs, and when the barking and shouting finally subsided, we posed for pictures.

Mine was no doubt one of the last mountain lions legally brought into California before the infamous vote that banned both hunting them in California and bringing them in from outside California.

I thought about that when, two years later, a moving van full of my mounts left California for Texas. If I ever move back, I'll have to leave a full-mounted mountain lion at the border!

I could carry the cat for photos, but I couldn't take a step uphill. We drug it out using ropes, and it was a good thing that there were four of us for that chore.

NORTH AMERICA MIXED BAG

10

ELK AND PRONGHORN

Elk and pronghorn are a strange pairing which is, of course, why I did it. Or maybe it's because opposites attract. On the one hand are elk: big, multi-sub-specied, and very difficult to hunt. On the other hand are pronghorn: fast, only one category for the record book, and not all that difficult . . . usually.

I've been on two North American elk hunts, both for the Rocky Mountain subspecies (the others being the Roosevelt of Vancouver Island, coastal Washington-Oregon, northwestern California, and various transplants; the Tule of California; and the Manitoba of Alberta, Saskatchewan, and Manitoba). My first elk hunt was a classic. Jim Zumbo was the on-camera hunter and expert with me to follow (as the hunter . . . not the expert). We packed into the Selway Wilderness of Idaho ("the Amazon of the north") by horseback. No place could be more beautiful. Also, no place could be more difficult to hunt, physically and visually.

The views aren't very long in the Selway, but the canyons make up for it by being steep and deep. The horses would accompany us out of the canyon where we camped if we walked them up, and they were good for riding on the tops, but they had to be hitched to a tree whenever we climbed down. Most of our climbing was down, or so I thought the first time we heard a bugle from down a steep, dark canyon.

We were hunting during the rut so Jim could impart his wisdom on how to hunt elk during the bugling season. Our outfitter and guide, Ken Smith, led us down . . . down . . . and down some more because the bull we had heard was hanging out in the bottoms and couldn't be enticed our way, despite Jim's expert calling.

I had just ordered one of the new BetaCams with three computer chips, one for each primary color (still the industry standard, but inroads are now being made by digital camcorders), but delivery would not be made until after the hunt, so we were using a three-tube BetaCam which included the handicap of having a 35-pound recorder linked to the 20-pound camera by an umbilical cord. Rick Morgan carried the camera, I carried the recorder, Jim carried his favorite rifle (a battered, old 30.06 that answered to the name of "Bertha"), and Ken Smith ("the other Ken") carried our food.

The scenery was beautiful and the terrain was treacherous.

As darkness fell, it was obvious we were not going to see this bull. Now came axiom number one when hunting the Selway: "The more you hunt down, the more you have to climb up." When the hunt was called off for the day, we all groaned in unison knowing that we had a long, steep, slippery climb up in the dark. Jim asked the other Ken what he would do if a client just couldn't make the climb. Ken said something like, "I'd tell him to find a big, fallen

Jim Zumbo packing into the Selway Wilderness.

tree and to lay on top of it, stomach down, with an arm and leg hanging over each side, and when he'd ask me why, I'd say, 'So when you freeze to death in that position, you'll be easier to pack out when we can get a horse down here in the morning.'"

Jim shot an elk, but it was on the last day, so I didn't get a chance to hunt. But I did get to see Jim's kill shot and that made the trip worthwhile. He set up on a rocky outcropping and bugled. The 6 x 6 bull he was after responded by moving through some trees below Jim's position. You could only catch a glimpse of the elk here and there. Jim bugled again and the bull took a step into an opening and started to let out

SPORT HUNTING ON SIX CONTINENTS

Cameraman Rick Morgan sleeping on the job as we waited for the afternoon bugling to start.

another bugle. Jim's shot pole-axed him in mid-bugle.

I got another chance three years later on the 1,000,000-acre San Carlos Apache Reservation, which is located east of Phoenix and south of the White Mountain Apaches who are known (among other things, of course) for having the finest elk management program and genetics for Rocky Mountain elk. Their elk are big and expensive. The San Carlos Apaches wanted to showcase their hunting opportunities, so they hired me to produce a video documentary on hunting black bear and elk on their reservation.

The 6 x 6 bull that Jim Zumbo shot on-camera in mid-bugle.

ELK AND PRONGHORN

The black bear hunt went fairly smooth in September. Tribe member Whitman Cassadore guided me to a nice bear after we passed several smaller ones, and I shot it. My cameraman for the trip was on his first hunt and performed adequately, but shall go unnamed. You will find out why when you read more about him, believe it or not, in the chapter on Namibia. As I posed for pictures with the bear, Whitman said, "Thank you for hunting this bear." Then I went home for a month.

You might ask why, as long as I was on the reservation in late September, I didn't go elk hunting during the rut. Before my bear trip, I asked the San Carlos game department officials the same thing and they said something like, "Oh, no. Come out in September and hunt bear while they're feeding on the prickly pears, but you'll have to come back after the rut to hunt elk because only tribal members can hunt during the rut."

With San Carlos Apache guide Whitman Cassadore and my black bear shot on an early fall hunt on the reservation.

Post-rut hunting is, of course, a completely different story than hunting during the rut when the bulls whistle, "Here I am," and actually show themselves once in awhile when driven to distraction by beautiful cows or smelly competitors. After the rut, the older bulls are so tired from fighting and fornicating that all they want to do is lay down in the deepest, darkest hole they can find and recuperate. They don't want to see females, buddies, or a video director carrying a rifle.

Whitman was my guide again and we tried everything we could think of for several days, without success. He finally said, "There's a waterhole in the pine trees a few miles from here that's the primary source of water for several thousand acres, so let's go there and see if the elk will come to us." An hour later, I was lying on a dirt berm with a view of about 75% of the waterhole. Steve Anderson, a very good studio and outdoor cameraman, was behind me and to my left. The wind was good, except for animals approaching directly behind us, but they would see us before reaching the water anyway. And our outlines were broken by trees next to us and behind us.

Just to prove our set-up was good, a flock of wild turkeys trotted down to the water, drank, and departed without ever suspecting our presence. After several hours, the fun and anticipation had long worn off, so Whitman said, "You stay here. If I creep to the right about 50 yards, I'll be able to see the rest of the waterhole." Half an hour later, he crept back to my side as silently as an Indian and looked as excited as Whitman can look. He whispered, "Crawl to your right and shoot the big bull." Steve started rolling and I started crawling. To my amazement, a huge bull elk was at the water's edge, head down, antlers up, drinking like he was going to empty the pond.

I was shooting a Weatherby .416 using 400-grain softs. I tried to put the crosshairs just behind the bull's shoulder, but the berm was too high so I moved back to a tree, raised up, and re-sighted. The bull was still drinking away. He was as stationary as a statue, absolutely broadside, and the distance was 100 yards. This is the shot that you dream about; the one they show you in shot placement diagrams. I put the crosshairs just behind the left shoulder. *Blam!!* Dirt exploded behind the elk and he was instantly off and running in a loop, left, up, and then right, but always farther away. I quickly jacked another round in the chamber while thinking that I better connect with this second shot after blowing that easy first one. Fortunately, I made it, and the bull collapsed onto his side and skidded to a stop in a cloud of dirt. Spectacular!

When we inspected the entry hole made by my second shot, we also found the entry and exit holes for my first shot. Later, when viewing the videotape, we could see my first shot blow through the elk just behind both shoulders and kick up so much dirt that, combined with the bull sprinting instead of flinching, it seemed to indicate a big time miss.

The main beams of this bull exceeded 58 inches and the antler tines were very heavy. Unfortunately, nine of the 12 tines were broken, so he didn't score very well, but he sure looks good on the wall. Whitman figured he would have scored 380 B&C without the broken tines. I sure would have liked to have ground-checked the bull

Two views of the elk that came to water after another hard day of fighting.

At the San Carlos Recreation and Wildlife Headquarters with the antlers from my elk. L to R: guide Whitman Cassadore, Director Jim Higgs, and tribe attorney Steve Titla.

My dad, Giles Wilson, joined me on a pronghorn hunt in Wyoming.

that broke that rack. In 1997, a hunter shot an elk on the San Carlos Apache Reservation that broke the non-typical world record. He was probably the son of the bull that beat up mine!

The fastest land mammal in North America is the pronghorn antelope. The only horned animal in the world that sheds his horns is the pronghorn antelope. And the animal that's the most fun to hunt when you only have a weekend is the pronghorn antelope.

As with elk, I've hunted pronghorn twice. My first hunt was memorable because the irrepressible Lad Shunneson was my outfitter and guide for the first time, and especially because my dad joined me as an observer on his first ever big game hunt.

As he had been doing for years, Lad had a tented camp erected in the middle of herds of pronghorn in the sagebrush hills of Wyoming. Unlike most states, Wyoming has a pronghorn season that is weeks long instead of days, so Lad was able to conduct several five-day hunts with lots of hunters, action, and commotion. Mine was the last hunt of the season, snow was on the ground, and the bigger bucks had already departed the area in the beds of pick-up trucks.

We finally spotted a wide-horned buck in one herd and I told Lad that I would settle for him, so we made a stalk over a snow-covered hill, but the little herd figured out what we were up to and started trotting off. I sat down for a shot, but lost sight of the buck I wanted, so I had to stand back up and freehand one. To everyone's surprise, including my own since Lad had called the shot as being 250 yards, my bullet punctured the buck's lungs. He ran a short distance and toppled over. His horns had a nice spread, but were only 14 inches long and thin. I had him mounted anyway, just to remember hunting with my dad, who really got into the fun of spotting pronghorn at long distance which, of course, is the first key to success.

Years later I decided to upgrade my pronghorn on a hunt in New Mexico with Roger Haley and Sam Patello, who had taken a Boone & Crockett pronghorn off Pow Carter III's cattle ranch the year before. As often happens, I was the cameraman and the last to shoot, so time was running out and the pressure was on when my turn finally came.

Time runs out quickly in New Mexico where the seasons are generally just two to three days. The good news is that Pow only takes six bucks a year off his 35,000-acre spread and 16 inches is a reasonable expectation. When it was my turn, I said, "Let's go look for 'Number 11.'"

"Number 11" was the name given a buck that we saw the day before the season opened. His horns were long and straight and looked like his name. The good news was that Pow thought the horns on Number 11 would exceed 18 inches. The bad news was that Number 11 didn't have much in the prong department, but that's

With Pow Carter III as darkness fell on the last day of the season.

SPORT HUNTING ON SIX CONTINENTS

why he was called Number 11. Oh well, time was running out . . . the sun was on its downward path . . . and it was the last day of the season.

I never saw Number 11 again, but in the course of frantically traversing the ranch, trying to beat the clock, we spotted a great buck with real good hooks and pretty decent prongs. Pow let me out and kept driving. I started crawling on my hands and knees, which wasn't bad duty since I had brilliantly remembered to bring knee pads for such an occasion and just had to pull them up from my ankles and I was in business.

As the sun reached the horizon, and while the buck had eyes only for his harem, I crawled into shooting range and dropped him. He had 17-inch horns. Dinner was especially enjoyable that night.

Posing with my field-dressed buck the morning after it was shot.

NORTH AMERICA MIXED BAG

11

BOATING FOR BLACK BEARS

There are lots of ways to hunt black bears and lots of places to hunt them. I have used spot and stalk in Arizona and dogs in Washington. On that Arizona hunt, I hiked about 50 miles with Whitman Cassadore, my San Carlos Apache guide, before spotting a good bear and successfully stalking him. In Washington, the dogs tried their best, but while they were resting one day, I spotted a chocolate phase bear in a deep canyon and shot it. It was spot and no stalk. On that hunt, I was with Billie Ritchey, the last of the mountain men, and he decided to show the whole bear to some of his friends to make them jealous. To accomplish this feat, Billie and I hoisted the beautiful little bear 300 yards up a 30-degree slope that was full of deadfall. Never again will I help someone make someone else jealous with a whole bear (even a "beautiful little bear"). The bear skin would have been just fine by itself, but it did serve as a nice package to carry out the bear meat. My son, Ryan, who was nine at the time, later told me that our bear meat dinner "wasn't as bad as the mountain lion meat Billie pulled out of his freezer for last night's dinner."

The point is that I like to experience different types of hunts if I'm doubling or tripling on the same species. So, for black bear, bait hunting or boat hunting were remaining possibilities. For bait hunting, I would probably pick eastern Canada and sit in a tree every afternoon over some bait that would clear the sinuses of a T-Rex and hope for a bear to end my agony and his life simultaneously. Or I could pick

Chocolate phase black bear that I shot in Washington with Billie Ritchey (who took this photo). Lad and I are left and right of a tired nine-year-old Ryan. Famous bear hunter Tommy Spears is behind Ryan.

Alaska, live on a 50-foot fishing boat, eat freshly caught crab, shrimp, halibut, and salmon, and cruise the coastline looking for bears. Consequently, I found myself in Wrangell, Alaska in May.

Wrangell is a fishing and logging town of about 2,500 friendly people located north of Ketchikan and south of Juneau along the panhandle of southeastern Alaska, just west of British Columbia. It is an island along the "inside passage" shipping route from Seattle and Vancouver north, and may be the most historic community in Alaska due to its rich Tlingit Indian heritage and its having been ruled under three flags: Russian, British, and American. The town was named after Russian governor Baron Ferdinand Petrovich von Wrangel and received its extra "l" when the postal service added it about the time of Wrangell's incorporation in 1903.

BOATING FOR BLACK BEARS

Black bear is one of the species that can be hunted without a registered guide in Alaska as long as no one provides guide services like assisting in the stalk or skinning the trophy. The boat captains are designated as "transporters." They can transport you to bear country, provide the skiffs so you can get to shore, and help you catch fish, but they can't help with the hunting except to keep you close to bear habitat as much as possible.

Beautiful Wrangell Harbor on the Inside Passage.

Lad Shunneson arranged the hunt and participated as a hunter but not as a guide. He arranges four consecutive hunts for black bear each spring, two spot-and-stalk hunts by foot in British Columbia, followed by two spot-and-stalk hunts by boat in Alaska.

My Alaska Airlines flight arrived in Wrangell the day before the five-day hunt, which gave me time to buy licenses and participate in two sightseeing spectacles: a jet boat ride up the Stikine River with Jim Leslie of Alaska Waters, and a "flightseeing" tour of the Stikine Icefields with Tyler Robinson of Sunrise Aviation. Both are "must do's" if you have the time.

Lad's transporters were Michael Lockabey captaining the *Chelsea L* (carrying Johnny Burke and Dane Heule and his son, Tim, as hunters, Steve McManus as an observer, and Lad's wife, Lenka, as cook) and Harold Bailey skippering the *Miss Kristie* (carrying myself and Paul Neuharth, Jr. as hunters and Paul's father, Dr. Paul Neuharth, Sr., as an observer). I wouldn't want to go with Harold again because his wife baked 48 huge oatmeal and raisin cookies for our trip. After subtracting how many cookies everyone else ate, it was determined that I was responsible for 43. I'm currently on a diet. Come

Our floating home for one week... small, warm, dry, and with great seafood.

SPORT HUNTING ON SIX CONTINENTS

to think of it, I don't recommend Mike, either, unless you can't stand poached halibut, boiled crab, and sautéed shrimp.

We all got to know each other pretty well because the two boats rafted together most nights for dinner so we could lie about the size of our fish and bears. Also, when you eat, sleep, fish, and glass for bears in an area the size of your kitchen back home, you get to know people in a hurry.

"There's a bear" are the magic words everyone works to hear or say. After you get jumped on for uttering those very words about black rocks and the blackened ends of tree trunks, you tend to wait for the objects to move about 20 feet before saying, "There's a bear."

In the spring, the bears come out of hibernation looking to get their digestive systems functioning again. Grass is generally their first food, although they search the shoreline during receding tides looking for whatever tidbits they can find. So the best chance of seeing bears is on the grassy areas along shorelines and the grassy flats that are often at the end of inlets. Also, spring hunts provide a lot more daylight than fall hunts, so we could literally hunt from 4:00 AM to 10:00 PM, but we generally slept in until 6:00 AM (5:30 AM if you wanted to be the first one into the cookies).

"There's a bear," Harold said while flipping sourdough pancakes with his right hand and steering with his left. We were a quarter mile from the shoreline and a half mile from the bear grazing at the end of a narrow, rocky inlet. Harold cruised *Miss Kristie* past the inlet without changing speed so the sound of the motor wouldn't change. Then Paul and his dad took off for the shoreline in a 16-foot skiff with me in the middle to video the stalk for Sportsmen on Film. Paul, Sr. motored the skiff to the rocky shoreline where Paul, Jr. and I jumped out. We found there was no way to make a stalk because the inlet formed a "V" of rocks with the bear on a small, grassy flat at the point of the "V." The surrounding forest was a jungle and, to add to the poignancy of the moment, the bear decided to leave. Paul dropped prone on the sharp and slippery rocks and urgently asked, "How far?" as he jacked a round into his .300. With the bear three steps from the jungle, I didn't have a lot of time to visualize football fields, so I blurted out, "200." Paul shot and the bear disappeared into the jungle. It looked like the shot hit low and, after inspection by skiff and on foot, we determined that the bullet hit a rock just below the bear's chest. We also determined that the shot was 350 yards. "Yards?" I said. "I was talking about meters." That way I was only 120 meters off instead of 150 yards.

Two days later, Paul made a long stalk along a proper shoreline and got within 90 yards of a big bear that he hammered while it was moving behind a log toward the forest. The bear wheeled toward the water and then back to the forest as Paul missed with his second shot and hit with his third before the bear disappeared into the jungle. I got it all on video except for the brown bear that almost walked over Paul while we were trailing the black bear. Paul moved out of the jungle in a hurry and called for me to do the same. I quickly retreated even though I was armed with

BOATING FOR BLACK BEARS

a video camera to record the brown bear eating me while I played dead. The mind does wander sometimes.

Paul located his black bear, quite dead, but he also saw the brown bear again and it was very much alive, so he decided to wait for high tide to retrieve his black bear by boat instead of on foot. This tactic allowed five of us (four to load the bear and one to thwart the brown bear) to motor within 20 feet of his black bear in the skiff. Fortunately, the black bear had not been dined upon during the intervening five hours.

Meanwhile, we received good news from the *Chelsea L* that 14-year-old Tim Heule had scored on a six-footer and Johnny Burke had returned tired and happy with a 6 1/2-footer. Their success allowed me to switch boats in order to video Dane's hunt which would start the next day.

Lad had told us that prime time for hunting was 6:30 PM to 9:30 PM and "magic hour" was 7:30 PM to 8:30 PM. We certainly saw the most bears during those hours (especially if it was sunny... which was rare), but that didn't mean that you quit

L to R: Dane Huele, me, and Lad with Dane's huge spring black bear.

looking the rest of the time. So, at 11:00 AM, after a black rock had moved, Dane said, "There's a bear." I already had my binoculars on the moving rock, but I hadn't said anything because, at the time, my mouth was full with a cookie.

Steve McManus, who had shot a monster black bear the week before in British Columbia, said, "That's a big bear." Steve doesn't exaggerate and that made us nervous because we didn't want this one to get away. I had already been on a failed stalk when the swirling winds had notified the object of our desire that something smelled bad on the shoreline and it wasn't a dead fish.

The big bear was eating grass like it was dessert on a small, grassy area by some deadfall. The wind was blowing out from the shoreline so we went straight to shore, landing about 500 yards from the bear. Then Dane worked his way along the edge of the forest and around a point as we tried to get to a big, fallen tree that, from the *Chelsea L,* looked like it would be a great place to shoot from. We closed to 50 yards, but still couldn't see the bear so we decided to wait, which was the right decision because the bear suddenly raised his head just on the other side of that fallen tree. We didn't move, the wind held, and the bear decided to move slowly off. Dane quickly got to his feet and fired. Even quicker, the bear ran into the forest. I never thought we would see it again because that forest was all trees and moss and half the trees were decaying on the ground. Bears usually don't leave much of a blood trail and they don't leave much in the way of tracks on moss, either. As we stepped into the primordial jungle, the bear was right there . . . waiting for us . . . stone dead. And he was a brute: an honest 7 $\frac{1}{2}$-footer with a head bigger than a basketball.

We waved everyone to shore to see the bear and photograph it before we took off its clothes. At the end of the trip, back in Wrangell, the skull was measured at over 20 inches when the skin and skull were officially sealed. Until then, we all thought that the length plus width of the skull would exceed the Boone & Crockett minimum of 21 inches. I can only imagine how big a black bear has to get to make B&C. This one probably weighed 450 pounds on his way to 700 in the fall. Of course, the skull easily made the Safari Club International minimum of 18 inches.

Lad, standing, as we glass the shoreline from a skiff.

Finally, it was my turn to hunt, with Lad taking over videotaping duties, but it was not to be. We spotted a bear that we determined to be too small by the size of its head (big compared to its body) and the amount of daylight between

BOATING FOR BLACK BEARS

ground and stomach (too much) and the way he walked (not enough effort; not enough shoulder movement). We did spot an eight-footer, but it was a brown bear that gave us a good video show by jumping in the water in front of our skiff and then quickly swimming back to shore when he saw us. Then he jumped in the water again, behind us this time, and swam 400 yards to another shore; an island-hopping bear breathing like a locomotive.

The island-hopping brown bear. When he first saw our skiff, I thought I heard him say, "Uh oh!"

Lad organizes his hunts for five hunting days for four hunters and usually has the transporters motor back to Wrangell the fifth afternoon but, with me being an extra hunter, and without a bear, we hunted all afternoon the last day before arriving in Wrangell close to midnight. The next day, the successful hunters had their bears sealed and flew out with big smiles. I was already scheduled to fly out the following day so I would have time to video the sights in Wrangell, which I did in the morning so Lad and I could give it one last try during prime time that evening.

Billie Ritchey had arrived a day early to go out on the next hunt so he was able to accompany us as we took the skiff about 10 miles around to the back of Wrangell Island. We stayed about a half mile offshore to minimize engine noise as we cruised in the light rain. "There's a bear," I found myself saying. It was true . . . it was black . . . and it was big. The bear was searching for feed but not finding much, so it was continually moving to our right. The wind was swirling and we couldn't get it perfect so we went straight to the shore, just 400 yards from the bear's backside. Lad and I scrambled to shore while Billie stayed with the skiff. We were now 500 yards away as the bear continued to move.

I raced to the treeline and then toward the bear as Lad rolled tape. At 250 yards, I flopped down but the bear moved between several fallen trees so I couldn't see him, and he kept moving away with only 15 yards to the forest on the left and 30 yards to the water on the right. I jumped up, scrambled over the slippery rocks, down a drainage, up the other side, and dropped to prone again with the distance back down to 250 yards. It was overcast with intermittent rain. I looked through my binoculars and found the bear as it reappeared from behind a log. Then I put my crosshairs on him and followed the moving bear out to 300 yards. When he turned right, I sent a 180-grain bullet on its way for a good chest shot. I had already decided to empty my rifle because the forest was so close and bears over-react when hit, even if the hit is only

My black bear, shot on Wrangell Island.

superficial. That over-reaction sometimes lulls the hunter into thinking he made a one-shot kill when, in fact, he may have only hit a paw. Billie later said he could not hear my three shots, but he saw each bullet hit the chest and turn the bear.

Lad got it all on tape and then we waved Billie to shore so he could video Lad and me walking up to the bear. He was a 6 $^1/_2$-footer with an 18 $^9/_{16}$-inch skull (I'm talking about the bear) . . . about average for this hunt . . . but the hunt, itself, is way above average!

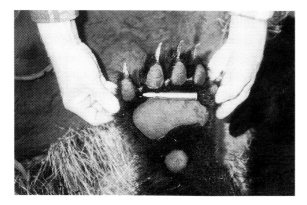 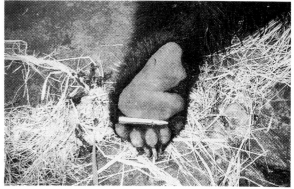

Front paw, left. Back paw, right. As different as hands and feet.

12

TATANKA

Their enemy, the Chippewa, called them "Nadouessioux" which means "little snakes." Today, the people of The Great Sioux Nation are also called Dakota, Lakota, and Nakota according to their language group. They were at the height of their power in 1803 when the United States bought present-day South Dakota from France as part of the Louisiana Purchase.

The Dakota Territory, encompassing present-day North and South Dakota and much of Wyoming and Montana, was organized in 1861. Seven years later, the U.S. signed the Fort Laramie Treaty creating The Great Sioux Reservation, which reached from the Missouri River on the east to the Wyoming-Dakota border on the west. In spite of the Treaty, the U.S. Army sent a flamboyant lieutenant colonel, a former Civil War general, to explore the Black Hills for a possible fort location and to determine if rumors of gold were true. His name was George Armstrong Custer and his expedition discovered gold in 1874. The city of Custer was informally organized the following year next to the first discovery, despite the Army's efforts to keep trespassers out of the Black Hills. By the spring of 1876, the rush of miners swelled the population of Custer to 10,000, but just a few weeks later, when gold was discovered in the northern Black Hills, the population plummeted to 14 (yes, 14, and that must have adversely affected the local economy!).

The United States ordered all Indians living outside the Sioux Reservation to return by the end of 1876. Among those who refused were groups led by Crazy Horse and Sitting Bull. When Custer marched against them in Montana on June 25, 1876, the Sioux killed him and his entire command of over 200 men.

From the time of the Louisiana Purchase to the achievement of statehood by South Dakota in 1889, bison numbers plunged from an estimated 60,000,000 to only a relatively few survivors. This left the Plains Indians without a primary food source and the prairie without its most influential animal. Bison are the largest land animal in North America. Big bulls can stand six feet at the shoulder and weigh 2,000 pounds. The Lakota call them "tatanka," which means "big or large thing."

In January 1998, I arrived in Custer, South Dakota to hunt a bison at Custer State Park after having been drawn for one of the nine tags. The Park was established July 1, 1919. At 73,000 acres, it is the sixth largest state park in the United States and is home to almost 1,500 bison plus many other species. The original stocking of only a few bison from the Scotty Phillips herd helped secure the comeback of the plains bison from near extinction to an estimated present population of 300,000.

Custer State Park is one of very few places from which a successfully hunted bison can be entered into the Boone & Crockett Record Book. I was the ninth and last hunter of the season. My goal was to hunt an old bull that would simultaneously have a big mop of hair on his head and horns large enough to qualify for both B&C and SCI. There to help me were J.D. Andrews and Vern Ekstrom.

J.D. is, among other things, an ex-policeman turned African professional hunter, a Custer taxidermist, and a whitetail fanatic. He would shortly add being a cameraman for Sportsmen on Film to his credits. I arrived three days prior to my hunt so J.D. could help me scout Custer State Park and also show me some of the sights for which the Black Hills are famous.

Vern Ekstrom is the Herd Manager at Custer State Park. Among many other duties, he guides all hunters drawn to hunt bison. I would meet him on the first morning of my hunt.

Prior to my hunt, J.D. helped me find and videotape bison, elk, pronghorn, bighorn sheep, and the occasional whitetail and mule deer. He also showed me Mount Rushmore, the Crazy Horse Memorial, and the inside of the Gold Pan Saloon and the Bavarian Inn Lounge where various liquid temptations were served.

At 6:30 AM on January 5, the day after my 55th birthday, J.D. picked me up at the Bavarian Inn (at my motel room . . . I wasn't still in the bar!) and drove me to Park Headquarters where we loaded camera gear, hunting gear, and ourselves into Vern's truck for a day of learning more about tatanka. The first Monday in October, the female and young bison are rounded up for vaccination, identification, and so excess animals can be selected for auction, since over 500 calves are generally born April to June each year. Mature bulls of four years or older are not sought for the round-up, and the older bulls are strictly avoided because they will tear up the pens and often kill other bison.

Some 80 to 90 mature bulls are believed to reside in the Park. Nine to 10 are usually hunted each year and another three to four die when fighting during the July breeding season. In order to maximize genetic traits, only nine-year-olds or older may be hunted. The system is working because the bison from Custer State Park are unsurpassed in body weight and magnificence of appearance.

How do you tell age? One method is by horn size. The older bulls, especially the aggressive breeders, rub their tips blunt so that their horns appear "fatter" throughout their length. Another method is by body size and coloration. But Vern has a third method. At their first round-up, the bulls are branded with a number on their right hip. If he could read an "8," for example, through all the winter hair, we were looking at a 9 1/2-year-old born in 1988.

Since Custer State Park is 114 square miles and varies from tree-covered mountains to grassland flats, a lot of country has to be covered to look over the bull population. The cows, calves, and young bulls are generally in easy-to-find herds, but the older bulls are usually off by themselves or in small bachelor groups, and they can be anywhere. So the routine was to drive and hike, drive and hike. Most of the driving was four-wheel-drive on tracks that are off-limits to the public, and the hiking was to inspect meadow after meadow not accessible by truck.

L to R: Washington, Jefferson, Roosevelt, Lincoln, and Wilson at Mt. Rushmore.

The Crazy Horse Memorial, only partially completed after 50 years. All four presidents' heads at Mt. Rushmore could fit in the head of Crazy Horse... and he's on a horse!

Occasionally we would stumble onto a few bewildered bulls who would look at us as if to say, "What are you doing here?" My rifle, a Sako .375 H&H Magnum shooting 300-grain Federal Nosler partition bullets, was never uncased that first day for two reasons. First, Vern believed there were about 10 legally shootable bulls and I wanted to see as many as possible before stalking one. Second, I wanted to sell the meat since I didn't have room in my freezer back in Texas for 800 pounds of steaks and burgers. To accomplish the sale, I had to select one or more candidate bulls, call

SPORT HUNTING ON SIX CONTINENTS

A breeding-age bull not yet huntable at Custer State Park. Note the pointed horn tips.

The Wrangler Restaurant in Custer, South Dakota has a full-mount buffalo on the roof. J.D. and I selected the inside dining option.

the State Meat Inspector, and then try to re-find those bulls and have him look at them from a distance in order to ascertain any health problems. The final challenge would be to stalk close enough to be able to place a shot 4½ inches behind the bottom of either horn on a broadside animal in order to drop it in its tracks and save all the meat for mercenary purposes.

During day one, we saw a good nine-year-old, a 10-year-old that was a little thinner-horned, and another nine that looked good until he turned his head and revealed a broken horn. We also saw a terrific seven-year-old with horns estimated at a whopping 24 inches by Vern, but two years away from being huntable. This bull epitomized the difference between the SCI and B&C scoring methods. SCI measures only the length and base of each horn so that this seven-year-old would be close to number one in their record book. B&C measures length and four circumferences on each horn (base and at ¼, ½, and ¾ of the length of the longest horn). Since the seven-year-old was still relatively thin at the quarters, Vern thought it would only make the bottom of B&C (115 inches being the minimum) even though it would make the top of SCI.

On day two, I was hoping to see some different legal bulls

and possibly get a look at an 11-year-old that had not been seen since the first November hunts. After lots of driving and hiking, Vern advised, "Let's go look at the herds. Maybe we can find an old one with the females."

The herds were easy to find feeding on the grassy hills, so we started driving through them. Occasionally we would stop and glass a big bull, but the pointed tips and thinner horns would usually betray them as five- or six-year-olds. After a couple hours, Vern exclaimed, "I'll be darned. I can see a cow that must be in heat and a big bull with her so we better check him out."

"If the breeding season is July, how can a female be in heat in January?" I asked.

"She may have aborted her calf and come around again," Vern explained. "You hear that bull vocalizing and showing his tongue? He won't let any other bulls get close to her. And look at those horns; all rubbed down, heavy to the tips. He's an old one."

Just then we got a call from Park Headquarters. The Meat Inspector, Dr. Peterson, was at the Park now and would not be available for inspection tomorrow. He would give us 24 hours to deliver any bull to the processing plant that he approved today.

First we relocated "The Breeder," who was judged medically sound despite being crazy for that cow, who must have had a great personality because she wasn't much to look at. Then we tried to find some other nine-year-olds and that elusive 11-year-old. With time running out, we came across five bachelors feeding at the edge of a long, narrow meadow.

J.D. said, "The second from the left is a good one; better than The Breeder." Then the one he picked started running and the rest followed.

"He's an old bull and solid B&C," Vern said with a smile.

Doc added, "I got a good look through my binoculars before they disappeared and he's got my blessing health-wise."

"I liked him," I said to everyone. "His horns looked long and fat and did you see the size of that mop? I would be very happy to get a shot at him, but why don't we spend the last hour of light looking for the 11-year-old?"

"By noon tomorrow," Vern replied, "it will be too late to shoot a bull and deliver it in time for processing. And at dusk tomorrow, your hunt is over regardless. So if you want 'The Runner,' we better put him to bed."

"Put him to bed" meant following tracks until finding the five bulls, waiting out of sight and downwind until they laid down, and then backing off. There was just enough daylight and patches of snow that J.D. and Vern were able to piece together the route. I felt like Capstick in Africa with his trusty trackers, Silent and Invisible. And we put those bulls to bed.

Early the third and last day, we returned to where we had last seen the bulls and then we started on their trail. It felt good to have my rifle with me for the first time. "They did spend the night here, but moved out earlier this morning," J.D. determined.

"There's only one thing to do and that's stay on their trail," Vern advised. So we started out . . . J.D., camera in hand, relying on his South African Professional Hunters School experience, pointing when he found sign; and Vern finding a track here, an overturned rock there, a piece of snow flung off a hoof, and the other signs he has learned over six years and 60 hunts for dozens of record-book bison.

At the second meadow up, we glimpsed the bulls, and The Runner ran while we tried to make sure he was the one . . . not easy with similar-sized animals moving at a variety of angles. An hour later, Vern said, "If we don't kill this one in an hour, we better find The Breeder if you want to make the delivery deadline to the processor."

We had already discussed the potential scores of both approved bulls and figured that The Breeder might make 115 B&C, but The Runner would score three to five points higher by both scoring systems. I finally said, "Let The Breeder do what he does best. Let's stay on the trail of The Runner until dark." Then I stuck my chin up and muttered, "On Silent. On Invisible."

"What?" Vern asked.

"Nothing. Nothing. Let's go," I said. J.D. smiled. He had read Peter Hathaway Capstick's books also.

Ten hills, five meadows, and two miles later, Silent and Invisible had solved every puzzle. Then J.D. pointed and started rolling videotape. Behind a dozen trees were three black outlines; then another and another. The bachelor bulls were standing, looking left and right, trying to detect us. I quietly chambered a round, placed my rifle on a branch of the closest tree, and cranked my scope up from $1\frac{1}{2}$ to six power in preparation for a possible 100- to 125-yard shot, depending on which bull was The Runner.

Vern finally whispered, "He's the closest one on the left."

I moved my scope left and found the old boy just as he swapped ends from right profile to left, which placed his head behind a tree and blocked the spine shot I needed to make in order to save 100 pounds of meat. "I'm going for a lung

L to R: J.D. Andrews, Vern Ekstrom, and me with my $9\frac{1}{2}$-year-old bull.

TATANKA

shot," I whispered just as the bull took one step forward, revealing his head. "What the heck," I thought to myself. "A hundred bucks worth of meat is a hundred bucks," so I moved the crosshairs to behind the bull's left ear, squeezed off, and the huge beast crashed to the ground.

As we walked up, I jacked another round into the chamber. The bull kept getting bigger as we approached . . . bigger body and bigger horns. I shook Vern's hand and smiled at the camera just as the bull gave three quick kicks causing me to backup and push the safety off my .375.

"They can kick even after they're dead," Vern said.

I touched the bull's right eye with my rifle barrel. Not a blink.

We waited a couple more minutes and then I cleared my rifle and posed for photos. He scored over the B&C minimum and well up in the SCI book. To make it even better, we just made the processing deadline.

We were all in a pretty good mood on the way back to Park Headquarters, so Vern told the story about the North Dakota farmer whose farm was surveyed by the government. "Your farmhouse is actually in South Dakota," the surveyor informed the farmer. "Thank heavens," said the farmer. "I don't think I could have stood another North Dakota winter!"

The older bull bison at Custer State Park are huge. . . pushing 2,000 pounds and yielding over 1,100 pounds of meat.

95

OOMINGMAK

In 1610, Henry Hudson was employed by England to find the Northwest Passage for the purpose of a shorter trade route to the Orient. He sailed into Hudson Bay and was frozen in. A mutiny followed in 1611, resulting in Henry and eight crew members being cast adrift. They were never seen again.

In 1845, England assembled a massive expedition, commanded by Sir John Franklin, to find the Northwest Passage. They sailed into what is now known as Franklin Strait, became ice bound for two winters, abandoned their ships in 1848, and marched south. The entire crew of 129 perished.

A century and a half later, Bill Tait of Adventure Northwest sent Lad Shunneson and Ken Wilson onto King William Island where many believe the bulk of the Franklin Expedition died. Sailing was out of the question at the time (April Fool's Day) because the ice was six feet thick, so we boarded a First Air flight in Yellowknife and flew northeast to Gjoa Haven, still in the Northwest Territories at the time, but to become the new province of Nunavut exactly one year hence.

Gjoa Haven is an Inuit hamlet of about 1,000 people located on the southeast side of King William Island. It was the key to unlocking the Northwest Passage when Norwegian explorer Roald Amundsen discovered "the finest little harbor in the world." It became known as Gjoa Haven in honor of Amundsen's 72-foot sailing ship, *Gjoa*.

After two winters in Gjoa Haven, Amundsen departed in August 1905 and, thanks to the small size of his ship and a little 13-HP motor to assist maneuvering, he passed through the straits south of Victoria and Banks Islands, circumnavigated

OOMINGMAK

Alaska, and arrived in San Francisco in October 1906.

Lad and I spent our first night in Gjoa Haven at the small but warm Amundsen Hotel. The next day we met our guides, Kanayok "Sam" Takkiruq and Nuliayuk "Jack" Ameralik, climbed into our respective kamotiks, and slid out of town behind Sam and Jack's snowmobiles. We were in pursuit of Oomingmak, "the bearded one."

Safari Club International recognizes two species of muskox: the Greenland variety of the arctic islands and the slightly larger (on average) barren ground muskox of the mainland. From Gjoa Haven, we headed south across the frozen Rasmussen Sea to hunt on the mainland. Sam and Jack were responsible for transporting us to the muskox herds and setting up and tearing down camp each day. Lad and I were responsible for staying alive long enough to shoot one muskox each. It was not an easy task.

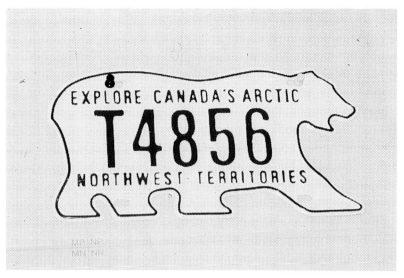

The distinctive vehicle license plate of the Northwest Territories.

In early April, the temperatures were still 20° to 40° below Celsius. At 40° below, Celsius and Fahrenheit are the same. Add in wind-chill and a kamotik being drug at 15 MPH, and you have a situation where exposed skin, anywhere, for more than a few seconds, is painful.

Evacuating liquids and solids must be accomplished quickly and efficiently. You might even practice protocol in your living room before your trip. Keep your face mask on and raise your goggles to your forehead. Remove your outer and inner gloves, unzip your parka, unzip your bib pants, unbutton your down outer long underwear, pull down your polypropylene inner long underwear, etc., etc., but don't leave those hands exposed for more than 15 seconds. The positions that you

The Amundsen Hotel in Gjoa Haven. Snowmobiles are the primary means of transportation most of the year.

97

Full traveling regalia. No exposed skin is the rule.

I'm with Nuliayuk Ameralik who is standing in front of the dreaded plywood box on the kamotik.

will find yourself in, especially if you have bad knees, are truly comical. Lad did come up with an important tip for the standing up procedure: "When your hands are numb, make sure, visually, that you have pulled out what you have intended and not just your shirttail!"

Most hunters spend 98% of their hunt in both the communal tent and their respective kamotiks. A tent, of course, is that canvas room that reduces temperatures from 40° below to 20° below for the purposes of eating and sleeping. A kamotik is a device created by the Inuit to torture the tourist hunter. Basically, it is a plywood box set on top of a pair of wooden runners with platforms fore and aft for supplies. The plywood box is then filled with additional supplies and one hunter.

To prepare for your muskox hunt, sit in a plywood box in the freezer at your local butcher shop with a fan blowing in your face and a crew lifting and dropping your box 12 inches to 18 inches every five to 10 seconds for 12 hours each day. Then get out of the box, crawl into a canvas tent, eat, and go to sleep. Take care of your "business" before dozing off because you don't want to put on cold boots and cold gloves and a cold parka (that's all, because you'll be wearing everything else while in your sleeping bag) to stumble out in the middle of the night.

Our goal on day one was to reach a plywood fishing shack to spend the night. We didn't make it. A rope broke on Lad's kamotik and the right side wooden runner collapsed. It was near dark and our guides were as tired as we were, so they put up the tent 12 miles short of our goal.

The next morning, Jack relashed the right runner and we were off to the south again. The runners are lashed to the cross supports with rope so the kamotik can undulate over the rough snow and ice. If nailed, screwed, or bolted, it would break apart.

The temperature dropped to minus 40° C and F each night.

On the afternoon of the second day, Sam and Jack came to a stop, as they did every hour or two, to let Lad and I out of our boxes for a few minutes. This time Sam said, "Muskox" and he pointed to some brown dots to my right. Then he motioned Lad and me to a little rise and pointed to a closer herd on our left.

Both herds looked like they had cows, calves, and bulls. We decided on the closest group of about 20 Oomingmaks and the chase was on. To my surprise, muskox can run a long distance and this herd showed no intention of circling as I had expected. Instead, they split, one or two at a time, until completely scattered, but we got a good look at the single mature bull through our binoculars and decided to pass. Its horn bosses had over an inch of separation and, from the side, didn't appear wide enough, but its horns did sweep down, out, and up . . . a definite trophy, but not a definite Boone & Crockett animal.

After a brief conference, we traveled about three miles and closed in on the second herd by pretending to be a pack of wolves instead of two guys in plywood boxes being pulled by snowmobiles. This herd didn't

Packing up camp in the morning before heading south again.

99

circle either. It had two mature bulls but neither were quite as good as the one we had already passed, so we headed south again and then westerly onto the Queen Maud Gulf where we camped just east of the McNaughton River.

On the third day out, we traveled to the west side of the McNaughton, but ran into near-white-out conditions and were forced to set up camp in the middle of the afternoon. The good news was we were finally where we wanted to be . . . within striking distance of the middle of the Queen Maud Gulf, possibly the most lightly hunted of all of Canada's prolific muskox habitat.

Day four dawned clear and beautiful with a blue sky, bright sun, and the usual 40° below warming to a sultry 30° below. We broke camp and traveled westerly across McNaughton Lake and made a stop. Sam walked back as I was climbing out for my hourly exercise. He said, "Muskox." I asked, "Where?" He pointed to some brown dots to the south.

Sam and Jack weren't excitable and they weren't very talkative, but they were insightful. The previous night, with all of us crammed in our tent, I turned on the video camera and asked Jack what he thought of his hunter, Lad. Jack responded,

With Sam Takkiruq and my barren ground muskox.

"He's all right, but he talks too much." Now, that's insightful.

Sam handed back my binoculars and said, "All bulls." So we started after them. Two or three looked good in this herd of bachelors, still friendly prior to the midsummer rut. Again, they would not circle in the classic defense posture, so when a good bull stopped to face us, I climbed out to approach with my bow, but he ran off. This happened time after time until we were both exhausted. Finally, I let fly four straight arrows over his back. Later I found that my sights had jarred loose and were way off.

For arrow number five, I aimed at his right front foot and lodged the broadhead in a rib! I don't know what happened with my sixth and last arrow, but I again aimed at the front foot but struck the right jaw, so I immediately grabbed Lad's .45-70 rifle and dropped the bull. It had been a poor showing and I announced that it was my last bowhunt. Bowhunters are wonderful folks, but Sam Takkiruq now has my bow and, as of 1998, I'm strictly a rifle hunter.

My bull made Boone & Crockett despite Pope & Young turning in their graves. His twin was running away so we decided to delay the skinning chores and find it. After a wild ride, we found it by itself. Lad made a long walk in the open, because it's all open up there, and impulsively decided to forego a 100-yard rifle shot or even a 50-yarder. He closed to 30 and his bull charged. Lad stood his ground and fired, but all we heard was a loud click. I was videotaping right behind him and this was not good news. Lad still held his ground, worked the lever action, and clicked again. In unison, Jack, Lad, and I started running. The snowmobiles and kamotiks were a long way off, but Jack and I knew we didn't have to outrun the muskox; we only had to outrun Lad!

Luckily the bull stopped his charge, Lad got the snow out of the rifle's action, and he killed the muskox. The excitement and kidding quickly turned to work. We had two muskox to skin, quarter, and pack and we had a day-and-a-half of bouncing back to Gjoa Haven. With Oomingmak, it's not the shooting that's the challenge (usually); it's the adventure of hunting with the Inuits on the frozen surface north of the Arctic Circle.

With Lad and his muskox . . . the one that almost got him.

THE SUPER SLAM

As I was duck-walking through the grass, I knew we must be getting very close to the big corsicans because Thompson signaled for me to get even lower and crawl to the oak tree in front of us. I held my rifle in my right hand and crawled to the tree that would break up my outline in case the sheep looked toward us. Then I raised to the kneeling position and placed the fore-end of the rifle stock in my left hand as I held onto the left side of the tree.

At first I could see only two sets of curling horns but, as I raised into position, the bodies of both sheep came into view. I eased the safety off and rested the crosshairs on the shoulder of the biggest ram, but then I took my eyes off the shoulder and looked at the horns to make absolutely certain that I was aiming at the largest corsican. Since Thompson had earlier estimated the horns at 40 inches, you would think that I wouldn't have any trouble picking out the biggest ram. But the one he was with had to go 37 inches.

My indecision didn't matter because the sheep were standing next to each other even when they occasionally changed positions, so I had no chance for a clear shot until they separated. As they playfully horned each other and grazed upwind, unaware of our presence, I couldn't help but reflect on my previous hunts in pursuit of the Super Slam of Exotics.

In 1985, I had produced, through Sportsmen on Film, a video on pronghorn hunting and another on mule deer hunting with Colorado outfitter and guide, Lad Shunneson. After those hunts, Lad suggested that I consider producing videos on hunting the various exotic animals. The idea intrigued me, and after considerable

THE SUPER SLAM

research, I decided to make two videos on hunting the ten animals of the Super Slam (a term coined by Thompson Temple for the Records of Exotics Record Book, meaning the successful hunting of axis deer, fallow deer, sika deer, red stag, corsican sheep, mouflon sheep, aoudad, ibex, blackbuck antelope, and Catalina goat).

I booked my first hunt in January 1986 with Lad as my guide. He selected a ranch near Waco, Texas because of the wide variety of exotics available. We arrived with Sportsmen on Film's full-time cameraman, Rick Morgan, on a very cold day in January and spent two days doing nothing but scouting and observing the various animals. Most of the game seemed used to vehicles but, except for moving from one observation point to another by vehicle, all of our hunting was on foot and the animals were quite wild wherever they detected us on foot.

On the third day, while I was trying to decide whether to make a stalk on a big spotted fallow or a big chocolate fallow, we located a white fallow with exceptionally long tines and wide palms. After a careful stalk down a ravine and a 100-yard shot from the prone position, I had my first exotic or introduced or non-indigenous trophy. In the case of fallow, they had been introduced to the United States over 200 years ago by none other than George Washington.

The next day, we frustrated ourselves trying to find a group of five aoudad rams that we had seen earlier and thought would have a chance of equaling or exceeding 30 inches each. While looking for that group late in the afternoon, we saw a single old ram climb up from a deep canyon and start to feed on some grass and cactus near the edge. When he finally raised his head, Lad and I both knew that he was a big one because his horns went out and then down below his jaw and then back in, almost to his neck.

An aoudad is biologically intermediate between a sheep and a goat. They are also known as Barbary sheep, but are native to many places in northern Africa besides the Barbary Coast. Now, thanks to the exotic ranching industry, there are many more aoudad in Texas than exist in Africa.

All of the aoudads had been so skittish that I was inclined to try a long shot, but I couldn't because of the number of trees between the ram and me. So every time he put his head down, Lad and I walked forward to the next tree until I worked my way

I wore a down jacket and Lad was in shirtsleeves for this photo with my white fallow.

The temperature warmed up for my aoudad, shot in the middle of the afternoon in January.

to a clear shot at 100 yards. When I got into shooting position, the ram was facing me with his head up, so I waited, motionless, until he went back to feeding. Then I drilled him where his neck met his back and he dropped in his tracks. He was a beauty with horns that averaged 33 inches.

The biggest trophy on the ranch was one of the red stags. We had seen him once while we were hunting fallow and, at first, thought he was a lot smaller than he really was. His horns were so heavy that it made the tines and main beams look deceptively small. We knew he was a natural 7 x 7 with a kicker on the left antler, and we finally decided that he had to have 40- to 45-inch main beams and that I should definitely try for him.

This stag liked to hang out in several hundred acres that were dense with trees, which made for very cold still-hunting in January, even with a down parka and heavy gloves. We spotted him twice more in the next two days, but once was in cover so heavy that I couldn't tell which part of his body I would be shooting at, and the second time we were in the truck, driving to another area to glass, and we happened to catch him out in the open at only 25 yards as we rounded a bend. I chose not to shoot under those circumstances, he quickly ran off, and we ended up running out of hunting time.

In February, I returned to Texas and hunted the Anderson Ranch, near Mountain Home, for sika deer. Lad was my guide again and he thought we might find a good sika because the ranch had the Manchurian or Dybowski sub-species which have the biggest bodies and the biggest antlers. After two days of hunting, Lad wanted me to try for the lead buck in one group. It was heavy-horned but had one broken tine. I ended up talking him into the lead buck in another group which was probably not quite as heavy but may have had longer tines and, luckily, had no broken points, which is especially unusual for sika in February.

During my stalk, the sika group ran off to about 200 yards and then stopped to look back and see where we were. That's where I nailed the biggest buck high on the shoulder and he dropped where he was standing as the rest of the group sprinted off. I was pleased that we had misjudged the antler length on the short side.

With two more hunting days left, we decided to make another try for the red stag. The drive to the ranch in central Texas took twice as long as we planned because of ice on the roads the last 100 miles. We hunted that day in well below freezing temperatures and didn't even get close to the big stag. But the following morning we were up before sunrise and out in the trees with a new hunting strategy. Instead of still-hunting, we would glass from several observation points in hopes of seeing him climb up from the canyon floor to one of the grassy mesas in order to feed at first light. Then we would make a stalk.

A decent sika stag, but the antlers are a little thin.

After about an hour of glassing, we saw "Big Red" climb out of one of the canyons. Not wanting to take any chance of being detected, we waited until he disappeared over the top and then we climbed after him. Near the top, I stopped to get my breath so I could take a steady shot. Then we slowly moved over the top and spotted him at about 200 yards. He was behind a tree, but when he moved a couple of steps, his head and neck were showing. I decided to try for a neck shot, a shot I usually don't like to take because the kill zone is greatly reduced. My rifle went *bang* and the stag jumped, reeled around, and ran back for the canyon.

I knew I hadn't hit him hard, so I ran forward to a point where I thought I might get a second shot. I guessed right. He was running down a game trail to my left and angling away. I mounted my rifle and swung with him until my crosshairs were riding his shoulder. Then I waited until I had a shooting lane between some trees and finished my squeeze. He dropped immediately and skidded forward on his chest. I looked around and, to my surprise, Lad was at my shoulder saying, "That's it, Ken," and Rick was right behind us confirming that he got it all on tape as he did for every animal. I'm happy to report that the stag did not suffer from ground shrink.

With axis being the only deer remaining in the Super Slam, I next booked to hunt corsican and mouflon in March, since I could hunt axis in May or June when more would be in hard antler.

I thoroughly enjoyed hunting corsican with L.V. Hubbard, an independent guide from Leakey, Texas, on the 15,000-acre Stowers Ranch near Mountain Home. The

With Lad and my red stag that required two trips and two shots.

Stowers Ranch has been under high fence since the early 1900s when an elk program was instituted. That fact and the witticisms of L.V. made for an interesting hunt. ("If you have luck, you can use mud for brains" and when I pulled out a $10 bill, "That's one of those South Texas hundreds.") I ended up taking an out-curling, 33-inch corsican with a Texas heart shot as he trotted away from me.

My mouflon hunt was with Thompson Temple, who was the perfect choice because of his being so instrumental in fighting for the purity of the mouflon species for both the Records of Exotics and SCI Record Books. I found the mouflon to be even wilder than the aoudad that I hunted and was fortunate to get up on a good trophy at 5:17 PM on the second day. I know the time, because we had agreed to hunt until 5:20 PM since I had to fly back to California late that night.

We made a short stalk through some cedar and ended up where we couldn't move in any direction for fear of being spotted. I took a shot that I really didn't want to take and, because of the recoil, couldn't tell if I hit the ram or not. But Thompson jumped up and started running toward where the sheep had been and he yelled back, "You got him." When I finally caught up with Thompson, he was holding the mouflon's horns. He could see that the point of impact was on the neck and he had seen too many neck-shot animals get up and run away because they were only stunned. But this ram was not going anywhere. His heavy horns were over 30 inches long and had the perfect heart shape. Thompson pointed out all the attributes of a 100% pure Mouflon and then further proved his point by picking up the small-bodied ram with just one hand.

In April, I booked into the Greenwood Valley Ranch with Finn Aagaard as my guide. At the end of the first day of hunting, Finn told me about his move to Texas from his native Kenya in 1978 after hunting was stopped in Kenya in 1977 (even though all of the game animals taken by all of the sport hunters in any one year in Kenya were less that the number of whitetails taken in his new home of Llano County, Texas in any one year). Finn also gave me his thoughts on exotic hunting (he loves it because of its similarity to African hunting), record books (he feels there is more emphasis on the record book than on the hunting experience and that it should be the other way around), and on rifle calibers and bullet weights for various exotics (the same as for similar North American or African game).

The next day we made a classic stalk on a herd of ibex, out of sight and with the wind in our face, until I got to a point where I could shoot from the cover of a stand of trees. But with the ibex bedded down, we had to wait several minutes for them to start standing before I risked a shot, and then I dropped what I thought was the biggest one at about 200 yards. As the rest of the herd ran off, I saw two or three others that might have exceeded the 37 inches that mine measured.

In May, I hunted the Cowden Ranch with Mark Cowden for Catalina goat. There were probably over 300 goats on the ranch but, since they were being raised primarily for *cabrito,* we had a heck of a time trying to find a trophy. Mark finally spotted a big billy running to rejoin a herd. As the goat ran to my right, I free-handed a shot under his belly and then nailed him in the shoulder with my second shot.

Later in May, I hunted axis deer with Thompson Temple, a hunt I had really been looking forward to since axis are prob-

A pure mouflon ram shot with Thompson Temple in 1986 when there were still pure mouflon around.

Former Kenya professional hunter Finn Aagaard with me and my "exotic ibex" that could pass for a bezoar ibex.

A great, pear-shaped axis, shot with Thompson Temple as my guide.

My daughter, Summer, was eight when she posed with my field-dressed blackbuck.

ably Thompson's favorite exotic to hunt and since they are such beautiful animals. We jumped a humdinger while still-hunting, but were only able to get a few seconds' look as the buck sprinted in heavy cover to our right and down into a big cedar break. Thompson said that he had seen that same deer before and that it had been unsuccessfully hunted on previous occasions. Therefore, we decided that our best chance would be a subtle drive. Thompson waited about 15 minutes in the location where we had last seen the buck while I walked to the far end of the cedar break. Then he slowly moved through the cedar in hopes of gently moving the axis out for a possible shot on my end.

The strategy worked perfectly and, when the buck walked quickly through a narrow shooting lane, I shot him in the shoulder. He leaped in the air like a high jumper and took off like a sprinter. I started to question my shot location, but he folded up after a 75-yard run and didn't move after that.

The last animal that I needed in order to complete the Super Slam was a blackbuck antelope. Back in March, I had met with Charlie Schreiner IV at the YO Ranch, and booked to hunt in June at the 4,400-acre Onion Creek Ranch which was operated by the YO.

THE SUPER SLAM

My guide was the ranch manager, Bo Wafford, and Bo knows that ranch backwards and forwards. Pre-hunt scouting is a continuous process for Bo, so when I arrived, he knew the approximate location of several dominate bucks. The first day, he was able to get me within binocular range of a 4 $\frac{1}{2}$- to 5-swirler that he said he liked the best. We then spent the rest of the day and part of the next morning trying to find a better buck.

I saw a heavy-horned buck that would probably match the first one for length, but didn't match the number of swirls. Since I was also interested in the SCI Record Book, which measures around the swirls, I decided to make a stalk on "Bo's buck." We parked the vehicle about a mile from the approximate edge of the buck's territory and still-hunted until we saw him. At this point, Bo and Rick split off to the left and I moved to the right where I thought I might get a clearer shooting lane and a closer shot. But the buck saw me and sprinted away. I didn't shoot because I didn't want to spook him with a low percentage shot. At that moment, the buck stopped to look at Rick and Bo, and I bowled him over. He measured 21 inches in a straight line and 30 inches around the swirls. My Super Slam was complete.

Thompson and me with "the B-52 bomber."

So what do you do when you complete the Super Slam? You can always go back and upgrade your trophy quality. Therefore, I booked a trip in mid-June with Thompson Temple and we agreed to look over a large part of Texotic's 35,000 plus acres and try to find one or two animals that would beat the score of animals I'd already taken.

One animal that I especially wanted to upgrade was my Catalina goat. Mine was not a classic trophy, because it had scored well due to horn weight instead of horn length. We finally located a goat that neither one of us needed to take a second look at because its horns were so long that it could probably take off in a heavy wind. We saw him running by us the first time at too great of a distance to shoot. After he disappeared, we made a stalk down a dry creek bed, which wasn't dry because of a thunderstorm the day before. Thompson spotted him first, the second time, and we both sloshed across the now very wet creek and up the far embankment where I was able to drop the "B-52 bomber" with a shoulder shot as he ran right. He had a 44-inch spread.

Thompson whispered, "He's on the right."

The two corsicans had finally separated and they both started walking towards the top of a rise. I moved my cross-hairs on the shoulder of the ram on the right as he moved uphill. He dropped at the shot. His horns measured $40\,^4/_8$ inches by $40\,^2/_8$ inches.

As I walked up to that ram on the first day of summer 1986, little did I realize that, except for a nilgai hunt, I would not hunt another North American-introduced animal for 10 years and that, during the middle of that period, I would move my family to the Texas Hill Country, buy a ranch with Roger Haley, and operate it as a drive-through wildlife park known as Kerrville Camera Safari.

With Thompson and a particularly long and heavy corsican ram.

NORTH AMERICA EXOTICS

15

THE BLUE BULL

The first time I heard of nilgai antelope in Texas was about the circus that went bankrupt during the Depression and released their animals on the King Ranch. It made me wonder what happened to their elephants.

Subsequently, I read that the nilgai were not let loose for free. The circus actually sold two males and four females to the King Ranch. This made more sense, economically anyway, and also explains why there aren't any tigers on the ranch. Bad for whitetails, you know... and Texans, too!

But when I asked Bill Kiel for more information about the bankrupted circus, I found out that that old rumor simply wasn't true. Bill started as a biologist on the King Ranch in 1961 and then became wildlife manager. He retired in 1989. His primary responsibilities were monitoring game populations and improving game habitat, but he also worked with Texas A&M graduate students doing research projects involving the King Ranch game animals, including the nilgai.

"Mr. Kiel, is it true that nilgai were released in 1930 by a bankrupted circus?" "No." "No?" "No." "What do you mean 'no'?" "In the late '60s and early '70s, graduate students from Texas A&M dug into all the old records. As near as could be determined, those animals came from the San Diego Zoo. They were brought in by Caesar Kleberg, who was the manager down at the Norias Division for a long time. There were probably less than two dozen released altogether in several releases between 1924 and 1930."

So, there you have it. From a few modest releases by Caesar Kleberg, the estimated population of nilgai today, even after periodic meat hunts to supply restaurants, is 6,000 to 7,000 on the Norias Division of the King Ranch and 10,000 to 15,000 in Kenedy and Willacy Counties.

I arrived on the King Ranch in April 1990 with my wife, Lorraine, my 12-year-old daughter, Summer, and my 8-year-old son, Ryan. I had booked a nilgai and turkey hunt with Amos DeWitt's Tio Moya Corporation. In the long history of the King Ranch, no commercial sport hunting had been conducted until Amos was allowed a modest test for the 1988-89 season. Apparently the King Ranch Corporation was impressed by his hunting operation, because Amos is now operating on a long-term contract.

From 1845 to 1851, Richard King made his initial fortune by moving supplies by steamboat for General Zachary Taylor's army fighting in Mexico and by supplying the growing economy in the Wild Horse Desert (the area between the Rio Grande and Nueces Rivers in South Texas).

King's ranch started with the purchase of a 15,500-acre land grant on Santa Gertrudis Creek. It became the cradle of the cattle industry in the United States.

By the end of the Civil War, the ranch had grown to 146,000 acres and, at King's death in 1885, it was more than 600,000 acres. His wife, Henrietta, inherited the ranch and turned its management over to Robert J. Kleberg, Sr., the husband of her youngest child, Alice. By the time of Robert's death in 1932, the ranch constituted 1,175,000 acres.

The King Ranch Corporation was formed in 1935. After the results of estate taxes and the Depression, the ranch was re-shaped to about 825,000 acres, which is about its size today and that means big . . . Texas big. It's bigger than the entire state of Rhode Island.

There are four ranching divisions, primarily because separate land acquisitions resulted in separated properties, although the Santa Gertrudis Division (the original division, where the main ranch headquarters is located) and the Laureles Division (the largest) are narrowly connected just north of Kingsville. The other two divisions are the Encino (the smallest) and the Norias.

It's almost 20 miles from the entry gates of Norias Division to the Tio Moya Lodge. "Tio Moya" is Spanish for "Uncle Moya" and is the name of a 15,000-acre pasture comprising part of Amos DeWitt's 36,000-acre hunting operation.

Amos chose his land well because it is excellent whitetail habitat as well as home to nilgai, turkey, and some quail, hogs, javelina, and rattlesnakes. Judging from the estimated 150 deer per day I saw while hunting nilgai, the whitetail population must be enormous. Bill Kiel said there is about one deer per 20 acres of whitetail habitat, but you can't divide the 825,000-acre ranch by 20 and arrive at a population because farmland and areas around structures or with sparse cover are not prime habitat.

Fortunately, I was at Tio Moya after all whitetail antlers had been dropped so I could concentrate on hunting nilgai, or so I thought. I had never shot a turkey and the big birds were everywhere, but they aren't allowed to be hunted around the

The Blue Bull

lodge, which is kind of cruel if you have a hard time filling your tag, because you can see big gobblers from the dining room.

I wore camouflage daily in case a set-up looked good for harvesting next Thanksgiving's main course. The first day we concentrated on nilgai, but we also tried calling in some long-bearded birds a couple of times without success.

Back at the lodge that night, I showed my family the beard from a turkey that someone had placed on the neck of the nilgai mounted in the lounge. When I quickly found out that nilgai do, in fact, have a beard like a turkey, I tried to pretend I had been kidding. I also made a note to pay closer attention through my binoculars the next day.

My guide was Bill Kiel's son, Jim, who certainly had the credentials to guide me. He had personally harvested over 600 nilgai in 1988-89 for the Texas Wild Game Cooperative in addition to guiding numerous trophy hunters. Even though meat hunting was primarily conducted at night with spotlights and the quarry was primarily cows, calves, and young bulls, head shots were required and a good knowledge of nilgai habits were mandatory. As sport hunters, we hunted during daylight, of course.

Before my hunt, I read an August 1986 article on nilgai in *Petersen's Hunting* written by Texas' own John Wootters. In later reflecting on my hunt, many of his comments were so perfectly similar to my experience that I received permission from *Petersen's* to quote from his article. I mean, why try to improve on the definitive observances?

Wootters writes, "Nilgai are as wild as turpentined turkeys! About seven-eighths of your nilgai will be running when first spotted." Jim and I found this to be so true that we abandoned the typical African safari method of spotting a trophy from the hunting vehicle and then making a stalk on foot. By the time we could climb out, there wouldn't be a nilgai to stalk. "Nilgai are born knowing what you're up to, and remember, they evolved [in India and Pakistan] coping very successfully with such varmints as Bengal tigers" (Wootters).

So we would drive to good starting points and walk into the wind, hoping to spot a blue bull ("nilgai" in the Hindu language) before he spotted us. The Tio Moya land is perfect for "fast still-hunting" because of the rolling terrain and intermittent cover.

That first full day, we saw three bulls with at least nine-inch horns. I'm not saying I could have shot them, but we saw them. I decided not to try for any of them, and after the last one, Jim said, "I don't think you're ready to shoot yet." He was right. I really didn't want to end my hunt when I was just getting to know the animal and how to judge its horns.

A mature nilgai bull can weigh 600 pounds and is a magnificent-looking animal with its muscular frame and sleek, dark hair (to me it seemed that the darker the hair and bigger the neck, the bigger the horns). "Magnificent" is saying something when an animal has shoulders higher than its rump and grows horns that average only about eight inches. Maybe part of it is the nilgai's attitude. Wootters writes, "If he carried a set of horns like a kudu's, he'd be considered one of the world's most desirable game animals, and if he had the temperament of a Cape buffalo, south Texas hunters would be afraid to leave camp in anything less than an armored personnel carrier."

On the morning of the second day, we were driving to a likely starting point when we saw a single Rio Grande turkey leave his roost. Jim stopped the Jeep and said, "Let's give him a try." I grabbed the shotgun and quietly chambered a 3 1/2-inch duplex shell. Then we walked half the 300 yards separating us and set-up in a good spot. Jim pulled a camo cover over his face and started talking turkey on his slate box. I sat in front of him wearing my tan, brown and camo nilgai outfit with camo war paint on my face just in case such an opportunity arose.

I really didn't think the big bird would come in. But after a few minutes he did, and when he got to 50 yards and kept coming with his 9 1/2-inch beard dangling in front, I started to get turkey fever. He played hide-and-seek for awhile, which allowed me to calm down so I could raise my shotgun the last few inches when he walked behind a bush at 35 yards. When his head and neck emerged, I fired and he went right down. I didn't expect the gobbler to be that heavy (live weight guessed at over 25 pounds). And he flapped his wings so much I asked Jim if I should wring his neck, but Jim assured me the bird was clinically dead.

Later in the day, we were walking back to the Jeep after a fruitless walk into the wind for nilgai, when Jim stopped me. I surveyed the horizon, but he pointed eight feet in front of us. A big rattlesnake was poised right in our path. We backed off and Jim killed it with a log. He carefully cut its head off and tossed the rest of it in the back of the Jeep where it coiled and uncoiled all afternoon. I kept looking back at it to make sure its head was still off. That rattler measured six feet nine inches and had 14 rattles. Jim skinned it for my son and, after tanning, it now adorns his bedroom wall.

The Rio Grande turkey that came to Jim Kiel's call.

The Blue Bull

Late that afternoon, we were walking over some sandy dunes near the Laguna Madre. As usual, I followed Jim single-file into the wind. Suddenly he dropped to one knee and I did the same. "There's a big, black bull over the hill. He's feeding about 120 yards away."

Jim carries two sticks, about four feet long, so his clients can cross them at the top while holding them with one hand to form a rifle rest in open country. "You won't have enough time to use the sticks. We'll crawl about 60 yards. Then you'll need to stand up, make sure the horns are what you want, and shoot." As we moved forward on hands and knees, I thought, "Okay, this is it. You know what nine-plus-inch horns are supposed to look like. You know to look for the big neck that separates the mature bulls from the younger ones. And . . . if you shoot this one, you'll have some extra time to take the family to South Padre Island. But . . . don't shoot a small one because the family won't enjoy you sulking on the beach."

Fortunately, the sandy soil was actually comfortable to crawl on and we closed the gap quickly. I already had a 400-grain soft point up the spout of

Ryan Wilson with the rattlesnake that measured 81 inches before its head was cut off. Note the pile of shed antlers in the tree.

my Weatherby .416 rifle, so I pushed off the safety, double-checked the variable scope setting at 1 3/4, and stood up.

I found the bull in the eyepiece with the crosshairs in the middle of his body. Elapsed time: 1.5 seconds. I swung left to check the horns, but they weren't there! So I swung right and found his big neck in feeding position and took a quick look at his horns. They where heavy, black, and long. Elapsed time: 3.0 seconds. I could see the neck of the bull moving up as I swung the crosshairs back left. Jim had told me to shoot low in the chest; that most people shoot too high. So I lowered my crosshairs to just above the crest of the hill as I aimed down. When they crossed the shoulder, the rifle exploded and the bull was literally blown off his feet. I jacked in another round as the animal kicked on its side and then lay still where it had dropped.

Wootters says, "The nilgai of Texas just might be the strongest animal you'll ever hunt. So far, I haven't heard of a nilgai bull that went down in his tracks and stayed down with anything other than a spine or brain shot . . . ." Credit my shoulder shot kill to Weatherby and Kiel. But credit my nilgai bull with keeping, in tact, Wootters observation of never having "seen an exit wound in a nilgai carcass, regardless of the bullet used." My 400-grain soft point ended up next to the skin on the far shoulder.

"What a bull," Jim said. "Look at those horns!" We looked at them, touched them, and measured them. Sixty days later, SCI master measurer Joe Krausz measured them as the new SCI #1 ($10\,^3/_8$ inches long with bases of $10\,^2/_8$ inches and $10\,^4/_8$ inches) after conferring with Jack Schwabland of the Record Book Committee. But, let's face it, the nilgai is an animal whose body outshines its horns and there are no doubt bigger horns out there. When I hunted, we couldn't find the bull that Jim called "the longhorned one."

The monster blue bull that Jim Kiel guided me to. Note the "beard" on its neck.

16

SUPER EXOTICS

I hunted the 10 species comprising the Super Slam of Exotics in the course of six trips from my California home to Texas from January to June 1986. Over the following 10 years, I hunted only one other exotic; a nilgai antelope. Maybe you read about it somewhere.

It wasn't that I didn't like hunting introduced species, but the six hunting continents are large and the number of species that can be hunted is great, and I enjoy the travel and adventure and generally greater challenge involved in hunting animals in their native habitat.

But I do love exotics, and not just for hunting. In 1992, I moved to Kerrville, Texas and, with Roger Haley, opened Kerrville Camera Safari, a drive-through wildlife ranch that we still own and operate. From among the hundreds of Texas ranches specializing in one or more species, I bought our initial stock of some 300 animals from some 30 species and stocked our ranch after completing the perimeter fencing. We have been open every single day since September 4, 1992. You drive through in your own vehicle and observe the animals at your leisure. Some come right up to you and some hang back in the trees, but they always put on a good show by just being themselves; whether from North America like bison and whitetail deer; or Africa like giraffe, zebra, eland, and scimitar-horned oryx; or the rest of the world like axis, fallow, sika, barasingha, water buffalo, and many, many more.

Our ranch is kind of a showplace for the North America exotic ranching industry and, as such, we have received the support of many legendary ranches and people involved in the industry, including the YO Ranch and Thompson Temple who, al-

SPORT HUNTING ON SIX CONTINENTS

The entrance to Kerrville Camera Safari, with the Gate House straight ahead and Interstate 10 on the right.

Customers looking at some of the hundreds of animals. These are addax. If they had been transferred directly from Chad, they would have wondered what all the green stuff was.

A view of part of The Wilson-Haley Ranch (home of Kerrville Camera Safari) which is located at the gateway to Kerrville, Texas.

Not just waterfowl use the lake!

though unrelated business operations, were the virtual founders of the industry.

The protector of the industry is the Exotic Wildlife Association, and the industry needs protecting because of the great benefit it has been and continues to be for so many species. Zoos are fine, but the animals are very confined and must remain limited in numbers. Ranchers allow their animals to roam freely and to maintain their wild characteristics and instincts. The animals can forage, fight, and breed on an exotic wildlife ranch. And, yes, at three to 10 years of age, a male can be harvested to help pay the bills.

Thanks to hunters, hundreds of ranchers have been given the financial incentive to provide the land, personnel, and capital to raise dozens of species so that many now exist in greater numbers in Texas than in their original native habitat. Examples are such Super Slam species as axis deer, blackbuck antelope, and aoudad. But there are even more species that were closer to extinction and exist in lesser but continually increasing numbers, thanks to the exotic ranching industry. These include Eld's deer, barasingha deer, addax, and scimitar-horned oryx.

So, ten years after I hunted the Super Slam, I hunted a few of the so-called Super Exotics in order to produce a video that would tell the success story of the exotic ranching industry while showcasing some very unique species and ranches . . . and not just in Texas.

First, to get my feet wet, or at least cold, I videotaped Dr. Truman Clem hunting a Tibetan yak on White Elk Ranch in the snows of Colorado with Tad Puckett. Yaks are certainly not endangered . . . millions exist worldwide. I saw thousands on one trip to Mongolia. But only the yaks in Tibet are considered wild and there are only about 2,000 of them so, as of this writing, you can't hunt any yaks outside the U.S. and bring the trophy and meat into the U.S.

White Elk Ranch has the second largest yak herd in North America. Dr. Clem looked over a lot of bulls on the 5,700-acre spread before dropping a big one in two feet of powder snow with one shot. It was so big that we needed a chain and a truck to complete the field dressing by pulling the guts out in 10-degree weather.

After that late fall yak hunt, I went on a winter Eld's deer hunt in Texas. Eld's deer were named after Lt. Percy Eld, the British Assistant Commissioner of Assam, who discovered them for European science in India in 1838. They are also known as brow-antlered deer because their antlers form a continuous sweep from the tip of their brow tines to the end of their main beams.

Eld's deer were endangered by the 1930s and all legal hunting was discontinued. Nevertheless, by 1951 they were thought to be extinct until a remnant population was found at Logtak Lake in India. A few animals were captured and, eventually, some were delivered to an endangered species facility in Florida. When the owner of that facility decided to go out of business in the early 1990s, two ranchers bought the 20-some Eld's deer and placed about half on each of their ranches in Texas. Under their stewardship, the herd numbers increased to about 50, but there was still one missing ingredient . . . income to offset the expenses. Income was missing until the U.S. Fish and Wildlife Service issued permits allowing the transport of Eld's deer trophies outside Texas. When this happened, I was able to interest a third rancher, A.R. Galloway, into buying some Eld's deer from the first two ranchers and participating in the breeding program. Herd numbers continue to increase annually so that the future of the Eld's deer is, I believe, secure.

In late December, just as the Eld's deer stags were starting to rub off their velvet, I hunted the third largest Eld's deer on Priour Ranch, saving the two largest for my clients scheduled to hunt the following month.

Front view of the brow-antlered deer discovered for European science in India by Lt. Percy Eld.

Then, in the spring, I hunted both addax and scimitar-horned oryx on the 10,000-acre Indianhead Ranch near Del Rio, Texas. Indigenous to the Sahara Desert in North Africa, each species has been on Appendix I of CITES since 1975. As of this writing, Chad is reopening for hunting several species, including aoudad, but not for addax or oryx because there are probably more of each (about 150) on Indianhead Ranch than currently exist in the whole of Chad. Maybe reintroductions from Texas will return these two greatest of desert dwellers to huntable numbers south of the Sahara someday.

The morning of my second day at Indianhead, Laurent Delagrange led me within 150 yards of a small group of addax in which a very good male was cavorting. When that bull stopped broadside, with his right shoulder fully exposed, I fired my .300 from a pair of shooting sticks and the bull looked to his left wondering what all the racket was about. I asked Laurent if I had missed and he said, "Yeah." So I shot

SUPER EXOTICS

This view really shows off the unique antlers of the Eld's deer.

again and Laurent said, "That one got it. I think it's right in the neck." I asked about the placement of my first shot and Laurent said, "I think you got that one in the rocks." When we approached the addax, I could see he was dead from a neck shot.

Since I still had oryx to hunt, I went to the rifle range at Indianhead and found that my rifle was shooting okay, which is always good news and bad news. The next day, we finally located a bull scimitar-horned that I wanted to shoot and we made a stalk, but the herd of eight to 10 ran. So we gave them time to settle down and stalked to some bushes where we could see the group walking to our left through a clearing of low foliage. I picked out the herd bull and fired, only to be shocked by having my 3 x 9 scope bounce off my chest and fall to the ground! Laurent was carrying my son's .243 (Ryan was the cameraman at the time), so I immediately grabbed it and killed the bull with a shoulder shot. He fell over backward as if I had been shooting a .416. Shot placement *uber alles.*

To complete my "Hunting the Super Exotics" video, I hunted water buffalo in Florida and barasingha deer in Texas. Water buffalo are the opposite of endangered.

121

Laurent Delagrange with my addax.

Laurent, cameraman Ryan Wilson, and Ryan's father with a scimitar-horned oryx.

The worldwide population is estimated at 75,000,000 and they can be hunted in Australia, South America, North America, and even Africa. I predict that some hunting will start again in Asia in the near future. I guess the main reason I hunted a water buffalo in the U.S. is because I wanted to experience the Brady Ranch in Florida. They have a small herd of water buffalo and a big herd of axis deer. By "big," I'm talking about 6,000 to 8,000 axis! Even Frank Brady, Sr. and Jr. don't know how many axis they have.

I completed my hunting of super exotics in the heat of a South Texas summer on the Galloway Ranch. Barasingha turned out to be a real challenge for me, requiring eight days of hunting. I've guided several hunters for barasingha on the Galloway Ranch and it's usually a two- to three-day hunt but, when the guide turned hunter, the hunt became difficult and I wasn't being overly selective, either.

Barasingha are also known as swamp deer and are indigenous to India and Nepal. There are now more barasingha on two ranches in Texas (Galloway and Priour) than in all of India. Maybe it's because of genetics, maybe it's the natural feed and abundant water on the ranch, but probably it's a combination of age, genetics, and nutrition that make the barasingha bulls at Galloway so big... some over 500 pounds.

The first year I hunted barasingha as a guide, I scouted them in late June when they were grown out in velvet. When I took my first hunter two months later, I was shocked to see that most of the bigger bulls had already broken one or more of their tines from fighting. So the next year, I took hunters in July, just after the bulls came into hard antler. But the temperature in South Texas in July is usually 90° to 100° F. and the deer rest in the shade throughout the day in very heavy cover so you either can't see them or you stalk too close trying to find them and scare them off. Even when you can locate them lying in the shade, you are rarely able to see all of their tines.

Frank Brady, Jr. was a kick to hunt with... in this case, for water buffalo.

In late June of 1997, I guided Jim Grookett to a monster barasingha that was fully grown out in velvet. He shot it on the last day of a three-day hunt in light rain following a downpour. A couple months later, I guided Roman DeVille to a nice bull that was laying in a thicket of heavy mesquite bushes. We approached to 30 yards and the bull turned his head just enough that I could see all of his points, so I whispered, "Shoot." Roman shot immediately and killed the bull.

Later that same day as we were hunting axis, I saw another pretty good barasingha bull emerge from one of the long ponds that make the Galloway Ranch so beautiful. I quickly asked Roman if he would mind if I shot that deer. Roman kindly agreed and suddenly became my cameraman. We made a fairly lengthy and circuitous stalk that got me in position to shoot the bull as he was casually walking from the water to the safety of the mesquite in the middle of the day.

With exotics, you remember the difficult hunts as being the most enjoyable.

Not as good as Jim's or Roman's, but still a big, beautiful barasingha.

17

KENYA

In 1975, eight years before my first big game hunt, my wife, Lorraine, and I went on a camera safari in Kenya. We landed in Nairobi, got in a zebra-striped van, and were driven from spectacular lodge to spectacular lodge in Amboseli, Masai-Mara, and Tsavo with game viewing in between. Most lodges had nearby waterholes so, after a hard day of driving up to prides of lions, pairs of cheetahs, and families of black rhinos, you could keep looking for game with a cocktail in hand.

One lodge was built on stilts and, at night, the stairs were pulled up like a drawbridge so the animals could roam underneath and the guests could not. In our room, over our bed, was a large switch that said "on" when pushed up and "off" when pushed down. I called the front desk and asked about the switch. The clerk said, "'On' means you want to hear the buzzer if herds of animals come to water. Then you can come to the bar and watch." So we pushed the switch to "on" and, sure enough, the buzzer went off about four hours later at two in the morning. Getting dressed and out to the bar was well worth the effort.

First, a herd of elephants came in and watered. When they departed, Lorraine and I decided to wait at the bar until morning. It wasn't very hard duty. We had had some sleep, the bartender made great Cuba Libras and Seven and Sevens, and the barstools had backs and comfortable cushions. We were about 30 feet above the waterhole and 30 yards away from the near side with enough artificial light to enjoy the view, like a bright moon. Next to arrive was a herd of Cape buffalo. The waterhole was less than an acre and there were probably 200 buffalo, but they had been through

SPORT HUNTING ON SIX CONTINENTS

A comfortable lodge built to accommodate tourists on camera safaris.

"Where's the money you owe me?"

this drill before and quietly took turns. One wave would drink and leave and the next wave would move in.

When the third wave came, Lorraine and I picked up our drinks and walked down a protected staircase to a tunnel out to an island in the middle of the waterhole where we emerged at ground level. We were within 20 feet of the nearest buffalo, but safely surrounded by a circle of iron bars and a solid ceiling over our heads. It was the only time I have ever drunk a rum and Coke in the middle of a herd of Cape buffalo!

We spent about a week at Masai-Mara and Amboseli. The breakfasts and dinners at the lodges were gourmet and we roughed it with a sack lunch while game viewing during the day. Outside of the likes of giraffe, zebra, and elephant, most of the species had to be identified for us. We could get fairly close to many animals; within 20 yards of lion and cheetah, although 50 yards was as close as our driver would get to black rhino and, in one instance, that was close enough to evoke a

KENYA

charge, but the driver was ready and quickly pulled away.

On one ride outside the parks, we drove past a tented camp. Our driver informed us, "This is a hunter's camp. They sleep in these tents here, eat in that tent over there, and they even have a shower tent. They can buy a license to hunt just about any animal except elephant; hunting them was just closed down."

After a week in the civilized bush, we returned to Nairobi for a night out at a French casino. The next day, we flew to

Lorraine Wilson looking for game from a VW pop-top.

Mombasa for a few days on the Indian Ocean. Mombasa was lively, warm, and beautiful, but we saw all we wanted to see in three days and, with a few days of vacation time remaining, we decided to return to the interior for more game viewing.

This time we traveled to Tsavo, but it wasn't as interesting as Amboseli and

Here's something that you won't see in Kenya today. . . a mother and baby black rhino out on the plains. In 1975, we saw about 20 in the open like this.

127

A pair of cheetahs photographed at 20 yards from the VW pop-top.

Masai-Mara. There was less vegetation, less game, and elephant carcasses could be seen every so often. Our driver said there had been a drought for about five years and many animals were dying in Tsavo. That evening, one of our fellow tourists informed us, "There has been a drought, but that's only part of the problem. Sure, elephants are very destructive, tearing down limbs and even whole trees for food, but the main problem is poaching. When the [Kenya] government ended elephant hunting, the ban reduced the number of hunting safaris and they were the main deterrent to poaching, either directly or by financing the game department's anti-poaching efforts. Word is the Kenyattas [the President of Kenya and his family] are using the national airline to transport poached ivory for their own financial gain. Camera safaris are fine in the parks, but the best way to control poaching is to encourage hunting safaris in the outlying areas."

Years later, after experiencing a few safaris in Africa, I developed three wishes relative to my camera safari in Kenya:

(1) Nairobi was the start and conclusion of most East African safaris from the days of Denys Finch-Hatton to the safaris of Hemingway and Ruark and Gates, Klein, Mullen, and McElroy. I wish I had soaked up more of the ambience of Nairobi. I wish I had listened to a few hours of hunting stories in the bar at the New Stanley Hotel.

(2) I wish I had developed a desire to go on a hunting safari in Kenya, but I would have had to move fast because, less than two years after our camera safari, Kenya discontinued all hunting safaris due to government involvement in poaching, pressure from a burgeoning human population for land schemes, and the financial clout of the preservationists who, themselves, are more interested in raising money and stopping hunting than in the welfare of the animals.

(3) I wish Kenya would reopen so I could experience the cradle of the safari industry with a rifle in hand instead of a camera (with both in hand, really). It's completely different, you know, when the game is wild from being hunted, you live in a tent amongst it, hearing it, feeling it, working hard to get close, making quick decisions and then having to shoot at a small target on a single trophy animal instead of at a whole herd with a big lens.

18

TANZANIA

Ten months after my first big game hunt, I was on my first African safari. I went to Alaska with Dave Harshbarger in September 1983 and got hooked. Then I booked a desert bighorn sheep hunt for January because it was an "off-season hunt." And, before my sheep hunt, I took my wife, daughter, and son to Texas for a whitetail deer hunt. When I returned from Mexico in January 1984, I asked Dave where we could go hunting before the fall season in North America. He said, "We could go to Africa, but I'll let you do the research. I've already been to Botswana, so I'd like to try somewhere different and about the only species I'm interested in hunting are leopard and elephant."

So I sent away to various agents and professional hunters for information on hunting in Africa. I tried to find videos or films on hunting safaris but couldn't. After considerable research, I made my decision based on a few photographs. I ran into a guy named Kitch Taub from Houston while on a trip there looking at real estate and learned that he had just taken his first safari a few months before. I asked him about his hunt and he whipped out about 20 photos held in a stack by a couple rubber bands. I removed the rubber bands and looked at the photos in disbelief. There was Kitch with a lion, a leopard, a buffalo, an eland, and lots of antelopes. A few answers to my questions and I was ready to book a safari in Tanzania with Luke Samaras. Kitch had booked through Frank Green of Safari South, so I called Frank and he sent me a packet of information and I had him send a packet to Dave, also.

While this was going on, I was astounded and frustrated that I could not find a video documentary of a hunting safari so I could see what it was going to be like. But

Videotaping the incredible sights and sounds of a first African hunting safari.

I couldn't, so I made a deal with Dave Harshbarger. We would both hunt with Luke, 2 x 1, I would have first choice on every species and would pay two-thirds of the daily rates and he would pay one-third, and we would videotape each other hunting so we could have a remembrance of our safari and show others what it was like.

The season opened July 1, and Dave and I would be Luke's first safari of the year. We flew into Dar Es Salaam on June 29 so we would have a couple of days to get used to the time change. It was a good idea and we relaxed into the eclectic coastal atmosphere of Dar. Time moved very slowly, but finally we were on a small charter plane into the Selous Reserve. We had already met Luke Samaras in Dar and he flew with us to a small landing strip near the Rufiji River. From there we drove about an hour and a half to camp. After about a half hour, Dave looked at me and said, "You've been awfully quiet. Have you been seeing all the game?"

"What game?" I hadn't seen a single animal. Dave and Luke claimed they had seen impala, zebra, and wildebeest. I didn't believe them, but for the rest of the ride into camp, they showed me how to look and where to look, and I started to see the same animals they were seeing. This safari was going to be fun!

We were on an old fashioned east African tented safari and it was everything that I had hoped it would be . . . a beautiful setting among acacia trees with a tributary to the Rufiji just a stone's throw away . . . good food starting with fresh lobster flown in with us . . . beautiful, amazing, immense starlit nights with a Milky Way several times milkier than I had ever seen, along with constellations that I had never noticed on my camera safari to Kenya nine years earlier . . . an experienced staff that knew their jobs and did them well . . . and those two areas of supreme importance: the dining tent and the circle of chairs around the campfire.

Dave and I tested our rifles before the afternoon hunt on day one. He put two shots next to each other about two inches above the bullseye with his .300 and two more almost touching the bull with his .375. I was nervous, inexperienced, and was uncomfortable with my rest and those were my excuses for spreading several shots around the paper at 100 yards.

About an hour before dark that first day, we got into a small band of Burchell's zebras and they disappeared into the long grass (I called it "tall" grass back then, but Capstick got me calling it "long"). Luke took a tracker and we followed him into the grass until we could see the head and top of the back of one of the zebras. Luke pointed at the animal and gave me a nod along with a movement of his index finger like he was pulling a trigger, so I raised my rifle, pushed the safety off, and fired. The grass exploded with running zebra and "my zebra" was running fastest of all. With any luck, he lived a long and productive life.

On the way back to camp, Luke said, "You shot over that zebra because only the top of his back was showing above the grass and you probably shot at what you could see of him. What you should have done was put your crosshairs on his back above his shoulder and then lowered them, into the grass, to where his shoulder was hidden or just behind his shoulder, and killed him. But every circumstance is different, every shot is different, and you just have to learn by watching and doing."

The next day we scattered a herd of Nyasaland wildebeest with the truck and then got out to follow the best bull. After several hundred yards, the bull turned and faced us. Luke said, "He's about 250 yards. Do you want to try this shot or take a chance on getting him broadside?" I said I'd try and, to everyone's surprise, I stuck

My first African trophy was a Nyasaland wildebeest with the distinctive white stripe below its eyes. Dave Harshbarger, on the right, later shot a better one.

Dave and me with our Burchell's zebras.

him in the middle of the chest and he went right down.

By day four, I had added a Lictenstein's hartebeest, an East African impala, and I had gotten even with a zebra. Dave shot a zebra out of the same herd and he also killed beautiful specimens of wildebeest and hartebeest. We were off to a great start by the time we spotted our first herd of elephants. Luke grabbed his rifle, I grabbed my .375 and swapped the softs for solids, and Dave grabbed the video camera. Then we started our stalk.

It didn't take long to look over all the bulls in the group and determine that none had big enough tusks, which we all agreed should be over 50 pounds per side. But on the way back to the truck, Luke spotted a couple of older bulls with three or four *askaris* watching out for the older gentlemen. The wind was good so we slowly walked straight to them. At 75 yards, Luke got a good look at both tusks on one of the older bulls and whispered, "That's the one we want. We'll try to get within 25 yards and then shoot him in the crease behind the front leg as many times as you can."

At about 40 yards, something alerted one of the *askaris* and all the bulls stopped feeding for over a minute as we froze. The closest *askari* raised his trunk and tried to get a whiff of scent in our direction, but the wind held. Finally, they all went back to breaking off tree limbs and we closed to 25 yards when the same *askari* figured something was wrong and moved toward us to investigate. As he did so, he blocked my beautiful broadside shot at one of the old bulls. When the *askari* cleared my scope, the big bull turned to face me . . . head on. In that instant, I remembered the frontal brain shot diagram from a Karamojo Bell book, calculated the short distance above the eyes to the line between the ear holes, and fired. At the shot, the bull crashed down on his stomach as dirt flew around him and the rest of the bulls exited instantly.

While rolling the video camera, Dave said, "Perfect . . . perfect . . . what a shot!" It was amazing what a little 300-grain solid bullet had just done, but before I could utter a word, Luke grabbed my arm and pulled me in a half circle to the fallen bull's right while saying, "Load-up." Then, when we got to about 10 yards, he said, "Give him a side brain," and that's what I did. We later determined that my first shot had been perfect but, with Luke, you always kill dangerous game twice.

Now, after 15 years of hunting on six continents, I can say that that elephant is

My brain-shot elephant in the classic position on its stomach.

L to R: Me, Luke Samaras, and Dave Harshbarger after my elephant was pulled onto its side by the hunting vehicle.

the only animal I felt sad about killing. I didn't feel bad and I didn't feel remorse and my sadness disappeared by the morning. I guess it was the fact that a single shot had felled such a large, magnificent animal. Luke says it happens to many hunters with elephants.

Since it was only day four of our safari and it was late in the afternoon, we decided to take what meat we could use in camp and just leave the tusks in the skull for a few days so they could be pulled rather than hacked out with an ax. Only in a huge, unpopulated area like the Selous would you dare leave tusks in the field. Unfortunately, the lack of population also meant no local villagers to use the meat. That didn't help old sad sack.

I had a few drinks that night and talked my way back to looking forward to the next day. Dave did say I was "walking like an old man" that next morning, but by our lunch break my head had cleared and I was in good shape. That afternoon, we found leopard tracks in enough abundance that Luke decided that I should shoot an impala for bait. By the end of the day, my impala was hung from a tree limb and Dave also had one up another tree.

The following morning, and each morning thereafter, we checked the baits until, on day eight, mine had been fed upon. Luke had a blind made a little farther from the bait than he would have liked, especially for a first time hunter to Africa (60 yards), but he wanted it in that location for the wind and light. He put in a couple folding chairs, had a front and back rest made for my rifle, and then had me sit in one of the chairs, place my rifle through the peephole and onto the outside and inside rests, and make sure that my crosshairs were just above the branch at the bait. With a few adjustments, all that was accomplished before noon.

We hunted elsewhere for most of the afternoon and then returned to the blind about three hours before dark, driving right up to it. Everyone got out of the truck, Luke and I and a tracker got settled in the blind, and I put my rifle in place and chambered a round. Then Dave and the other tracker and a game scout got back in the truck, slammed the doors, and quickly drove off about a mile to wait until dark or a gunshot as the signal to return.

Luke motioned for me to slide my safety off and then we waited . . . and waited. Just as I started to get bored, it got real quiet and then, to my absolute shock, a leopard was in the tree! I started to hyperventilate. It may have been the worst case of leopard fever ever contracted. I slowly moved my right eye to the scope and could see the eyes of the leopard staring right through mine. Somehow that helped control my breathing, so I moved my right index finger from the trigger guard to the trigger. At the same time, the leopard walked along the limb from the trunk to the bait. When it stopped, I picked out a rosette on its left shoulder and fired.

Luke said my shot literally blew the cat out of the tree but, nevertheless, he had me wait in the blind while taking the tracker for a closer look. About a minute later, he yelled for me to come out and see my cat. It was directly under the bait. I was overjoyed. I was also too inexperienced to realize that I had shot a female, but Luke later told me that it was my first safari and he felt I should not pass up the opportunity. I agreed with him then and I agree with him now. Besides, anyone can hit a big target, but it takes a good shot to hit a small target. Right?

Dave's leopard was really exciting. We were going to check a bait and actually saw the leopard walking in the early morning. Dave piled out of the passenger side, the left side, of the truck and belted the cat, knocking it flat. Everyone yelled congratulations until the cat jumped up and ran into the thick stuff. Uh oh!

After a little preparation, we went in after the cat with more people than Luke cared to have along, but Dave wanted to be there and I insisted on videotaping the action. Luke felt I needed a couple extra people with me so the leopard would have a choice of who to eat.

Dave and me with my leopard . . . the first cat of the safari.

Two trackers were slightly in front of Luke and to his right. Luke was carrying a side-by-side 12 gauge shotgun loaded nine BBs to the shell. Behind him was the game scout (a government observer), an apprentice PH (a government requirement), both carrying well-worn rifles, then Dave with his rifle, and me with the video camera rolling. The trackers moved very, very slowly until one stopped and pointed. Luke took a step to get in front and then knelt down as he tried to spot spots. The bush was all green and yellow and dappled by the rising sun.

Then the cat growled and everyone moved back three steps in unison. Finally, one of the trackers could see part of the leopard. He put his left hand on Luke's back and, with his head in contact with Luke's, he pointed with his right arm to where Luke should aim. The cat growled loudly and Luke shot where the tracker was pointing about seven yards away. Then he shot again, broke open his shotgun, dropped in two more shells, and snapped the gun closed. Dave could see part of the cat and said, "I got him," and shot his .375.

Then the leopard charged and Luke shot twice more at point-blank. While Luke

A leopard was one of the few animals that Dave wanted to hunt, and he got a good one.

reloaded again, the game scout fired his rifle. The leopard was now on its side but still breathing, so someone fired an insurance shot. Still the cat panted for another half minute and then stopped. The elapsed time from the first shot to the sixth (according to the video) was 26 1/2 seconds. The insurance shot was made 15 seconds after that. And the leopard was a good 6 1/2-foot male with lots of holes.

We returned in triumph to our camp as the staff chanted, *"Chui,"* and carried Dave around while still chanting. I had experienced the same ritual after returning with my leopard, so Dave and I could be a little cynical knowing that the joy was more for the beer that would be allocated to the staff that night than anything else.

Next on the agenda was retrieving my tusks, but first we checked a watering area and, sure enough, elephants were filtering in and out of the bush and down to the mostly dry riverbed. We were several hundred yards off and well above the riverbed so we had a good view as several bulls appeared and disappeared. Luke rejected a couple candidates for Dave even though their tusks seemed plenty long enough. Finally he spotted one he liked and pointed it out to Dave. As Dave looked through his binoculars, Luke said, "Why don't we walk down and shoot that one?" After the stalk and kill, Dave started calling our PH "Cool Hand Luke."

I captured the stalk and kill on video. For the next 10 years, I was told by literally hundreds of hunters that it was the most spectacular kill scene ever filmed. After those

Tanzania

10 years, I started to hear that Mark Sullivan's buffalo charge footage was more spectacular and then, in 1997, I was told by many that the leopard charge footage Hal Ahlberg gave me for my "Leopard Charge" video was even more spectacular.

So here's what happened on the third most spectacular stalk and kill ever filmed. We made a cautious stalk to within about 50 yards of the bull, but it slowly moved away so we circled below it to close the gap which put us in grass above our heads. The elephant was on an embankment about 20 feet above us, but out of sight. Luke was in front and slightly to the right, then Dave, and then me as we took a few steps closer to the bottom of the embankment at which time we could see a vague outline of the elephant but nothing to shoot at. For 18 seconds, the bull didn't move and neither did we. Then, in three short seconds, the elephant moved to the edge of the embankment with his ears outstretched and his head visible above the long grass. Dave looked at Luke, who nodded, and then Dave looked back at the bull and fired at a point below the eyes due to the severe uphill angle. The bull threw his head up as his back legs crashed, revealing both tusks, and then he collapsed forward, over the embankment, and rolled down 10 yards to our right. Luke rushed forward in case an immediate second shot was needed, but it wasn't, so he had Dave take the insurance shot.

Dave's elephant expired from a perfect brain shot, but still ended up on its side.

We spent four hours hacking out the ivory, removing the nerves, and axing bone off tusks or, more accurately, watching the crew take care of those chores. Then we hiked back to the truck with both tusks and as much meat as we could carry. Next stop was my elephant about 10 miles away. When we arrived I could see that the meat hadn't gone to waste after all. After the hyenas had eaten everything they could, the vultures had picked the bones clean. All that was left was the skin that looked like a deflated hot air balloon colored white by watery vulture droppings, and the head with tusks in place. Without much effort, the tusks were simply pulled from the skull and the nerves flipped out with a knife. We loaded the tusks in the truck with Dave's tusks and returned to camp with over 250 pounds of ivory.

We saw buffalo almost every day but I had set an unrealistic goal of a 48-inch spread which the Selous produced once every blue moon, but mine was a white moon safari so, as the 21 days started to slip by, I substantially lowered my goal. One eventful day, we tracked four old bulls until we could see three of them. Luke picked out the one with the biggest bosses and I emptied my rifle of a soft and three solids, 300 grains each, and we took photos.

With the Cape buffalo that Luke determined to have the biggest bosses of the three bulls that we could see.

So this left lion for me to finish the Big Four on my first safari. I had had two chances up to that point. One was a beautifully maned cat that we saw for an instant in a dry river bed at about 200 yards, but never saw again. Tracking that lion in six-foot grass with three feet of forward visibility was nerve-wracking and it didn't take Luke long to call off that insanity. Several days later, a pride came to a bait, but the big male was shaved bald. So, on day 20, we decided that spot and stalk might be our best chance, and we started driving.

L to R: Luke, Dave, and me with my east African eland bull; the kind for which the Selous is famous.

Since we weren't looking for them, we naturally ran into a herd of eland. They were fairly spread out in medium cover and didn't bolt. Luke left the motor running and led me downwind. After a short distance, I could see a big eland standing broadside and motionless at about 100 yards. I raised my rifle but Luke whispered, "Don't shoot unless I can see it's a bull." Luke moved left and right and finally said, "It's a good bull." Just as he said, "Good," the bull started walking and when he said, "Bull," I fired. The bull crashed off about 75 yards and dropped. We walked up and admired him. He was a great eland. Everyone was happy. Luke said, "I'll go get the truck and drive back with the still cameras for photos and loading." I was standing about five yards from the eland, admiring him as he lay on his left side. He had been down about five minutes without breathing when he suddenly stood up and I dropped him with shot number two.

When I glassed these two lions, I felt they weren't big enough. Then the farthest one stood up!

We winched the huge antelope into the back of the truck and started back to camp when the game scout said, *"Simba."* There were actually two *simbas* lying on

139

their backs under a tree. They were apparently sleeping off last night's meal in the middle of the afternoon. Luke and I jumped out and moved as close as we dared. The cats must have known we were there, but they didn't seem to care. Finally, they both rolled over. They were big-bodied but their manes weren't great, so I reluctantly decided not to shoot and lowered my rifle. Then the farthest one stood up and really looked big and his hair didn't look too bad so I whispered, "I'm going to shoot the far one." Luke said, "Shoot him in the shoulder and keep shooting."

At my first shot, the cat did a complete somersault and struggled away from us while his companion departed instantly. I shot twice more and killed the cat. He was huge. He was nine feet four inches between the pegs and Luke thought he weighed 450 to 500 pounds. When we brought my lion back to camp on top of my eland, there was a wild celebration, which I later discovered was because the staff knew they would have the best steaks in Africa from my eland along with their beer that night. I know I did.

Luke Samaras took this photo of Dave and me with cat and trackers.

19

ZAMBIA

In August 1987, I flew 500 miles northeast of Zambia's capital of Lusaka by private plane to what is affectionately known as Waka-Waka International, a dirt landing strip in the Luangwa Valley. The Valley lies about 2,500 feet below the surrounding escarpment, but it is 40 to 60 miles wide and 250 miles long so, once you are in the Valley, you don't have the impression of being in a valley because of its great size.

For an hour at Waka-Waka, I was the center of attention of the native kids who visually examined me and my equipment until the next charter plane circled the little airstrip and then landed. Disembarking were my professional hunter, Ronnie Sparrow; my hunting companion, Wayne Pocius; and my cameraman, Rick Morgan. They had flown in after a great week in the Bangweulu Swamps where Wayne had shot a Zambezi sitatunga, black lechwe, oribi, and tsessebe. The plan was for Wayne to hunt Cookson's wildebeest and Nile crocodile for three days in the Luangwa and then depart, leaving me as the sole hunter for another week.

During the 2½-hour drive from Waka-Waka to camp, I could see the vegetation varying from riverine, where the Luangwa River runs through the Valley, to dense scrub and mopane forest, to the hill country. Camp itself, was constructed of grass and thatch with our sleeping huts each having a shower "ensuite," as Ronnie would say. The centerpiece of camp was a picturesque thatch dining pavilion overlooking the Luangwa River.

Wayne shot a good Cookson's wildebeest the second day; the Valley being the only place where what is generally considered the most beautiful of the wildebeest

Backlit in the dining pavilion, L to R: Wayne Pocius, me, Ronnie Sparrow, and cameraman Rick Morgan.

sub-species can be hunted. On the way back to camp, we saw dozens of vultures spiraling, so Ronnie suggested that we take a look because we might find a lion kill. When we arrived, we found that the lions had killed a hippo. What they hadn't finished the hyenas had, because all that was left was a skeleton recently picked clean.

We walked single-file back to the Land Rover through the long grass. Sakala, our tracker, led the way, then Ronnie, me, Wayne, and Rick. Suddenly Ronnie turned, and since I was next in line, motioned me forward and pointed to a hyena standing broadside and looking over his right shoulder at about 60 yards. I raised my rifle and fired. The hyena ran through the grass in a half circle and dropped. Many people that have viewed the full mount of this animal in my trophy room say it is the biggest hyena they have ever seen, but the skull measurements place it only in the middle of the SCI Record Book.

L to R with my spotted hyena: Ronnie, Wayne, Sakala, and me.

ZAMBIA

The next day, Wayne concentrated on hunting crocodile. We saw hundreds, but most were only nine- to 10-footers, and trying to get within rifle range of the few bigger ones was proving to be difficult. It is surprising how well crocs can detect motion or sound. They have to be stalked with great care because they can disappear into the water in a flash.

Sakala and Ronnie finally led Wayne to a few trees on an embankment overlooking a 12-foot croc lying next to the water with his tail toward us and his head angled slightly right at 80 yards. Ronnie whispered, "Just put it [your bullet] in at the end of his jawline and it will go right through his brain." Then he nodded and Sakala placed the shooting sticks clear of the trees, Wayne balanced his rifle on them, and squeezed off.

At the shot, the croc's head snapped up and fell back down; the tail wagged for 15 seconds, slower and slower, and stopped.

Ronnie and Sakala shook Wayne's hand and we all walked down the embankment to claim the croc. It was out of our sight for maybe 20 seconds, but that was long enough for it to come back to life and disappear. We inspected the blood and drag marks in the sand, but never did find the croc. Wayne would fly back to the States in the morning, so that was his last chance.

That night at dinner, Wayne was in a pretty good mood, despite "the incident with the crocodile," and it was a good thing because Rick and I had a little going away ceremony for him. At that time in the evolution of Safari Club International, some hunters would walk around the Annual Convention with sashes and merit badges, like the Boy Scouts, and this spectacle culminated in the "parade of sashes" at one of the gala evening events, generally accompanied by a combination of applause and snickers. Wayne was working his way up the political ranks of SCI at the time and would, in fact, become president of what I believe is the world's most productive hunting and conservation organization.

That night, in the Luangwa Valley of Zambia, several members of the staff made a great deal of commotion while carrying a makeshift sash to the dining pavilion. The sash was placed over the right shoulder and under the left shoulder of a bewildered Wayne Pocius. Then, with a quick series of speeches, Rick and I awarded Wayne various bottle caps and buttons to attach to his sash for the trophies he had collected in Zambia. (The button for the croc was, of course, given and then retracted.) Ronnie was literally rolling on the floor as we made Wayne parade around the dining table. It didn't take long after that for the sashes and merit badges to disappear from the SCI Convention.

After Wayne's departure, I shot a puku, hippo, Cookson's wildebeest, warthog, crocodile, and impala; everything I wanted to shoot except a Cape buffalo and lion. The puku, which is also known as Vardon's kob, was a must to collect because almost all record book entries are from the Valley.

We wanted the hippo for lion bait since they had already shown an appetite for the river horse. And as long as I was going to shoot one, I wanted a good trophy

My puku was shot after a long crawl to get in position to see its shoulder.

because there were plenty around.

I preferred to shoot a bull on land, but we kept finding them bunched together on the other side of the river. Twice we made stalks and were detected which caused a rush of dozens of hippos to the water followed by lots of splashing and snorting. After the second time, Ronnie said, "With everything else you want to shoot, you better shoot one [hippo] in the water or we'll run out of time to go to Lochinvar [for Kafue Flats lechwe]." I agreed.

"The herd bull is moving downstream with a few cows, so let's back out of sight, move downstream, and reapproach the embankment," Ronnie advised while looking through his binoculars.

When we reached some trees, we stalked back to the edge of a 30-foot drop-off where I could see the hippos looking around about 100 yards out. Ronnie picked out the herd bull: "The one with the big bump on either side of each nostril where his tusks are pushing up on his upper lip; do you see him?"

When the herd bull turned to look at us, I placed a 300-grain solid between his eyes. He immediately submerged and we didn't see him for 45 minutes by which time his stomach gasses caused him to float to the surface.

Ronnie asked our trackers, Sakala and Chogalola, to retrieve the hippo. They looked at all that dark water, visualized the hundreds of crocs we had seen the past few days, and wisely declined, so we hired three local fisherman for the job at a cost of 25 cents U.S. each. I fired a round across the water and then the fisherman entered with wooden poles to both feel the bottom and slap the water. When they reached the hippo, they put a rope around it and then swam for shore . . . fast! Then the fishermen and our trackers floated the hippo downstream to where the embankment ended and the Land Rover could be hooked to the rope and the hippo pulled out.

Once about 75 yards onshore, we all helped roll the hippo on his ample stomach and then Mooney, our driver, used an ax to chop openings on both sides of the hippo, just in front of the hindquarters. He removed two pieces of skin, each about 16 inches long by eight inches high and 1 1/2 inches thick. Ronnie wanted the openings to be small enough to discourage the hyenas and to force the lions to take longer to feed.

That afternoon I shot a warthog. We also crossed paths with a truck with five guys standing in the back, three with rifles at the ready. Another three guys were in the cab and two of them got out with their rifles. They said they were looking for poachers and the stickers on their door backed them up; but those rifles were still pointed in our direction. The head man said they were glad to have us in the area to report any poaching, but the real reason they were glad to see us was for the beer and biltong we were encouraged to give them when they accompanied us back to our camp.

When we saw two good warthogs from the hunting vehicle, Ronnie had the trackers drive off while we made a stalk.

Early the next morning, we returned to the hippo, parked about a mile away, and walked through the long grass to reach it. We spotted several lionesses along the way at close enough proximity for Ronnie to caution, "You watch the lion on the left and I'll watch the two on our right."

When we could see the hippo, we caught glimpses of three lionesses and a young male at the carcass before they ran. At the hippo, we found the cats had not even torn the thick skin, but had just reached in the convenient openings and pulled out the stomach. To discourage vultures, we covered the hippo with thornbush and our men built a four-sided blind. Then we departed.

I shot a Cookson's wildebeest in the middle of the day by hitting him hard in the chest as he stood facing me at 150 yards, but he still ran off. Since I was five feet up a tree when I shot, I handed my rifle down to Sakala, jumped down, grabbed my rifle back, and then ran a short distance before dropping the beast with a 200-yard shot through a forest of trees. After photos, we ate lunch and returned to our newly built blind, quietly entering at 4:00 PM.

At about 5:00 PM, a big lioness appeared, looked around,

A Cookson's wildebeest, which I first shot while up a tree (me, not the wildebeest) and then, again, from the ground.

145

and wiggled into the thornbush to start feeding. After awhile, we could see other members of the pride hanging back in cover, so Ronnie decided we needed to remove the thornbush, which we did without incident. Eventually several more lionesses started feeding, but no big male. We stayed until dark and then returned to our Land Rover and drove 1 1/2 hours back to camp.

At first light, we were back in our blind, quietly looking through the viewing holes. We could see several lionesses and year old cubs at the carcass, some feeding and some just lolling around with big stomachs and bloody faces. After an hour of seeing no new lions, Ronnie said, "We'll give it 30 more minutes and if a good one hasn't come in by then, we'll leave because there may not be a shootable male here."

After 30 minutes, Ronnie said, "Let's go chase the lionesses off the hippo." As we walked out of the blind, 11 lionesses and cubs ran for cover, but the 12th one, the dominant female, immediately came for us. We were 20 yards from the blind and 60 yards from the hippo. I was on the left, Ronnie in the middle, and Sakala on the right. Ronnie and I immediately raised our rifles. Sakala was unarmed, but knew not to run. We held our fire until the lioness was at 20 yards. Just as I started my trigger squeeze, she veered off and disappeared in the bush.

"She wanted to give us a go," Ronnie said with a smile. I smiled back . . . bravely.

As we approached the hippo, we could hear a tribe of baboons screaming as the lion pride passed them. The hippo had a good set of tusks, but it had not sat long enough for them to be pulled so the men hacked off the jaws and, back at camp, the skinner boiled out the tusks.

That evening the skinner presented me with the warthog and hippo tusks. The warthog's measured 12 inches, of which four inches had been in the jaw, and the longest tusks from the hippo were over 24 inches, of which nine inches were in the jaw. The hippo tusks were big enough that, when I unwrapped them a year later upon delivery to the U.S., the two biggest were missing, stolen by someone along the way.

The next afternoon we made a stalk among the piles of deadwood on the shore of the Luangwa River until I crawled into a pile 150 yards from a sandbar at a bend in the river. There a big crocodile lay at the water's edge, facing me straight-on. Using the wood as a rest, I shot the croc between the eyes. His head jumped up in the air and fell back down as his tail wagged weakly and stopped. But I had learned from Wayne's experience of a week earlier, so I killed the croc twice more.

This time our crew felt a little braver (I don't know why, because the river was absolutely infested with crocs), so they waded out to the sandbar, ran along it, and whacked the croc with a pole to make sure it was dead. Since it didn't turn around and eat them, they put a rope around it and dragged it into the water and then back to us where Sakala said it was a male. When I asked him how he knew, he had his men roll the croc onto its back. Then he reached into a slit near the back legs and pulled out the pure white evidence of manhood.

The trackers waded across a croc-infested river to retrieve this one for me.

Our last day in the Luangwa Valley, I shot an impala, of which we saw hundreds but none over 20 to 21 inches. And we had not seen a Cape buffalo, which was disappointing. Nevertheless, it was a great 10 days, counting the time spent with Wayne. When we returned to camp that last night, the staff was waiting with a celebration of singing and dancing.

The next morning as we drove out of camp, Ronnie said, "It's about a 12-hour drive to Lusaka. We'll overnight there and leave early the next morning, about 4:30 AM, to get to Lochinvar at about 7:30 AM, where we'll have four to five hours of lechwe hunting, which should give us enough time to come back to Lusaka, clean up, and for you to catch your flight." In other words, we were going to cut it very close.

No sooner had Ronnie finished explaining the logistics of making a try for Kafue Flats lechwe than, in an amazed voice, he said, "Ken, there's some buffalo!" He swatted away a tsetse and added, "Get your rifle, get ready, and let's go after them because they're in our concession."

With the bottom tusks from my hippo and many of my trophies from the Luangwa Valley.

I was dressed in traveling clothes and my rifle was in a locked case at the bottom of a pile in the back of the truck. Chogalola kept his eyes on the buffalo while I uncased my .375 and grabbed some ammo from the glove box. Then we were off at a run. After several hundred yards, Ronnie stopped and Chogalola pointed. There were five bulls of equal horn size looking around the thornbush at about 200 yards. I put my rifle on Ronnie's left shoulder and fired. The buffalo thundered off and we sprinted after them.

When we reached the spot where the bulls had been standing, we slowed to a careful walk until Chogalola pointed again. Fifty yards ahead, my buffalo was lying on his right side, stomach toward us, trying to get up. I shot him in the chest and he let out a death bellow.

As we walked closer, the bull started kicking, so Ronnie said, "Be careful!" Just then the bull raised his head and Ronnie added, "Give him another one just for insurance." So I shot him for the fourth time and told Ronnie, "I'm down to my last round" (since I had grabbed only five cartridges out of the glove box). "If he charges, you take over," I said jokingly . . . I thought.

We watched the bull carefully from 30 yards. He wasn't breathing. Ronnie said, "I'll tell you, these things are tough." I walked a little closer and commented on the nice spread. Ronnie stopped me and warned, "It's not impossible that he gets up and comes for us. I had a case where a guy shot a buffalo, put his camera on top of it and, the next thing, it gets up and runs away, so it always pays to be careful."

As if on cue, the buffalo, who had been on his right side for about five minutes, rolled onto his stomach, facing us, and started to get up. Ronnie immediately shot twice below the eyes and, with the buffalo's head down, I shot him in the spine.

L to R: Ronnie, Rick, Chogalola, and me with my last-second Cape buffalo.

"See what I mean?" Ronnie asked. "He was exactly trying to get up. He was just building his strength to give us a go."

Due to the buffalo detour, which also entailed loading and delivering it back to camp, we didn't reach our hotel in Lusaka until after midnight. Then, as planned, we were up at 4:00 AM and on the road a half hour later.

About an hour outside of Lusaka, we ran into a roadblock that put us behind a long line of cars and trucks. Ronnie looked at his watch and then had Sakala walk to the front of the line and find out how much it would take to get us through without waiting. Sakala returned 10 minutes later, spoke to Ronnie in Fanagalo, and then jogged off to the roadblock again. Ronnie filled us in: "They won't take money. They want meat. We don't have any, but I sent Sakala to tell them that if they let us through immediately, we can bring back a lechwe."

Sakala returned with what looked like an army officer who scrutinized us and our truck and then escorted us around about 20 vehicles.

Two hours later, the Kafue Flats transitioned from brown grass to greener grass where the nomadic cattlemen had their herds. About 50 zebra sprinted in front of our Land Rover as we drove the edge of the wet grassland until we saw a herd of over a hundred male Kafue Flats lechwe, the longest-horned of the lechwe species. We got out of the Land Rover and started zigzagging through the ankle-deep water to within 400 yards of the herd. Ronnie picked out a good one . . . I can't say it was the best because there were probably 20 with horns over the magic 30 inches.

Sakala placed the tall shooting sticks by me as Ronnie and I talked back and forth until I was sure I was on the same lechwe. Then I shot. Ronnie called out, "Low!" As the herd ran, I shot once more. Ronnie said, "Low again. Let's leave these now and go after another herd because if we go after these, they're just going to be skittish."

I looked at my watch and saw that there was less than two hours until our predetermined latest possible departure time. By the time we sloshed our way within shooting distance of the next herd, we had less than one hour remaining. Ronnie finally said, "Do you see that white egret there, on the extreme left of the herd? He's to the left of that white egret and he's a good one."

I fired and the lechwe jumped and ran. "Good shot. No need to shoot again, that was a good lung shot," Ronnie observed. I exhaled with relief. At that point, I was not even shooting for a trophy. I was shooting for meat in order to get out of Zambia!

I shot my Kafue Flats lechwe, where else, but on the Kafue Flats?

AFRICA — CENTRAL

20

C.A.R. (BINGO ON BONGO)

A diary of hunting with the Pygmies of the central African rain forest

May 27-29, 1994 (Friday - Sunday)
The journey starts — Kerrville, Texas to San Antonio to St. Louis to Boston to Paris to Bangui, capital city of the Central African Republic (C.A.R.). Bangui is located just north of the equator on the north side of the Oubangui River. On the south side is Zaire. The C.A.R. is a part of what used to be French Equatorial Africa, along with Chad and Cameroon. The native tongue is Songo (for the non-Pygmies), but French is also commonly spoken.

For several reasons, I booked this safari with Alain Lefol, a French citizen who has hunted the equatorial rain forest with great success for over a decade.

First, for the shear adventure of hunting with the Pygmies who are the Kings of the Jungle because of their great knowledge of the flora and fauna, which they use daily to survive. By agreement among the C.A.R., Cameroon, and Congo-Brazzaville, the Pygmies are classified as Citizens of the Forest and may wander through those borders and use the resources of the rain forest as they need. I, of course, would be confined to the C.A.R. and bound by its hunting rules and regulations.

Second, because the bongo lives in the rain forest. The Safari Club International

Record Book of Trophy Animals (Edition VIII, Volume I) states that the bongo is "... [O]ne of the top game trophies of the world. Many consider it the premier African game animal. The bongo is a large antelope (a mature bull weighing about 600 pounds) with a humped back and rather short, stout legs. It is bright chestnut red with 10-14 white stripes on each side. Both sexes grow horns, those of the female usually being smaller and straighter."

Third, because of the title of a chapter in a book I read 10 years ago ... the *only* chapter title I can remember out of all the hunting books I have read. The book is *Hunting in Africa* by Frank C. Hibben and the last chapter is titled "Bingo on Bongo" (title and quote by permission of the publisher, Hill and Wang, New York). A few sentences on the opening page of that chapter inexorably resulted in this safari, "The bongo antelope of Africa is shyer than the most blushing wallflower that ever refused a dance. 'Rare and hard to get' are gross understatements as far as the bongo is concerned. I ought to know. I spent over nine weeks of hunting, on four separate African safaris, before I shot one."

In Bangui, I am whisked off the plane by Bette Delsarte, who is probably the friendliest and most efficient whisker in the business. Born and raised in Milwaukee, she married a diamond buyer and has lived in Bangui or the surrounding rain forest for the last 10 years. She coordinates Alain Lefol's safari operation while Alain and his wife, Eliane, are in the jungle. My passport and visa are checked, my international inoculation card is checked, the serial numbers on my rifle (a .375 H&H magnum) and my shotgun (a 12 gauge over and under) are checked, and each round of ammunition is counted, since I will be taxed on each round missing when I return to the airport in 15 days.

At the airport, I meet Dominique and Serge Simon, a French couple who, unbeknownst to me, have flown in from Paris on my Air Afrique flight. They are on assignment to cover my safari for *Connaissance de la Chasse* ("Knowledge of the Hunt"), a respected French magazine. Serge is the photographer and Dominique the writer and they have traveled the world covering hunting, wildlife, and adventure.

Base camp consisted of several chalets. Mine is on the left.

I am on assignment to produce a video for Sportsmen on Film. The Simons and I will share video duties. Serge speaks no English and I speak no French, so Alain or Eliane or Dominique will need to say everything in two languages.

C.A.R. (Bingo on Bongo)

Bette puts us on a bushplane for the one-hour flight to base camp located in Alain's concession in the southwest corner of the C.A.R., 300 miles southwest of Bangui, 60 miles east of Cameroon and 75 miles north of Congo-Brazzaville. Our pilot is Frenchman Jean Paul Mangeon who, when we land near the Sangha River, informs me (upon hearing I am from Texas) that he received his pilot's training in Fort Worth. He learned well because he had to drop in over a huge tree to put down on the landing strip recently carved out of the jungle.

Base camp is located on a hill overlooking the surrounding rain forest. To reach it, we drive through the small villages of Adebori, Bandoka, Lobi, Mekanda, and Motao where automobile travel is so rare that the children wave to us like we are a passing train. The camp consists of thatched roof chalets for living quarters, a large dining room-lounge, bathroom and shower chalets, plus chalets for the kitchen, mechanic, skinner, trackers, and servants.

After lunch, I sight in my rifle (using 300-grain solids to penetrate the limbs and vines and leaves of the rain forest where visibility is often just a few feet or yards), and we drive a winding dirt track for about an hour and then walk along a trail to inspect a huge limba tree with a star-shaped base at least 20 feet wide at the tips. Bats are using a hollow in the tree and, since their droppings are very salty, bongo sometimes visit to lick the salt. Alain calls it a "saline." There, in the moist soil, are bongo tracks belonging to a big male (as judged from the size, especially the width, of the track) but they are over a day old, so we don't follow them that late in the afternoon.

At dinner that night (where I ate my first bongo meat, which is absolutely delicious . . . even better than eland), Alain tells me we were fortunate not to find a fresher track and shoot a bongo on the first day because I wouldn't have experienced the hunt or appreciated the trophy. Twice he has had clients see 30-inch trophies on the first day and he could not let those unfortunate souls pass them up. Of course, the earlier you get a bongo, the more time you have to hunt other unique game such as western forest sitatunga, dwarf buffalo, and several duikers.

May 30 (Monday)

In the morning, we hike in and inspect two salines north of camp. No fresh tracks, so we drive a logging road to a point where we hike in about two hours to what is called a "mineral" or salt lick. This mineral is about one-quarter of an acre and, at the time, is mud with a fallen tree over it. In the mud are tracks of elephant, buffalo, and bongo, but nothing fresh enough to follow.

Some bongo hunts are conducted by sitting in a machan, or stand, over a mineral hoping that a bongo will show up, but Alain's hunts are conducted as the Pygmies hunt them which is by tracking close enough to a feeding or sleeping animal to release a pair of small dogs to distract the bongo long enough to allow the hunter to advance the final yards for a shot (the Pygmies use poisoned arrows). In the thick cover of the rain forest, I will need to get within 10 to 20 yards just to see a part of the animal through my scope set at $1\,^1/_2$ power.

Alain Lefol with Mekama at the Sangha River.

After lunch, we set up for duiker calling by walking to an area with good visibility (15 to 20 yards). Mekama, the head tracker, sits down with me next to him. I'm holding my shotgun loaded with BBs. Mekama then mimics the sound of a duiker in distress by holding his nose and emitting a sound through his mouth like a cat meowing with a bad cold. Within seconds, a duiker charges up behind us and departs as soon as I start to turn. We try again in two other places with no luck.

Late in the afternoon, we walk out at three miles per hour for the first hour which is a pretty good clip over the slippery footing of wet leaves, clay, and roots. Vines are everywhere to trip and strangle (although each Pygmy carries a machete to ease the way). The pace for the next half hour is increased to four miles per hour. I am following Alain with Mekama in the lead. Next are my two gunbearers (who carry my guns in soft plastic cases to protect them from the wet leaves and scratching vines), three more trackers, eight packers (who take turns carrying lots of water, a little food, rain gear, binoculars, and camera gear sealed in plastic to prevent the high humidity from rendering them useless), plus Dominique and Serge.

Alain says something to Mekama and the pace quickens to five miles per hour, and we separate from the group behind. Then Alain and I pass Mekama who doesn't realize we are in a race. When we reach the Land Cruiser, Alain turns around for the first time and says, "Good exercise, yes? If you don't lose 15 pounds, your wife will think you spent two weeks in Paris!"

May 31 (Tuesday)

Daylight is about 6:00 AM to 6:00 PM where we are hunting between three degrees and four degrees north of the equator. Our usual routine is a 5:00 AM wake-up, breakfast, and departure by 6:00 AM. We usually return by 8:00 PM, shower, eat at 9:00 PM, and retire by 10:00 PM with the generator turned off shortly thereafter.

By agreement, my professional hunter for this day is Alain's nephew, Jean Christophe Lefol, just turned 21 and already a licensed assistant PH in both the C.A.R. and Tanzania.

We drive about three hours northwest to inspect a "savannah," a meadow in the

C.A.R. (BINGO ON BONGO)

rain forest. The dirt road that we drive for 60 miles is part of 150 miles that Jean Christophe and a team of 50 Pygmies cleared with chainsaws and machetes before the start of the season. Most of the original clearing for roads is done by logging companies who are authorized to remove one tree per acre. When they are finished, the jungle reclaims the roads except for those Alain salvages.

As we walk into the savannah, we find a promising set of bongo tracks but, after following them a short distance, Jean Christophe surmises they belong to a female with one swollen hoof that gives the impression of the wider track of a mature male.

Upon reaching the savannah, we walk the perimeter for about a mile and find buffalo sign but no buffalo and we see a young sitatunga but no bull. All they have to do is lie down in the tall grass or submerge in the waterways and they become invisible.

On the way out, we set up to call duiker several times (I call it "walk a mile, call awhile hunting"). On one occasion, Mekama points and I move my barrel in that direction. Then he points frantically with his whole arm. Visibility is maybe 15 yards as I struggle to see the duiker that Mekama can see so clearly. Finally, I shoot at where he is pointing . . . or, I guess I don't.

June 1 (Wednesday)

Near the Lobi River (where we hunted on the first afternoon), Alain sends Mekatijo (Mekama's brother), Lipoupa, and me on a two-mile roundtrip to inspect a saline. No tracks.

Good news. While I was getting my morning exercise, Mekama found fresh bongo tracks. Alain decides it is a group of four and not to follow them, because it's tough enough to track close to one without the added problems of three more. But the tracks were made that morning and one set is large, so Alain is persuaded by his trackers to follow them.

Mekama takes the lead with two assistants, followed by Alain, me, my rifle gunbearer and the rest of the crew. We follow the tracks in the moist leaves at a fast pace, pausing only occasionally where the bongos have milled around. Then three or four trackers cast out until the direction is again determined. Rarely does a track show clearly in the red clay of the forest floor. Usually leaves have to be removed to see the impression.

Gombo, smiling before he was run over by the bongo ("bongo on Gombo").

When the trackers sense we are close, the two little dogs (10 to 15 pounds each), Mipa and Yalo, are sent trotting in circles in front of us trying to see a bongo before it sees us and bolts. Finally, the dogs make contact and let out a bark. Then we see a patch of red hide in a sea of green leaves. Alain signals Bencque to uncase my rifle and hand it to me. I slide a round into the chamber, lift the scope covers, and carefully crawl forward with the safety on while waiting for Alain's trophy assessment. When the bongo turns, I find its left shoulder in my scope, but Alain says, "Female." The herd bull has escaped. We back off and, when the dogs follow us, the five to six year old female bongo runs through our Pygmy packers and hits Gombo in the shin as he tries to climb a vine that fails him (it will take Gombo a week before he is able to rejoin us).

On the way out, Alain points out that, without the use of the dogs to give time and opportunity to view the body size and horns, many hunters would have shot at the patch of red and ended up killing an 18-inch female.

June 2 (Thursday)

In the morning, the Pygmies are excited because we will take 25 of them, cross the Sangha River by barge, drive northeast for 2 ½ hours and fly camp for three days. We need the extra manpower as porters and to set up the temporary camp. As we are doing just that, one of the trackers finds bongo tracks that fill the four prerequisites that I now realize are required for success (bull tracks, large, fresh, and alone).

We find that it hasn't rained here in several days so, even though the soil is sandy, the tracking is difficult. We follow the tracks for three hours before we come upon a well-defined track in some clay. The track is studied intently by Mekama and Alain before both conclude it is over a day old. Furthermore, Alain feels the dryness of the area will hurt our chances so he orders the construction of the fly camp halted, and we re-cross the Sangha and return to base camp quite late.

June 3 (Friday)

Today we drive south 20 miles to a plateau known as Songho 2 and walk into a mineral where we find bongo tracks which we follow for five hours over the wet and slippery forest floor.

In the middle of the afternoon, Serge badly sprains his ankle when he falls and successfully saves his expensive camera. Alain tapes the ankle and then takes a satellite reading on his GPS (Global Position Satellite navigation instrument) to determine the most direct route for Jeannot to lead Serge back to the Land Cruiser while we continue the hunt. (Serge stays in camp the rest of the safari. I take shorter and higher steps from then on in the interest of self-preservation).

While Serge is being tended to, we have walked over the bongo tracks so the Pygmies cast out in all directions, but can't relocate the trail. Alain calls off the hunt so we can return to the Land Cruiser in daylight.

C.A.R. (BINGO ON BONGO)

I am wearing French-made high-top, soft leather boots, polypropylene inner socks and wool outers to keep my feet dry, long pants with ties on the bottom to protect my legs from the clinging vines and crawling insects, a T-shirt and baseball cap. The cap is optional, but it keeps the water off my glasses and the bill serves as an early warning device for the higher vines that the Pygmies don't cut through.

Because we are continually wet from sweat or rain every day, I have three sets of clothes, all in Bushlan's spring camouflage which seems made for the rain forest. Laundry is done every day, but does not dry on the days it rains, so three sets of clothes are better than two.

The Pygmies are about the smilingest, jokingest bunch I have ever met. They like working for Alain and some have been with him for 12 years during his two months of hunting the rain forest each year plus assorted work like road clearing. The rest of the year, they hunt with spears and poisoned arrows, eat manouk root, and live off the land, building a hut in a few hours out of sticks, vines and leaves, and moving on when they feel like it or moving back to small permanent Pygmy villages. They stay clear of the towns where, unfortunately, they are subjects of derision and are often conscripted for labor.

Posing for a photo after a long hike.

Typical housing in a Pygmy village.

A Pygmy lady returning to her village after a day of leaf gathering.

Our trackers appear to average about four feet four inches in height and I believe they will always be small because, if I am any indication, the taller ones must be too tired to breed when they return from a day of ducking through the vines.

June 4 (Saturday)

A 30-mile day; 48 kilometers by the map to Gelele and Niam-Tanga but no doubt farther because of the winding trails and steep terrain in some places. We check three minerals with no luck. When we are 15 miles down the narrow, slippery trail, a broken leg would probably result in the Pygmies having to bring you food until you healed.

On the trail, we hear gorillas (as we did on three other days) and find knuckle imprints and droppings. At one mineral, there are thousands of butterflies. On the way back out, we run into several sets of fresh elephant tracks, but the most welcome sight is the Land Cruiser at the end of the trail.

June 5 (Sunday)

I took my weekly anti-malaria pill last night. We don't have many mosquitoes, but we do sleep under mosquito netting. Most bites seem to be from ants encountered while brushing against vines and trees. Anti-itch cream keeps the bites from becoming infected.

C.A.R. (BINGO ON BONGO)

This morning we return to the Lobi River and find fresh tracks. Alain thinks they are medium and belong to a young bull or old female. Mekama thinks they are large so he and his men follow them errorlessly. When the dogs finally bark, we spot the bongo across a deep ravine. By the time I reach Alain, my rifle is already uncased and he motions me half way down the ravine so I can have the most unobstructed shot. When the bongo turns, Alain says, "Too small; over 30 inches [which is big], but small bases. It's a female."

The Pygmies killed this lizard and spent most of the night cooking and eating it.

Mature females have a horn circumference of six to seven inches at the base whereas mature males average 10 to 11 inches. Females are legal to shoot, but Alain and I have agreed that I will only settle for a male so we walk out. Half the safari is now gone and the problem with going seven days with nothing is you now know the same thing can happen for another seven.

On the drive back to camp, we talk about how expensive it is to outfit in the C.A.R. which is landlocked and where almost everything is flown or barged in from other countries. Alain's Land Cruiser cost $60,000 in Bangui where gas is $8 per gallon.

June 6 (Monday)

This morning we drive 65 miles north/northwest to Komi 3, a three-hour drive. At the second saline, we find a set of huge bongo tracks. They are the biggest Alain has ever seen. He calls them "buffalo tracks." They are judged to be two days old which is confirmed when we find droppings partially covered by the dirt brought over them by the insects that eat the droppings. But the tracks are so big, we decide to follow them anyway in case the bull crosses his own trail and we can pick up a day. We track all day to droppings made the night before, and then race out for 80 minutes as it rains in the gathering darkness.

We drive back three hours and make plans to arise at 4:00 AM and return to Komi 3 to set up a fly camp.

If you like playing in the rain, walking in the mud, sweating, and the color green, this is the place for you.

June 7 (Tuesday)

Up at 4:00 AM and on our way at 5:00 AM. We go straight to the plateau at Komi 3 while Jean Christophe takes a team to set-up the fly camp near the Napongo River.

Since we are again two days behind the "buffalo tracks," Alain decides we should walk the perimeter of the plateau and try to cut fresh tracks but all we find are medium tracks made by another bull. Alain concludes that "our" bongo laid up during last night's rain and won't move again until tonight.

We have walked for six hours but, if we cut straight across the plateau, Alain figures we can get back in three hours. He takes a satellite reading but can only pick-up two in the narrow opening we find in the forest canopy and we need three to get a fix. The Pygmies want to return the way we came but Alain references his compass and guides us up and over the plateau and straight to the Land Cruiser. Even then, darkness beats us, and we use flashlights the last half hour.

June 8 (Wednesday)

We check two dirt roads and two salines for tracks. Nothing. We make a two-hour round trip walk to check three savannahs and find dwarf forest buffalo tracks but no bongo. We drive near the plateau and hike in. After an hour, we find bongo tracks and follow them to a clear print. Too small. We walk another hour and find large tracks, but they lead to a group. Fifteen minutes later, we find more large tracks. Alain has two trackers follow them while we break for water and a sandwich. This may be it!

Bad news. The bull was part of a group, so we walk out. On the way, we find the carcass of a duiker that is hanging from a snare trap. The Pygmies are saddened by this waste of meat. They run duikers into vine nets and eat everything they kill.

It rains enough to force us to suit up and then it stops which allows us to make it back to the Land Cruiser with an hour of daylight left so Alain drives near a savannah we haven't yet hunted. Binoculars are useless in the rain forest, but now we unpack them for the first time in anticipation of needing them in the failing light and openness of the savannah. We quietly walk from one island of vegetation to another as we approach the waterways and tall grass at the end of this big opening in the jungle. Sometimes bongo feed along the forest edge.

As Alain glasses the perimeter, I see a male sitatunga through my binoculars as it emerges from a waterway and walks along the edge of the tall grass. Alain sees him also and says only, "Use my shoulder." I quietly chamber a round, put the fore-end of the fiberglass stock on Alain's left shoulder as he plugs his ears, find the sitatunga in my scope (now set at six power), and fire. The bull drops hard and then jumps up and disappears into the swamp. My crosshairs were square on the shoulder when I squeezed off but, without the animal lying before us, there is some doubt.

Alain sends Poupee back to get the rest of the men to aid our search. We walk through three-foot-high grass and three-foot-deep waterways in the gathering darkness. Then Alain lets out a yell. He sees the head of the sitatunga above the water . . .

very dead from a heart shot. The Pygmies laugh and each shake my hand. On the way back to fly camp, they sing thanks to Manganui, their hunting God, for providing them with this meat.

The western forest sitatunga is rarely shot by trophy hunters primarily because most of your time is spent hunting bongo. Sitatunga are usually taken with luck and patience. On the other hand, bongo require hard work and, with just three days remaining, I will also need luck to get one.

With Alain Lefol and Pygmy staff by my western forest sitatunga, shot while hunting bongo.

June 9 (Thursday)
Our easiest and most disappointing day. We drive from saline to mineral to saline to mineral and drop off trackers to walk in, inspect, and walk out. Nothing. We check for tracks on the logging roads. Nothing. So we pack up and return to base camp for the last two days.

Our trackers and porters are from two different Pygmy tribes. West of the Sangha River is the Bangombi tribe, while east are the Pandjele. Tomorrow, we will again cross the Sangha River, drive 2 $1/2$ hours, and hunt near the Pandjele villages.

June 10 (Friday)

We look all day and find nothing, but it has rained and tomorrow should be a good day to find tracks, so Alain leaves two trackers at each of three Pygmy villages with instructions for them to check the salines, minerals, and trails at daybreak and to return to the villages by mid-morning. We re-cross the Sangha and return to base camp, arriving at 9:00 PM.

June 11 (Saturday)

Today's the last day. We will make an all-out effort, arising at 3:30 AM and departing at 4:30 AM.

At first light, we inspect the salines and logging roads close to camp, because the earlier we find tracks, the better. Nothing.

We return to base camp at 8:00 AM and check with Jean Christophe, who has checked the plateau below camp, but also found nothing. So we drive to the Sangha River where we will once again barge across and drive to the Pandjele villages that are now our last three chances.

The tugboat captain can't be found. We wait half an hour. At 9:30 AM, the captain's assistant says he can operate the tugboat. He walks upriver, hitches a ride on a pole canoe to the tugboat, motors down to the barge, and pushes us across. We arrive at the first village at 11:30 AM. The trackers haven't returned, which means they have found nothing and are still looking.

We drive to the second village, but a large tree has fallen and blocks our path. Alain chainsaws it in three places and the Pygmies roll two sections out of the way so we can pass. The trackers have found nothing around the second village.

Crossing the Sangha River after a precious hour was wasted waiting for the tugboat captain.

We drive to the last village in silence as the sky turns dark from impending rain. The trackers are there waiting. The Village Chief says they have found a track. We walk for 45 minutes and find two sets of tracks. The biggest tracks are small, but the Chief leads on for 15 minutes more and shows us another set of tracks. They are from a single bull and are medium. It's our last chance so we follow them in the sandy soil. The bull wanders through heavy cover. We find his bed . . . still warm. The thunder turns to rain and then it pours, wiping out the fresh tracks.

C.A.R. (BINGO ON BONGO)

But one of the dogs barks so we crawl through the vines and thick cover toward the sound. Alain sees the bongo as it turns to face one of the dogs. My rifle is uncased and a round chambered. Mekama drops back and Alain and I crawl forward. My glasses have been ripped from my face twice by vines, so I carry them in my left hand as I move the rifle along the ground with my right hand. Then Alain points. I put on my glasses, open the scope covers, raise my rifle, and look through the scope. The

More obstacles. . .logging roads have to be cleared of fallen timber.

With the rain stopped and the area cleared, pictures could be taken.

rain is so heavy that I see nothing. Alain is pointing at two patches of red at about 25 yards. I pick out the patch on the left, rise to the kneeling position, sight over the top of the scope, and fire, hitting the bull in the right thigh (I picked the wrong patch!). He turns and I see shoulder, but the vines keep me from aiming that far right, so I shoot at the back of his lungs. Alain pulls me left. I see my crosshairs for the first time, put them on the bongo's right shoulder, and fire again. He goes down and the Pygmies run up and start singing. They each grab a small branch with leaves and circle the bongo, waving their branches up and down as they thank Manganui. The rain pours down until the end of the song, and then the rain stops.

Three hours later, with the skin and all of the meat loaded in the Land Cruiser, the trackers sing for an hour straight as we drive through the villages whose inhabitants hear the singing and line the dirt road and cheer as we pass through.

May there always be a rain forest for the bongo and the Pygmy.

Alain Lefol skinned my bongo for a full-mount but, because of its small size, I ended up having it shoulder-mounted. Nevertheless, it's one of my most-prized trophies.

ZIMBABWE (LEOPARD CHARGE)

"Leopard Charge" visually documents the hunt for a big, male leopard that resulted in a charge and mauling. The charge, itself, is electrifying and riveting. It stops convention traffic in its collective tracks and rivets it to the aisle as viewers squirm and contort in open-mouth amazement at the quickness of the charge, the size and agility of the leopard, the total engulfment of its human target, and the speed and proficiency of the man who rushes forward and shoots the leopard off its victim.

Leopards are abundant throughout most of Africa, but they are not often seen in the daytime, because they usually hunt at night when cats are king. To offset this problem, professional hunters have developed a protocol something like this: find leopard tracks, shoot bait animals, drag the areas of the tracks with the bait animals, hang the baits in trees, inspect the baits each morning, build blinds when baits have been fed upon by leopards, and sit in the most promising blind from mid-afternoon to dark-thirty (unless you have a morning feeder).

Many are the clients who have spent half their hunting and sleeping time watching bait in a tree. A few clients have managed to avoid this tedium by hunting with Bushmen in the Kalahari Desert. Some Bushmen are able to track leopards on foot at a trot while the client and pro follow by truck. If everything goes right, the leopard tires of the exercise and charges. The Bushmen run back, past the truck, and the client is supposed to shoot the leopard before it jumps in the bed of the truck and shows everyone how it uses its teeth and claws.

A third method to hunt leopards is with dogs. The idea isn't new but, until recently, has generally been unsuccessful because the dogs have not been properly trained. By 1996, several leopards near Bulawayo, Zimbabwe had become notorious as stock killers and the landowners were frustrated. They weren't being helped by local safari operators because there wasn't enough plains game around to interest clients in hunting on their land. And the landowners weren't having much success hunting the leopards themselves, because the cats had become smart enough not to come to bait or return to their own kills.

While stock killing leopards were creating problems in Zimbabwe, ranchers in the Cape Provinces of South Africa were having problems with jackals and caracals, as well as the occasional leopard, eating their fawn crops. But the ranchers had found help from dog handlers with dogs trained to track the predators. Roy Sparks was one such dog handler.

Back in Zimbabwe, Mark Butcher, a professional hunter with Matapula Hunters, thought, "Why not enlist help from Roy Sparks and go after stock killing leopards with dogs? We can help the local ranchers without having to endure the boredom of watching dead meat rot [the traditional method of hunting leopards from blinds]. The risks are higher than with baiting, so I prefer clients who are experienced in Africa, know how to use their rifle, and who will follow instructions. This was especially important for my first experimental hunt."

Hal Ahlberg was Mark's choice as his first client for hunting cats with dogs. Hal is a veteran of 15 African safaris and has hunted with Mark six times. They met Roy on a ranch two hours' drive from Bulawayo, cut a big leopard track, and released the dogs. Hal had hired Buck Rogers to videotape the hunt for his personal remembrance, and what a remembrance it was going to be!

When the hunters jumped the leopard, it ran for rough country and into one of the multiple openings in a rock *koppie*. Hal couldn't get a clean shot, and then the leopard escaped. The dogs ran him down a canyon and into another rock *koppie*. This time Hal took two quick shots with his 7mm magnum. The leopard had not shown its chest, but Mark thought that it was hit well enough that he and Hal should hold their positions 10 yards from where they could see the leopard.

Roy Sparks, however, was concerned about the safety of his dogs, so he walked up to the rocks with a single action .41 Ruger handgun and took a shot from close range. The leopard charged and Roy missed him with his next shot from six inches under duress. As Roy fell backwards and threw up his left arm, the cat engulfed him and they tumbled downhill. In the ensuing five seconds, Roy was bit to the bone in four places and his left wrist was fractured by one bite. But it could have been much worse. When Roy and the leopard tumbled, the cat was turned so its claws faced away and could not be used for raking. Instantly, Mark Butcher ran forward with his .458, placed the muzzle on the leopard's shoulder, and blew the

ZINBABWE (LEOPARD CHARGE)

Hal Ahlberg's leopard charges Roy Sparks and slaps Roy's handgun.

Middle photo: As Roy falls back, the leopard engulfs him and bites his left shoulder.

Bottom photo: Roy and the leopard roll downhill.

Instantly, professional hunter Mark Butcher rushes forward with .458 in hand.

leopard off of Roy. Any hesitation or any other action, such as standing back and shooting, could have been disastrous.

For insurance, Mark shot the cat a second time. Then the work began. He sent a tracker for the first aid kit, he had Hal hold a compress on Roy's worst bite, and he sent the cameraman, Buck, for the truck. Then, cognizant of the high chance for infection, Mark pulled the wounds open and poured antiseptic into each bite and scratch.

After being treated for shock, Roy was able to walk to the truck. And he recovered enough to insist upon a picture with Hal, the leopard, his staff, and his dogs before departing. Then Mark drove Roy to the hospital in Bulawayo while Hal stayed behind to use the closest phone to make sure that a doctor would be standing by. With the team effort and his inherent toughness, Roy Sparks quickly recovered and continues to pursue stock killing leopards with his dogs. He is older and wiser.

My thanks to Hal Ahlberg for allowing me to edit his video footage into "Leopard Charge."

Hal Ahlberg standing with rifle. Roy Sparks standing with bandages.

AFRICA RSA

22

ZULULAND SAFARI

A one-on-one safari is the best way to trophy hunt because you're always the hunter, but it can be expensive and lonely. A two-on-one adds a hunting companion, but divides your hunting time and can create conflicts and jealousy. If three or four hunters want to share the same camp, two professional hunters will create more hunting opportunities, but the hunting area is divided as well as the hunting time. Knowing all of the above, I departed on a five-on-one safari . . . and it turned out great!

My wife, Lorraine, accompanied me as an observer and we brought our 14-year-old son, Ryan, as a co-hunter on his first safari. Lad and Lenka Shunneson joined us as a hunter and observer, respectively, and they brought Lad's 15-year-old son, Drake, as a co-hunter on his first trip to Africa. And Greg Summitt, long-time national marketing manager for Sportsmen on Film videos, was the fifth hunter.

Saddled with the responsibility of trying to fill each hunter's wish list was Bill Wille of Professionals of Africa. Bill thought he could make everyone happy because we were two father-son teams and because Lad's only interest was the elusive Natal red duiker and Greg also wanted to hunt only one animal, a southern nyala, the Lord of the Zululand woodlands.

Surprisingly, Bill Wille is a taxidermist in Colorado nine months of the year and a licensed professional hunter in South Africa each June, July, and August. His wife, Donna, rounded out our group so she could take Lorraine and Lenka sightseeing at the famous Hluhluwe and Umfolozi Game Reserves and so she could drive the hunting truck the last few days of our 11-day adventure.

SPORT HUNTING ON SIX CONTINENTS

L to R: Lorraine, me and our son, Ryan, relaxing in Durban before the start of the safari.

Zulu dancers in full regalia.

The new South Africa is divided into nine provinces instead of the previous four. The Cape Province is now the Northern, Western, and Eastern Cape. The Transvaal is now Northwest, Northern, Gauteng, and Mpumalanga. The Orange Free State is the Free State and Natal was renamed KwaZulu-Natal in 1994 in recognition of its Zulu and English populations.

We landed in Durban, the largest city in KwaZulu-Natal and South Africa's busiest port and beach resort. From there, Bill Wille drove us north, along the coast of the Indian Ocean, to Richard's Bay and then inland to the heart of Zululand. From 1788 to 1828, Shaka built the Zulu tribe into a mighty war machine and caused the death of at least one million people as he conquered all of Natal.

Bill's head tracker, Joseph, is a Zulu with great eyes, ears, and nose for hunting. He could feel changes in the wind so well that I abandoned using my little plastic bottle to puff talc in the air to see the direction of the air currents. With a pair of Swarovski 8 x 30 binoculars, which I loaned him for the safari, Joseph became the ultimate tracker.

Generally we would drive to an area and then walk in search of game, following Joseph as he continually walked into the ever-changing wind. Occasionally we would spot game from the vehicle and then make a stalk. That's how Ryan shot the first trophy of the safari. Bill spotted a good impala ram standing to the side of a herd of ewes. He and Ryan and Joseph piled out of the truck, with me following with the BetaCam, and made a careful downwind stalk. Joseph then placed my Tripod Systems shooting sticks to the side of a thornbush and Bill placed my Sako .300 WM on the sticks as Ryan peered through the scope turned to nine power. The ram was facing straight toward us at 150 yards, but appeared ready to bolt, so Bill instructed Ryan to shoot now without waiting for a broadside opportunity. At the shot, the ram stumbled and took flight, disappearing in the heavy cover in just a few strides.

Where the impala had been standing, Bill found a large splash of blood about three feet up on a green bush, but it took 20 minutes and several hundred yards for Joseph to track down the ram to where it had died. Ryan had just clipped enough of the impala's left shoulder to earn his first African trophy, a nice 21-incher, which is good for Natal.

Drake's impala was dropped on the fifth day of the safari after an intense period of waiting for the herd ram to clear a large group of females and present a shot between two closely set trees. Drake's first African animal, a warthog, had been shot three days earlier.

Greg Summitt was booked for only seven hunting days, so it was agreed that he would have first shot at nyala, which is a fabulous animal and generally considered to be one of South Africa's top two trophies, along with southern greater kudu (although southern white rhinoceros, vaal rhebok, and others will pick up some votes).

Because nyala like thick woodlands where they can disappear in one to two steps, Bill calls them the bongo of South Africa. The bulls are certainly one of the most unique-looking animals in the world. They are one of the spiral-horned antelopes, with anything over 24 inches considered a trophy. Older bulls are slate grey in color with eight to 14 vertical white stripes on their sides, a long mane of erectile white hair along their back, a long fringe of dark hair hanging from their neck and along their belly to between their back legs, and to top off their wardrobe, their legs are orange from hocks to hooves. They are one of the few examples of design by committee

L to R: Joseph, Bill Wille, and Greg Summitt with Greg's nyala shot in a jungle.

that worked. The bulls probably average 250 pounds, but the cows weigh only about half that and they look like a completely different species since they are almost completely orange with up to 18 vertical white stripes. Baby males start out looking like females and, in a period of about two years, transform into completely different looking animals.

Bill had us hunting prime nyala habitat so that we were seeing up to 30 bulls per day, of which a few had horns in the mid-twenties, but none were shootable until the third day when Greg was able to down a good bull with one shot in the thickest cover imaginable. He was a tired but happy hunter, so we immediately made him return to his driving duties.

Lad and I were both hunting for Natal red duiker, a real specialty animal because they are difficult and, as we found out, sometimes time-consuming to hunt. We each finally got ours on the 10th day, which drove Lad crazy because he was to have the first shot while I videotaped him. We usually saw several red duiker per day as we walked through the dense woodlands, but the difficulty is that both the males and females have horns and you can only shoot males in Natal. This meant that we had to spot the 30-pound animal before it spotted us and search for "evidence of maleness" before the constantly wandering animal disappeared. The "evidence" was hidden by grass most of the time, so Lad had to refrain from taking the few shots he had.

It rained on our ninth night and stopped the next morning, so more animals than normal were out wandering. Since the 10th day was our next to last, Lad and I split up and, instead of still-hunting, we each took a stand, about a mile apart, and where dirt hunting tracks crossed the jungle of vegetation preferred by our small adversaries. I shot my red duiker that morning as he crossed one of the tracks at 85 yards and Bill was able to spot maleness in time. Luckily, he was a fine trophy with 2 3/4-inch horns. Lad got his shot later in the day after he abandoned his stand in favor of ultra-slow still-hunting. He made good on a 30-yard shot as his duiker fed away from him. Each of those little animals will be full-mounted and placed in special places in our respective trophy rooms.

I also wanted a bushpig, and that turned out to be an interesting hunt. Since they are

L to R: Bill Wille, me, and Joseph with my hard-earned Natal red duiker.

mostly nocturnal, bushpigs are generally hunted over bait at night or during the day with dogs. Dogs weren't allowed where we were hunting, because the chase greatly disturbs the other game, so I found myself sitting behind the wall of a ground blind on the first night of the safari, just 20 yards from an area of bushpig activity that was baited with bread and table scraps for the omnivorous animals. Bill and Joseph and I arrived at the blind a half hour before dusk and then sat like rocks for three tedious, boring hours before quietly leaving empty-handed.

The next morning we inspected the bait and found it untouched but, that night, the bait was cleaned up while we slept in our tree house accommodations a few miles away. So we replenished the bait and, when it was hit again on the third night, we were back in the blind the following night, sitting quietly and slowly going out of our minds while occasional mosquitoes whirred, itches came and went, legs went to sleep, and the cold night air of the July winter seeped through our layers of clothing. Bill nudged me as a dark form appeared 20 yards away and then a second form. I slowly moved my right eye to my rifle scope, but found nothing as both pigs had run off. But one ran back just as quickly and started eating. It appeared to be the biggest of the two. My rifle rested on the top of the wall of the low blind with a 180-grain bullet already chambered and the safety off. I could almost see the outline of the bushpig well enough to shoot in the moonlight but, at Bill's signal, Joseph eased up the rheostat on a small, battery-operated spotlight. Instantly, I sent the shot 20 yards and dropped the bushpig in its tracks or, more precisely, on a loaf of bread.

The solid portion of my bullet passed through both shoulders, but the soft portion ricocheted through the length of the body and exited at the right hip . . . a vicious shot that kept Bill from having to follow up with a 12 gauge shotgun because, unlike warthog, bushpig will come for you. He was a big boar with 5 1/2-inch tusks. He will be mounted with the back half in the hall that divides my trophy room and the front half on the other side of the wall in my African trophy room.

The wildebeest in Natal are the blue or brindled subspecies. "Brindled" means "brown-streaked" and refers to the vertical markings that are present

With the bushpig that didn't come to bait on the first night, but did on the fourth.

Lunch in our tree house dining room. Lorraine and Ryan are in the foreground. Lad, Donna Wille, and Bill Wille, in back. Lenka Shunneson, with her back to the camera, talking to our cook . . . oh well.

from the neck to the front of the hindquarters. A big, bull wildebeest is a load to bring down. Bill calls them "the poor man's Cape buffalo" and Drake found out why. He took a 90-yard shot at a lone bull with his dad's .350 Whelan shooting 250-grain bullets as the beast stood quartering away, but missed the far shoulder. The bull dropped from the shock of the bullet, but quickly jumped up and ran left. Bill drilled the wildebeest in the left shoulder with a good running shot and dropped him again, but as we continued our walk-up, the bull struggled to his feet and ran straight away. This time Lad shot him and then Drake put in the insurance shot. He was as tough as a Cape buffalo, but he ran like *he* owed *us* money.

Ryan learned from that experience. When he got a broadside shot at a good blue wildebeest, Ryan broke both of the bull's shoulders with my .300 WM and dropped the beast where he stood. Bill still made an insurance shot at 10 yards.

Lad and I had previously shot nyala, but Ryan and Drake each wanted one badly. Drake got his on the sixth day when he made a fine 150-yard shot across a small valley following a bush-to-bush stalk as the nyala fed on the other side near dusk.

Ryan with his blue wildebeest, which Bill Wille (right) calls "the poor man's Cape buffalo," because of the punishment they can take combined with the lower trophy fee.

Ryan kept passing on nyala, with a little encouragement from his father, until Bill spotted a terrific specimen on the ninth day as Donna was driving us back to camp for lunch. We jumped out of the truck and set up the shooting sticks as Donna drove away, but Ryan couldn't see the bull as it walked straight away into the forest. So Bill moved Ryan up to a convenient fallen log where he could still see the back side of the animal. Bill said, "Shoot him." Ryan whispered, "All I can see is his rear end." With confidence in Ryan's shooting and the 180-grain partition bullet, Bill said, "Shoot him at the base of his tail . . . now." Ryan shot and the nyala went down. Everyone whooped it up. I was ecstatic because Ryan had shot a great trophy with the classic bell shape to the bottom half of the horns that then spiraled and tipped well out with excellent ivory tips.

Bill, Drake Shunneson, Lad, and Joseph with Drake's nyala.

When Lad and I finally collected red duikers on the next to last day, everyone had filled their wish list except for the last animal on mine . . . the southern reedbuck which is about the size and color of a Texas whitetail deer, but with forward-curved and partially ridged horns. We had seen a good trophy with 12-inch horns late on that 10th day, but he detected our stalk through the three-foot-tall grass and made a getaway. Late in the afternoon on the 11th and last day, we saw the same buck again. He was with a female and about a half mile up a canyon. We made a crawling stalk through the grass from tree to widely-scattered tree, and just when we had closed the gap to about 250 yards, a smaller male whistled and the already nervous larger buck and doe took off running up the far side of the canyon.

Bill said, "You're going to have to shoot him from here." I put my rifle on the shooting sticks and cranked the scope to nine power. When the buck first stopped, he was about 400 yards off and facing straight away in the tall grass. My crosshairs were jumping erratically so I waited until the buck almost reached the top and, when he turned sideways, I let my shot fly. Bill said,

Ryan bagged his nyala with a Texas heart shot.

"I think you hit him"... then, "He's down"... then, "He's up but I think I see red"... then, "He's lying down, so we'll have to walk down, cross the drainage, and climb up to him."

Several minutes later we reached the spot where the redbuck was last seen. Then Joseph pointed and the buck was running at 80 yards. I shot and missed. Joseph said, "His back leg is broken." When the buck stopped, I took my time and dropped him. It was 30 minutes until dark on the last day. What a great ending to a double father-son safari.

My common reedbuck is almost out of the picture, but the cast of characters is more important anyway. L to R: Lenka, Lad, Donna, Drake, Bill, Ryan, Lorraine, and me (4 x 1 with three observers!).

AFRICA RSA

23

KUDUS AND CARACALS

The southern greater kudu is the most sought-after big game animal in Africa for good reason. It is one of the most magnificent looking animals in the world with spiraling horns that twist three times and attain lengths of four to five feet along those curves; sometimes even more. A big bull will weigh 650-800 pounds, but its gray body and white stripes allow it to disappear when it doesn't move in the thick thornbush country that it loves. It is the largest subspecies of kudu with the longest horns and it lives in Africa's least expensive country to hunt... South Africa (in addition to Angola, Botswana, Malawi, Mozambique, Namibia, Zaire, Zambia, and Zimbabwe).

On seven previous safaris to Africa, I had not shot a kudu because I wanted one that was unrealistically large and, thus, virtually impossible to find, let alone shoot. And, on those seven safaris, I had seen only one caracal, the beautiful African lynx with the long hairs growing from the tips of its ears. On that occasion, the professional hunter, who was driving, said, "There's a caracal!" I was a cameraman at the time. The hunter and I both frantically searched the bush out to 200 meters, but neither of us saw the cat until it bounded away just off the starboard side of our Land Rover. If only the PH had said, "There's a caracal lying down 10 meters from us at two o'clock!"

Around the campfire on a previous safari with professional hunter Bill Wille of Professional of Africa, I revealed my desire to hunt kudus and caracals with my son, Ryan. Bill said, "I've got the place to hunt caracals in the eastern Cape. They hunt them with dogs, like mountain lions, in order to limit predation on their wild and domestic stock. It's a lot more productive and exciting than spotlighting. We could take 10 days and hunt caracal for half and then move to the Transvaal for kudu. And, if you really wanted to push it, we could also hunt Cape greater kudu before moving north for his big brother."

"How big do Cape kudu get?"

"A big bull won't quite reach the weight of a southern greater kudu and his horns average seven to 10 inches less, but the Cape kudu is a great trophy because it's hunted in rolling to mountainous terrain with very heavy cover so you can often see it at a long distance, but you usually only see its head and horns. And, when it walks on a hillside, it's out of sight more than it's in sight."

"What's a reasonable trophy expectation if we put in 3-4 days?"

"The high 40s, with a little luck."

So I said, "Okay, next year we'll hunt Cape kudu and caracal in the Cape and then southern greater kudu in the Transvaal. Kudus and caracals. The high 40's will be fine for a Cape kudu, but I still want a monster in the Transvaal."

"How big?"

"58 or better."

"Then you better book 14 days instead of 10."

"Consider us booked." It was a nice feeling to be in the middle of one great safari with the next one already planned.

One year later, my son, Ryan, and I flew into Port Elizabeth, South Africa's fifth largest city with a population of over one million. P.E. is located in the Eastern Cape about halfway between Cape Town and Durban. In 1820, Britain shipped 4,000 settlers to Algoa Bay on the Indian Ocean. On June 6 of that year, the Acting Governor of Cape Province, Sir Rufane Donkin, directed that the settlement be named after his late wife, Elizabeth.

Our first hunting concession, known as Blaauwkrantz ("blue cliffs"), was only one hour's drive inland. Arthur Rudman, the owner, was our host and shared professional hunting duties with Bill Wille. Each evening, we dined with Arthur and his wife, Trinette, in their Victorian dining room complete with operatic background music. It was all very sophisticated except for the hunting and the memorable evening we all yelled and screamed while watching the South African Springbok-New Zealand All Black rugby game on television.

Hunting methods included baiting with oranges which brought in a $1^1/_2$ horned kudu, spot and stalk, and organized drives, which are usually more productive than the unorganized ones. Ryan shot his Cape kudu with the help of a drive. Arthur and Ryan and I walked along a steep hillside where we could see 160 yards across a narrow canyon (according to my Bushnell laser rangefinder). Bill then drove our crew of eight beaters about a mile distant and had them walk slowly toward us. Arthur said this technique works when the same area is seldom beaten and when the kudu are laying down in the middle of the day. If they are up feeding when the drive takes place, the kudu often figure out what is happening and

Kudus and Caracals

they quickly determine where not to go.

"Grab your rifle and get ready!" Arthur urged Ryan and pointed to a kudu bull appearing and disappearing as it picked its way along the opposite hillside. When Ryan was set and the bull was almost to a small opening, Arthur gave a short yell. The bull took another step and stopped in the opening with his ears alert. Ryan nailed him high in the shoulder and then had to shoot twice more to put him down.

Once down, the 600-pound animal disappeared in the thick bush, so Arthur stayed at our shooting position while Ryan and I hiked down, fought our way across a small drainage, and then back up the other side. Following Arthur's hand signals, we found the kudu before the beaters arrived. I took photos, one man gutted the animal, and the rest rolled the bull onto a stretcher consisting of two long poles with wire in between. With much jabbering and effort, the beaters hoisted the stretcher to their shoulders and muscled their way down the hillside to the canyon floor and

Ryan Wilson with his trackers, drivers, and Cape greater kudu hunted with Bill Wille and Arthur Rudman.

then along the drainage to a spot that Bill could reach with the hunting vehicle.

I shot my kudu from a high seat built on the back of the truck. Instead of building elevated blinds all over the concession, Arthur drives to an area, parks the truck, and glasses, which sometimes results in either spotting an animal and planning a stalk or in conducting a drive toward the truck. While we were parked and glassing a hillside, a big bull kudu stood up and looked at us from 378 yards (per the rangefinder). All I could see were his horns and head, but that was a small miracle since I had missed two previous opportunities in other locations when everyone in the back of the truck could see a shootable bull, but I couldn't until it was too late to shoot.

This kudu wasn't going to wait around for a stalk, so I fired through the cactus he was standing behind and at a point where his chest should have been. He wheeled and ran uphill. I let fly twice more and the bull fell over on his back. My first shot had hit the brisket. My next two were ineffectual shots high on the back legs. Before loading the animal on the stretcher, Bill measured the horns at $48\,{}^{6}/_{8}$ inches per side; a fine Cape kudu trophy and a memorable hunt.

Bill Wille is kneeling just in front of the horns of my Cape greater kudu. Arthur Rudman is standing, back right.

From Blaauwkrantz, Bill drove us about two hours to Rex and Carol Anne Amm's concession known as Aloe Ridge. Rex had a dog team lined up for us to hunt caracal and permission from virtually every landowner in the area to track caracal on their property since the 25- to 45-pound cats are accomplished hunters that decimate small animal populations with a special love for bushbuck. The latter were to prove our allies because there are two ways to locate caracal and neither involves finding tracks. One method is to turn the dogs loose with a number of handlers and systematically cover an area in search of fresh scent. Another way is to place spotters at lookout points in order to listen for bushbuck barking early in the morning. When a caracal is on the prowl, the bushbuck will invariably make an alarm call. Then the dogs can be moved to that area to search for scent.

Glassing to keep track of the dogs and their handlers in caracal habitat.

When scent is found and verified by the more experienced dogs, the chase is on and you can bet that the cat will go a long way in thick cover. I shot my caracal out of a tree just above a drainage. All I could see was part of the cat's stomach which I hit with buckshot. He dropped 40 feet to the ground and fought off the dogs as I moved in for a second shot. It was absolute pandemonium. The dogs were bark-

My caracal was shot on the second day and required two shots.

Ryan shot his caracal at mid-morning, but it looks like night because of the jungle habitat.

ing, the handlers were hitting the dogs with sticks to keep them away from the cat, Bill Wille (who is also a taxidermist) was yelling for me not to shoot the caracal in the face, and Rex Amm was yelling for me not to shoot the dogs. With a shell up the spout and the safety off, I managed to end my hunt with a shot to the side of the cat when the dogs and handlers gave me some momentary room.

Ryan shot his caracal two days later and got it with one shot. On the climb back out, one of the spotters reported that he had heard a bushbuck barking in a canyon about a mile away. It was only 10:00 AM so Bill and

Ryan's southern greater kudu had a nice spread.

KUDUS AND CARACALS

Rex figured we still had two hours before the scent would dissipate in the heat of the July day. We all agreed to try moving the dogs and handlers if Bill's wife, Donna, wanted to become the hunter . . . and she readily agreed. Three hours later, covered with sweat and blood, Donna watched, with a big smile, as one of the handlers gingerly climbed a cactus tree and removed a nice, male caracal from where it had been shot. As luck would have it, all three of our caracal were good-sized males.

Next stop was the Thabazimbi area of the Transvaal and home to the legendary southern greater kudu. In only a couple days, Bill was able to put Ryan on a beautiful, wide 53-incher whose horns flared out after the third twist. This gave me six days to hunt for the 58-incher of my dreams. I would be hunting for a 12- to 14-year-old bull, probably in the last year of his life, but with the genetics for the deep curls that add those extra inches.

In the course of those six days, Bill and I looked over at least 15 bulls that were magnificent trophies of 53 to 57 inches. A couple might have made the magical 58, but I decided to pass. On each occasion Bill mumbled something about it being no wonder I had never shot a kudu before this safari.

L to R: Richard Herholdt, Bill Wille, Lee Cannata, me, and Ryan with my southern greater kudu, photographed where it fell.

183

There have been exceptions, but most giant kudu obtain their horn length by flaring widely at the base, sometimes past their 21-inch ear spread, and by forming deep curls. If you look down a kudu's horn from the tip to the base, you can slide a pipe down the opening. If the pipe won't pass a golf ball, the horns probably won't reach much over 50 inches. But if that pipe will pass a tennis ball, the horns have a chance to reach the 60-inch mark when fully grown.

"Shoot that kudu as soon as you can!" My mind snapped to attention as Bill urgently whispered and pointed. I could see the outline of a kudu's body behind a thick thornbush, so I moved to my right and fired through the outer edge of the bush. The bull ran 20 meters, stumbled, and went down, but I shot him once more anyway. One shot kills are fine, but if the animal is still moving, I take a second shot just to make sure; especially when the cover is heavy and he can disappear in one or two steps.

We admired this kudu, and photographed it, and then Bill measured it. "I guess you'll need to keep hunting for that 58-incher," he said. "This one measures 60 $^2/_8$!"

My southern greater kudu posed on top of a berm.

AFRICA RSA

THREE OF A KIND – TWICE

In Seven Card Stud, it's possible to get two sets of three of a kind, but you can only declare the full house. When trophy hunting in South Africa, you can declare all six if they're big enough to make the book. One set of three is the common blesbok, white blesbok, and bontebok, and the other set is the common springbok, black springbok, and white springbok.

The bontebok is one of the great success stories of African game conservation. Historically they were indigenous to only a small area of southwestern Cape Province and were almost exterminated by over-hunting in the early 1800s. Fortunately, enough were saved and protected by local farmers that their numbers are now secure and a limited number may be hunted each year with proper export and import permits. If you hunt a bontebok yourself (and why not, because the airfare to Africa, the daily rate, and the trophy fee add up to less than the cost of a caribou hunt), be sure to take the full skin, because it is one of the most striking of any animal. The facial blaze, rump, base of tail, lower legs, and underside are all pure white. The rest of the body varies from a dark brown with iridescent purple to silvery fawn. The horns are all black (unlike the male blesbok) and fully ringed.

Bill Wille of Professionals of Africa guided me to my bontebok by water and then by land. We used a canoe to cross a river that was a couple hundred meters wide and then we staked out a hillside meadow where we knew bontebok liked to feed in the afternoon. Both the males and females have horns, but those of the male are heavier. Not wanting to take a chance on shooting a female for both breeding and trophy reasons, Bill took his time and we made three different stalks before he gave me the green light to shoot. My 180-grain bullet entered behind the right shoulder and the solid portion exited in front of the left shoulder. The bok never knew what hit him.

The scientific name for bontebok is Damaliscus dorcas dorcas and for blesbok is Damaliscus dorcas phillipsi. They are classified as conspecific subspecies. The blesbok is slightly smaller than the bontebok and is much duller in coloration. Its horns average about an inch longer than the bontebok's (16 inches versus 15 inches for the middle of the SCI Book), are whitish on the front part of the rings for older males, and the rings do not encircle the horns as is the case with the bontebok. Blesbok are animals of the open range, relying on eyesight and speed for protection, but they readily run to cover when threatened. They are inexpensive and quite popular to hunt as attested by the 22 pages of entries in the Ninth Edition of the SCI Record Book. I had shot a blesbok years earlier in the Transvaal, so I let my son, Ryan, out of his cameraman duties to hunt one with Bill Wille in the Eastern Cape. Bill picked out a good male, then told Ryan to hold fire as a couple females stepped in front. Apparently Ryan took his eye off the scope, then didn't hear Bill, then put his eye back on the crosshairs and fired. Unfortunately, he dropped one of the females. Fortunately, he only killed one and he was able to return two days later and take that same male, which proved to be a good trophy with 16-inch horns.

Bill Wille, right, made absolutely sure I was shooting the biggest male bontebok in the herd.

Ryan's blesbok required two shots, two days apart.

Three of a Kind – Twice

A few days later, with a tracker nicknamed Vet Boy, I was able to ambush a very nice white color phase of the blesbok out of a group of more than 20. They had all paraded by my position, including several decent males, but Bill felt the biggest would be last. When we finally saw the best one, he was so far behind the herd that I thought we had already let all of our chances trot by. I opted not to take the closer running shot and ended up hitting him twice when he finally stopped at 225 meters. He measured 16 1/2 inches and completed my first three of a kind.

L to R with my white blesbok shot out of an all-white herd: Bill, me, and Vet Boy.

L to R: me, Rex Amm, and Bill Wille. The common springbok on the right has the longest horns by 1/2 inch.

The second three of a kind involves the springbok, which is the national animal of South Africa and the symbol and name for South Africa's world champion rugby team. The largest subspecies with the largest horns is the Kalahari springbok of Botswana and Namibia. It takes about 13 inches to make the book. The South African or common springbok is about 25% smaller so that 10-inch horns can make the book.

Springbok are much like hunting pronghorn antelope in North America, with the same long range shooting, but at half the body size of the pronghorn. I shot mine at about 250 meters. I don't know how, but with a big hole through its lungs, the buck ran behind a bush. Bill said, "You hit him good." Then he said, "He's pronking now! How could that be? Wait a second." But I didn't wait. We later figured out that the first one (the biggest in a bachelor herd of six) ran behind the bush and died just as another springbok came bounding out. So I killed two; a 12-incher and an 11 $\frac{1}{2}$-incher, but the trophy fee was low and the farmer was happy to get the meat.

Black and white springbok are color phases of the South African springbok. The three mounted next to each other, or on a single pedestal, make a beautiful display. I managed to shoot both color phases in mountainous terrain on the same day. The black one (dark brown, really) was a tribute to our tracker, Sampson. With Rex Amm conducting a drive through several thousand acres of foothills, Sampson predicted exactly where the herd would pass. I stayed hidden behind a

Black springbok are really dark brown with white facial markings.

Three of a Kind – Twice

tree as they came by. Bill said, "Shoot the last male," so I moved around the tree trunk and got my shot at 80 meters. In the excitement, I had left my scope set at nine power so I considered myself lucky to have picked the correct animal out of the herd. His horns measured 13 inches.

The white springbok was a different story. The population is less because they are less hardy, and their horns are smaller so that nine inches will make the book. We could find only one worth shooting and he was with a group that was very wild. I finally took a shot at 400 meters with a good squeeze from a good rest, but the wind blew the bullet right. (I couldn't have missed, could I?) Now the herd was double wild, so Sampson picked another ambush point and Rex conducted another drive. Bill said, "They're coming our way. They're turning toward us. They may run us over!" I turned the scope down to three power and waited for the herd to appear from a gully. Suddenly, the buck I wanted emerged and stopped in tall grass at only 50 meters! I lowered the crosshairs and put a red spot on his right shoulder. He ran uphill and dropped. Out of that whole, big mountain, he chose to stop almost next to me. But that's what happens when you're lucky enough to draw three of a kind — twice.

White springbok generally grow the shortest horns of the springbok color phases and mine was no exception. Sampson, the psychic, is in the middle.

SOUTH AFRICAN MOUNTAIN GAME

Most southern and east African countries have enough big game species that it is not unusual for a hunter to bag 10 or more on a 14- to 21-day safari. What makes such mixed bag hunting interesting is that virtually every species requires different hunting techniques, and often times the habitat is also unique. The animals don't just roam around your tent or hang around in a big mixed herd. You have to go where they live and hunt them the way the professional hunters have learned to hunt them over generations. This means that, for vaal rhebok and mountain reedbuck, you head for the mountains. Some may call them hills, but there are a lot of them, they're rocky, the wind blows, and it's a long way to the top.

The vaal rhebok, in my opinion, is one of the Republic of South Africa's top three trophies in terms of desirability, uniqueness, beauty, and difficulty to hunt. The other two are the southern greater kudu and the southern nyala. There are 31 pages of entries for southern greater kudu in the Ninth Edition of the SCI Record Book, 16 pages for southern nyala, and only five pages for vaal rhebok. There are several reasons for this, with the main one being that you generally have to dedicate several days plus travel to specifically hunt the vaal rhebok.

Incidentally, the distinction for the three species with the most entries in the African portion of the Ninth Edition of the SCI Record Book goes to the southern impala (27 pages), the Cape buffalo (29 pages), and the aforementioned kudu (31 pages). But those three species can each be hunted in nine or more countries whereas the vaal rhebok can only be hunted in South Africa and nowhere else.

The gray rhebok, as it is also known, because *"vaal"* means "gray" in Afrikaans, is certainly one of the most unique-looking big game animals and it is the only member of its subfamily. Its horns are needle-straight, virtually parallel, and very slim for their length. Its body is small (only 40 to 50 pounds, which is another reason that it ranks only number three) and is covered with soft, woolly hair. The end of its nose is large, flattened, and glandular. And its eyesight is extraordinary due to its oversized, bulbous eyes. Add "fast," "wary," and "smart," and you are down to only five pages in the record book.

L to R: Lorraine, Ryan, and Summer Wilson shopping for souvenirs. Ryan's T-shirt is from the Hard Rock Cafe-Cape Town.

Professional hunter Bill Wille escorted me to vaal rhebok country in the mountains of the Eastern Cape Province after having arranged for the assistance of two other professional hunters, Rex Amm and Noel Ross. Rex was the driver of our truck, dropping off Bill and me and Noel's head tracker, Sampson, in the foothills of likely mountains and later picking us up at predetermined locations. And Noel was the driver of the second truck, which he used to locate rhebok so that Rex could drive Bill and I to whatever location Noel suggested whenever we returned to the first truck empty-handed.

My first chance actually came in the flats of some foothills where Bill spotted a decent male with seven- to eight-inch horns at about 200 yards between some trees. I didn't have time to use my rangefinder before I shot, so I probably overestimated the distance because of the smallness of the animal, and I shot over him. I had to sleep on that mistake.

The next day we were on another mountain at daybreak. Bill and Sampson and I had crawled to a ridge and were pinned down at that location by three groups of vaal rhebok that would see us if we moved. When, after considerable glassing, we couldn't locate a trophy with at least seven inches of horn, we hiked back down as the rhebok scrambled away from us. None were closer than 600 yards, but they ran, anyway, just as soon as we moved.

When we returned to the truck, Rex informed us that Noel had spotted a rhebok herd with a good buck and they had already worked out a plan. Rex drove us to the

L to R: Bill Wille, Noel Ross, Ryan, and me with the unique vaal rhebok that can only be hunted in the RSA.

other side of the mountain from Noel so Bill and Sampson and I could walk to a vantage point. Then Noel showed himself to the herd, still on the opposite side of the mountain from us. Just as we had hoped, the herd ran over the top to our side. But I couldn't get a good shot at the big buck, and the herd of about 12 quickly disappeared in the brush not more than 200 yards from us. At that point they stopped to look around. We were certain they had not seen us, so we decided to change positions to see if we could get an angle on the buck.

Sampson finally spotted the one we wanted as it was standing between some bushes thinking it was out of sight. I backed up to where I could see him and slowly put my crosshairs on his chest at 110 yards and waited for the cameraman to get on him. And I waited and waited some more. The cameraman whispered he still couldn't see the buck through his viewfinder. Bill urgently whispered for me to shoot, and Sampson tried to help out the cameraman as the buck started to nervously look around. I decided to wait for the sooner of the cameraman to say "okay" or the buck to take a step. The risk was high, but I was mesmerized by the beauty of the animal as he looked left and right with those stiletto horns flashing in the sunlight.

Suddenly three events occurred at once: the buck bunched his muscles to jump, I heard the "okay," and my rifle went *bang!* The buck went straight down but, when I walked up, I saw how lucky I had been because my bullet had just clipped enough

South African Mountain Game

of his brisket to anchor him. He was a beautiful specimen with 7 1/2-inch horns and 2 3/4-inch bases. This is the kind of hunt that, if you dedicated a week, you would have a good chance of shooting a monster nine-incher.

Now it was on to mountain reedbuck. They shared the same range as the vaal rhebok we had just been hunting, but we had been away from our base camp long enough that we decided to return and hunt the population that lived close to Rex Amm's lodge.

All the entries for southern mountain reedbuck in the SCI Record Book, as of this writing, are from South Africa even though there are limited populations in Botswana and Mozambique. The mountain reedbuck is the smallest of the reedbucks (being about the same size as the vaal rhebok) and with six inches of horn making the record book. Only hard horn is counted and the bases are not measured because it is too easy to confuse hard horn with the large, pasty swelling at the bases that is, in fact, green horn.

For my mountain reedbuck hunt, Bill brought Lucky along as our tracker. After Rex dropped us off at the bottom of a likely mountain, we played hide and seek with several trophy candidates among the trees and bushes in the foothills, and then turned our attention to a group higher on the mountain. My laser rangefinder showed they were feeding at about 750 yards so I searched for a spot with cover about 500 yards closer and found a brushy area that looked good.

We walked, crawled, and then squirmed on our stomachs to stay out of sight. When we raised up to glass, Bill picked out a good male as the herd turned as one to look at us. I shot and missed, but continued to track him through my scope as I jacked in another cartridge. He ran uphill another hundred yards and stopped. This time I dropped him. Bill said, "You like hard shots don't you?" I replied, "I'd rather be good than lucky." Lucky laughed. We all laughed.

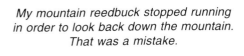
My mountain reedbuck stopped running in order to look back down the mountain. That was a mistake.

26

BUCKS AND BOKS

"Bok" means "buck" in Afrikaans. Of the indigenous species of South Africa, there are five bucks listed in the SCI Record Book and ten boks. On previous safaris, I had collected all ten of the boks, although my Kalahari gemsbok was shot in the Kalahari Desert of Botswana and not in South Africa, but who cares, because there is no bok slam anyway. And there is no buck slam either, but I wanted to complete one nevertheless, so I booked a South African safari with professional hunter Bill Wille of Professionals of Africa. My battle cry was, "The buck stops here." Bushbuck are the smallest of the spiral horned antelope and are ubiquitous south of the Sahara Desert. SCI recognizes eight subspecies including two in South Africa: the Limpopo bushbuck and the Cape bushbuck. All bushbuck are challenging to hunt because the most effective hunting method is to walk slowly into the wind, in areas with cover and water, early and late in the day.

Cape bushbuck occur in the Cape and KwaZulu-Natal Provinces of southeastern South Africa. I hunted mine near Grahamstown. For about two hours, neither Bill Wille nor I had seen any bushbuck before they saw us so, with only a half hour until dark, Bill suggested that we climb into an elevated blind overlooking a large field and hope for the best. No sooner had we settled in than three Cape bushbuck males started running around the clearing that measured 300 yards by 800 yards according to my Bushnell laser rangefinder. The bucks weren't fighting and they weren't fleeing, so maybe they were just having fun. One made the mistake of trotting by our stand so I put a bullet into the front part of his silhouette. He measured $12\,^5/_8$ inches, which placed him about one-third up from the SCI minimum.

When we changed camps to the Thabazimbi area of the Transvaal, I told Bill that I had shot a 12-inch Limpopo bushbuck years before, but I wanted to try to upgrade to a 15-incher or better. The bodies of the bushbuck of the Limpopo River drainage tend to be much lighter than the dark brown Cape bushbuck, and the Limpopo's horns tend to be longer with the median entry in SCI being $14\,^4/_8$ inches whereas the median for the Cape is 13 inches.

For the Limpopo subspecies, Bill and I hunted with Renier Els whose family's property encompasses the headwa-

This Cape bushbuck has quite a dark cape; particularly the neck and face.

This Limpopo bushbuck has a light coat, but its horns only appear light because of dried mud. L to R: Bill Wille, Renier Els, Ryan Wilson, and me.

ters of the Limpopo River that separates South Africa from Botswana at that location. Naturally, we walked into the wind (Renier first, then me, our cameraman, and Bill), but in fairly open country and about 200 meters off the river; first the Limpopo River and then the Crocodile River.

We stopped and glassed. I could see a bushbuck feeding at 150 yards so, as pre-planned, I put the front end of my rifle on Renier's left shoulder. It looked like a male, but I couldn't see horns because Renier kept putting his hand in front of my scope. Later he told me that he does that on purpose to prevent the client from shooting before he has time to judge the trophy. Suddenly Renier plugged his ears and whispered, "Shoot!" It took me a few precious seconds to steady the crosshairs by which time all I could see was the back half of the buck, but I figured a 180-grain bullet should anchor a 100-pound animal. At the shot, the buck went down, but he struggled back up so I shot him again.

When we walked up, Bill Wille, who is also a taxidermist, said, "I see you saved the cape," referring to the two holes in the middle of the body. As is my habit, I touched the buck's eye with the end of my rifle barrel to make sure he was dead. On contact, the buck swung his horns halfway up my barrel as I retreated! Renier loaned me his handgun and I put a small hole in the right place, and I made sure the eye didn't blink before we posed for pictures. He was a great trophy with $16\,4/8$-inch horns and very heavy bases. So now I have two Limpopo bushbuck in the record book; one near the bottom and one near the top.

The next buck I didn't want to pass (because I had on previous safaris) was a ringed waterbuck, also known as a common waterbuck; the one with the target on his rear end. The four other sub-species of waterbuck for recordkeeping purposes (Sing-sing, East African, Crawshay, and Angolan) all belong to the defassa group which have solid white patches on their rumps.

Bill and I spent two days following up rumors of a 33-inch monster but, hunting early and late, we never saw anything bigger than 26 inches. After our Limpopo bushbuck hunt, Renier had told us that he knew the general whereabouts and habits of an old, heavy-horned waterbuck that would make 29 inches. With my time running out, we made arrangements to hunt with Renier again and that proved to be a good decision.

We met at first light, but Renier thought we should wait another half hour because I would only have one chance and he wanted to make sure there was enough light for our video camera before we started. Our cameraman, my son Ryan, quickly turned on our camera and showed everyone its light-gathering ability. We could see better through the viewfinder than through our binoculars, so the hunt started right then.

We saw about 20 waterbuck in the next hour, but they were at the back edge of a large meadow with tall grass and it looked like they would disappear into the surrounding cover if we started a stalk. Bill felt the herd wanted to walk across the meadow and that we should back off, keeping the wind from them to us, and allow the waterbuck to move more into the open.

When the biggest buck showed himself, he looked one-third bigger than the satellite bucks and his horns looked long and heavy. This was the waterbuck I had been looking for on so many safaris. "They're starting to move across the meadow," Renier whispered. "You're going to have to shoot from here." We were 250 yards from a small tree in the middle of the meadow according to my rangefinder. Bill whispered, "When he passes that tree, you better shoot, because the herd is getting nervous."

The scope on my .300 WM was on nine power and the crosshairs were steady. When the buck came into view, I found his back, moved the crosshairs toward his shoulder, and fired. *Whump!* He dropped in his tracks. I hadn't moved the crosshairs down far enough to reach the shoulder, but had luckily hit the spine.

The ringed or common waterbuck that completed my South African buck collection.

After the congratulations, I touched the buck's eye and admired his size. He easily weighed over 600 pounds and his 29-inch horns were heavy throughout with 10-inch bases. I thanked Renier and Bill for helping me stop this buck. In fact, counting my common reedbuck and southern mountain reedbuck, I had stopped all five of South Africa's bucks with Bill Wille at my side.

Bill with his Cape grysbok and me with the one that completed my South African bok collection.

The bucks: Limpopo bushbuck, Cape bushbuck, common waterbuck, common reedbuck, southern mountain reedbuck.
The boks: Kalahari gemsbok, Cape springbok, white springbok, black springbok, blesbok, white blesbok, bontebok, Cape grysbok, steenbok, vaal rhebok. An 11th bok, the Sharpe grysbok, is found along the Zimbabwe/Mozambique border.

FIRST MEETING/LASTING IMPRESSION

In November 1985, I read *Death in the Long Grass* by Peter Hathaway Capstick. I couldn't put it down. I read it straight through. It was the most compelling book I had ever read.

The next day I wrote Mr. Capstick in care of St. Martin's Press, New York. I said I was a producer of hunting videos and suggested that we do one together. St. Martin's forwarded my letter to Peter at his residence in Verwoerdburg, South Africa. After receiving the letter in December, he called me at my office in Los Angeles. "Ken Wilson?" "Yes." "This is Peter Capstick calling from South Africa. Listen, old boy, if you want to talk business with me, you need to do it here, in person. I don't want to make a deal by phone or mail or FAX."

I collected my thoughts and said something intelligent like, "You mean you'll meet with me?"

"Yes, here at my home."

I thought some more, "How about next week?"

"Fine, fine. Just let me know when you'll land in Joburg and I'll pick you up. Don't worry about a hotel room, you can stay with Fifi and me."

When I arrived at Jan Smuts Airport in Johannesburg, I discovered that Peter doesn't like meeting people at the airport. He talked his friend, Gordon Cundill, into transporting me for the one-hour drive back to his house located in a suburb of

L to R: Peter Hathaway Capstick, me, and Gordon Cundill at our first meeting.
(Location: the Capstick patio near Pretoria.)

Pretoria. And when I arrived and first met the man himself, I also discovered that Fifi was not the name of his pet dog (that little rascal being a spoiled brat named Boris). Fifi was Peter's wife, Fiona, who is a very striking and sophisticated woman (which shows how opposites attract), a former officer in the South African Army, and extremely intelligent (for example, she translates five languages professionally and speaks several more).

Gordon had been invited for two reasons. First, Peter had only recently completed a lengthy safari with Gordon as professional hunter, during which they had both come very close to being eaten by a lion. That story and many more were the basis for *Peter Capstick's Africa: A Return to the Long Grass*. Second, Gordon was general manager of Hunters Africa, one of the oldest and largest safari operators in Africa.

Prior to that 1985 "return to the long grass" safari, Peter had not hunted as a pro for 10 years and, in fact, had hardly hunted at all except for occasionally matching wits with cattle-killing cats on friends' ranches. But that 1985 safari had rejuvenated him. He called it "absolute mayhem" and "a generally marvelous time." He lived it again while writing his sixth book. And he was desirous of going on another safari when my letter arrived. So he had decided in advance that if he liked this guy Wilson, this "Hollywood producer" who dropped everything to fly over and meet him, he would go on another safari next winter (December being summer in the RSA) with Cundill and Wilson.

Peter and I hit it off right away as we sat in his backyard talking hunting and drinking Lion Lager. The second day of my three-day stay, we signed an agreement on a napkin. It was a small napkin, but as it turned out, we only needed small napkins for each of our projects over the next 10 years.

By the third day, Peter and Gordon and I were old buddies, had already made a deal, and just sat around and planned that greatest of the world's adventures, a safari, for April-May 1986 in the Chobe, Okavango, and Kalahari regions of Botswana. When we completed that safari, we planned another and another and then more. Between safaris, we traded FAXes, hundreds of FAXes, and I always enjoyed his salutations, such as:

To: Ken Wilson, Great Lord of the Nile, Life to Lepers, Writers, and Tax Collectors, and not a bad all-round kid for a Honkey.
From: Abu Ben Capstick, credits to follow on separate parchments, cuneiform tablets and papyri for lack of space.

To: Ken Wilson, Savior of the Unworthy, Keeper of Lions, Fine Credit Risk, Shy and Understated Paladin of the Fallen.
From: The Fallen.

To: Ken Wilson, Beloved of Allah, Lotus of the pool, Land Merchant. Boy Genius. Nice Guy. Producer. Director. Worthy.
From: His Humblest Supplicant, the Most Needy and Least Deserving Peter Capstick.

Of course, the content of his letters was just as creative. Following are the openings of two:

To: Ken Wilson, Mogul of the Skies, Patron of the Mis-scheduled, Champion of All Undertrodden Travel Agents.
From: Undertrodden Travel Agent (Amateur Status).

Dear Ken:

Happy August Seventh, in which during all of history nothing of the SLIGHTEST importance happened but this FAX. Frame it.

I have spent literally all day trying to square things away as to the current trip. You know, I never knew that elephants died THIS hard! You'd think Cleveland Amory was my agent.

To: Ken Wilson, Inventor of the Zipper, Yo-Yo and Easy-Finance.
From: Boris Capstick.

Dear Uncle Ken:

My assistant is busy slopping my warthogs and asked me to drop a note. Something about South West. Wait, I hear him screaming now....
Sorry, Ken ... Goddam dog plays with all my toys!"

Shortly after Peter died in March 1996, I re-read *Death in the Long Grass*. It is still the most compelling book I have ever read.

CAPSTICK/BOTSWANA

Nowadays I go on hunts with just one cameraman because entourages overload outfitters and scare animals. But I didn't know that in 1986, so in April, I arrived in Johannesburg and overnighted in Pretoria with cameramen Rick Morgan and Dennis Gerber and soundman Chip Payne. We also arrived with two 25-pound BetaCams, two studio-size tripods, babylegs tripods, assorted playback equipment and monitors, 60 videocassettes, lighting equipment, wireless and handheld microphones, reflectors, and three weeks of luggage for each member of the crew, not to mention the rifles, ammo, and duffel bags for Peter Capstick and me.

It took two charter Cessna 210s to transport us from Jan Smuts Airport in Johannesburg to our camp by the Chobe River in northern Botswana after a stop for customs in the capital of Gaborone. When we arrived in camp, I counted all the people and all the equipment and everything had arrived except for the 60 videocassettes! Someone had left that box on the tarmac in South Africa! I felt like Knute Rockne had given us a brilliant locker room speech before the big game and then screamed for us all to run out on the field and kick ass, but when we reached the door, it was locked from the outside.

This situation did not impress Gordon Cundill who had flown ahead to make sure our camp and equipment and staff were prepared, but Capstick took it right in stride. He called his wife, Fiona, by shortwave and asked her to remedy the problem and to add some Triscuits (his favorite snack). This required her to drive from their home in Verwoerdberg to Jan Smuts, locate the missing box, and convince the highly suspicious customs officials that she had the right to depart with the cassettes. Then

SPORT HUNTING ON SIX CONTINENTS

Capstick on the plane from South Africa to Botswana. Cameraman Rick Morgan rides in the co-pilot seat.

Jeff Rann and I dragged my red lechwe out of three feet of water for this photo.

she had to drive one hour to Lanseria Airport and place the box (with the Triscuits) on a charter plane to Chobe camp so our safari could begin.

After an evening around the campfire that involved too much liquid and too little sleep, someone (I hope it wasn't me) decided we should all go lion hunting the next morning to break in our crew who had never before been to Africa or seen a wild impala let alone the King of Beasts. Step one (finding big, fresh tracks) was soon accomplished so we could move onto step two (following the tracks for a few hours until the heat of midday when we would walk up to the sleeping cat and dispatch him for the camera).

For step two, we had our two head trackers, then Gordon, another tracker, then Peter and one cameraman, the assistant PH, then me and the other cameraman, and then our soundman and three guys carrying water for us and sticks to protect themselves in the event they were assaulted from the rear. Folks, 13-man stalks just don't work.

Incidentally, the assistant PH on this adventure was a young man named Jeff Rann who was an American citizen with the distinction of having been born in Afghanistan and duly licensed to hunt dangerous game in Botswana with clients in tow. The next day, when we wised up and split up, Jeff became my PH for the rest of our stay at Chobe. I'm happy to report that, not long thereafter, "Rann Hunting Safaris" became one of the top hunting operations in Botswana and, years later, Safari Club International named him African Professional Hunter of the Year. But if you ever get a big head, Jeff, I still have footage of you very much under the weather one morning after a tough night with Capstick.

Jeff and I warmed up with a red lechwe hunt. We made a nice stalk and I shot a good male in the right shoulder. He ran about 75 yards and disappeared. After a 10-minute search, we finally found him submerged in a five foot wide channel of water. Jeff and I dragged him out. The official cause of death was lead poisoning complicated by drowning.

Actually, the very first afternoon in camp, before the 13-man lion hunt and before the lechwe hunt, Gordon could see I was going crazy waiting for the delivery of the videocassettes, so he suggested, "Why don't we take two trackers and go look for something interesting close to camp?" I was ready before he finished his sentence. And when we came back with good specimens of tsessebe and blue wildebeest, the safari was off to a great start. When the videocassettes arrived that evening, the "Botswana Safari" series of videos could also start.

Sometime during the post-lion business meeting, complete with campfire and refreshments, it was decided that Capstick and I would concentrate on Cape buffalo; and when we were both successful, we would move to the Okavango Swamps for a few days while Gordon would set-up our Kalahari camp; and then we would hunt lion in the Kalahari.

For the next several days, Peter departed camp in one direction with either Gor-

My first Botswana trophy was this tsessebe hunted with Gordon Cundill.

Gordon is on the right, with my blue wildebeest.

don as his PH or Robert Ramajaga (the first black African licensed as a PH in Botswana) in search of buffalo, with Dennis Gerber handling the videotaping; while Jeff and I left in a different direction with Rick Morgan as our cameraman. In the back of my mind was Capstick's now famous on-camera comment about hunting Cape buffalo: "It comes down to one very, very simple axiom . . . either you're going to die or he's going to die . . . so you better do your job right."

I remember one stalk in particular, because it is the only time I have been afraid for my life. I've been in other situations made dangerous by animals, including charges by lion and elephant, but I was not afraid because I was confident I could protect myself. And I've been afraid in a couple climbing situations I got myself into when hunting sheep and goat. But a Cape buffalo on this safari scared me alive. This, after such Capstick comments around the campfire as: "The worst thing about the Cape buffalo is you can do some very rude things to him with a big bullet in the right place and he doesn't seem to pay any attention once he's got his adrenaline and other high-powered additives rushing through his system. He's like an express train without a driver."

L to R: me, Capstick, and Cundill relaxing at camp.

So this particular morning, Jeff and I cut fresh tracks early and followed a herd into heavy scrub. Several times we got close enough to hear them feeding, but the wind would change so a few animals would get our scent and run off, taking the herd with them. Then we would have to circle to the side of the herd, get the wind right, and move in again.

One time, we unknowingly moved between the herd and three or four bulls feeding on the periphery when the wind swirled and they all started running. Trouble was, they didn't know where to run and we couldn't see them running because the combretum and terminalia were so dense that our visibility was four to five yards. Jeff was on the left, Rick in the middle, and I was on the right with our two trackers behind us, but we were all within touching distance. At this point the herd was dispersing in every direction and some buffalo were knocking down 10-foot-high bushes within yards of us, but we couldn't see them as they ran by.

Suddenly a big bull broke through the bush directly in front of us and charged past within arm's length. When the bush disintegrated, Rick took two steps back. The bull flashed passed before either Jeff or I could aim our already raised rifles. Jeff turned to Rick and hissed, "Hold your ground." He wanted us in a small protectable group; or maybe he wanted us to all go down at once like a five pin pick-up with a bowling ball. What Jeff hadn't seen was me taking four steps back while Rick took his two.

Then the herd was gone. Before, during, and after the near miss, I had been afraid because I knew that, even if I had been able to make a killing shot, a dead-on-his-feet buffalo, running right at us, would still have run us over.

Later, we stalked up on a herd in more open scrub, but the buffalo were so spread out and feeding so continuously that we couldn't see the headgear on most of the bulls. Jeff said, "It doesn't look like any are over 40 [inches of spread], but I can't see all of them with their heads down grazing, so let's walk straight at them. If a good one raises his head, be ready to shoot." So we walked into the middle of the very surprised herd and they all raised their heads. Jeff frantically searched for a big one, but couldn't find any, and then they were gone.

The next day that tactic worked perfectly. The buffalo stopped feeding and raised their heads, Jeff said, "Shoot the one on the right of that opening," and I stuck a 300-grain solid in his shoulder. A second later, Jeff put a 400-grainer in the same spot, and then the bull was swallowed by the thundering herd.

We followed until the trackers found a single bull's tracks veering off, and then they found blood . . . so the trackers started moving very cautiously while Jeff and I followed at port arms, safeties off. This was a good time to remember Capstick's warning: "There's a great tendency among hunters to see a dim outline in the bush and shoot the wrong one. Then you turn around to shake hands with your professional hunter for a job well done, only to find your wounded buff bearing down on you."

Fortunately, our trackers spotted my buffalo at 50 yards. He was on his stomach with head up and starting to get up, because he saw us at the same time. I shot him in the neck and he toppled onto his left side and gave out with a death bellow. When I touched his eye with my rifle barrel, he blinked, so Jeff had me back off and stick one in his chest from three yards. Then we took pictures.

It was a two-hour wait for the trackers to retrieve the hunting vehicle. When they returned, we hand-cranked the gutted buffalo into the back and departed. Within seconds, literally hundreds of vultures converged on the entrails. Quote Capstick: "Africa doesn't waste any protein. Everything eats everything else."

The next day, Peter got his buffalo on-camera and the day after that we flew from the Chobe to the Okavango where my wife joined us for the rest of the safari.

Etsatsa Camp in the middle of the Swamps was beautiful. Capstick had been there the year before and had become so enthralled with fishing for tigers and bream that that's all he wanted to do at Etsatsa. I was there to hunt an aquatic antelope. Ronnie Blackbeard, whose family settled in Botswana in 1820, was my PH. We would hunt from dugout canoes, known as *makoros*, with a poler in each (the poler standing at the front and pushing against the bottom of the waterway with a long pole while the passenger sits in the middle).

PH Jeff Rann on the right side of my Cape buffalo.

Because of the heavier than normal rains that preceded us, the water level was high, much of the papyrus and reedbeds were covered, and the sitatunga were dispersed. In fact, the first several safaris through had yet to shoot one. This was not good news.

The main channels of the Okavango were 10 to 20 feet deep while the side channels were only two to four feet deep. The *makoros* moved quietly, but were difficult to stand up in without falling. That first afternoon, my poler saw a sitatunga and, thanks to previous practice, I was able to stand without testing the depth of the water. Then I could see the sitatunga, but Ronnie, who was standing in his *makoro*, couldn't see if it was a male or female.

My poler passed his pole back to me and I stuck it in the channel bottom, grabbed it with my left hand, and placed my rifle on my outstretched thumb. Then I caught a glimpse of horns with ivory tips and decided to shoot. I was using my .375 loaded with 300-grain solids; more than enough gun for a 150-pound animal, but that was Ronnie's recommendation in case I had to shoot through papyrus or the like.

Cameraman Dennis Gerber, far left, takes a break to watch the skinners work on the Chapman's zebra I shot.

Capstick poses with my buffalo horns on the bottom and his on the top the morning we moved to the Okavango.

At the shot, the sitatunga went right down and we poled forward to retrieve him. He was in three feet of water, so Ronnie and I jumped in and floated him back to my *makoro*. He was mature and beautiful, but not quite a record book animal. Nevertheless, the first sitatunga of the year was a good excuse to have a four-hour

The first sitatunga of the season. Ronnie Blackbeard is to my left.

Lorraine and me at the Duck Inn in Maun. It was owned by PH Soren Lindstrom who almost lost his life in a lion attack.

party on the houseboat back at Etsatsa Camp that evening.

The next day we flew to Maun so our plane could refuel at the airport and we could refuel at the Duck Inn before flying into the great Kalahari Desert, really a waterless savannah as Gordon pointed out. When we arrived and inspected the camp, we found that a pride of six to eight lions had passed through the night before, and one or more had torn up the canvas shower enclosure.

As might be expected, lions were the main topic of conversation around the campfire that night. Their roaring in the distance only added to the ambience. Quote Capstick: "At night they [lions] completely change character and when you hear that soft pad outside your tent, it will send a feeling through you that I'm sure is the same one that someone sleeping around a campfire a million and a half years ago felt."

About two that morning, my wife woke me. "I hear lions outside our tent," she said. I calmed her down while thinking that Capstick's stories had gotten to her. Then I heard the quiet padding of the King of Beasts right outside the zipped-up entry to our tent. I picked up my .375 and jacked a round into the chamber. They were not going to tear through canvas and take us without a fight. Then I remembered Capstick's written words about a sleeping Peter Hankin: "His friends will later decide that even if he had the rifle now he would still have less than one minute to live."

The padding around camp was non-stop for the rest of the night. Lorraine and I sat in our cots looking at the thin walls of our tent for the next four hours. Finally the dim light of false dawn gave me enough courage to unzip the tent flap a couple feet and peer out, rifle at the ready. It was then that I saw that the King of Beasts were two donkeys that had gotten away from the nearby Bushmen village and had spent the night walking around camp.

That morning, Ronnie commented that I didn't look very rested. I just said that my wife had kept me up most of the night. He smiled lasciviously.

The quantity of game in the Kalahari was amazing if you knew where to look and Ronnie knew where to look. It didn't take me long to shoot good gemsbok, red hartebeest, and springbok. But Peter and I still needed a lion.

Kalahari lion hunts are unique. You drive until you cut track and then a Bushmen follows the tracks at a run . . . for miles and miles and miles . . . until the tracker sees the lion. Then it's up to the hunter to kill the lion before it eats someone. Capstick: "The primary source of liquid for lions in the Kalahari is the blood of its victims."

Just when I thought the donkeys had scared all of the lions out of the desert, Capstick had good news when Ronnie and I passed through camp late one morning. He and Cundill had found fresh tracks and Peter had decided that, "Wilson is such an eager chap . . . let's let him and Blackbeard try for this one." So he placed some toilet paper on a bush by the dirt driving track where the lion and his mate had crossed a few hours earlier. Then he and Gordon returned to camp, ordered lunch to

Lorraine poses with my old, red hartebeest that we found wandering around by himself.

Lorraine poses with husband, trackers, and husband's gemsbok.

go, and gave it to us, along with directions, when Ronnie and I returned.

An hour later, we found the "signal" paper and, in the interest of visual ecology, removed same and started tracking. Two Bushmen followed the tracks at a run as Ronnie and I followed in the truck. There were two reasons for this procedure. First, the tracks were easier to follow by the Bushmen at ground level. Second, clients aren't expected to run a marathon in soft sand and then shoot straight when charged.

After a few miles, we came upon a freshly killed gemsbok ... a very good male. Ronnie said, "This bull was just killed. He backed himself into this bush and gave a good fight. The lions haven't even had time to feed. They both ran off just before we arrived. The male will split from the female and we'll follow the male. If he charges, shoot from the vehicle."

Less than a mile from the gemsbok, the trackers suddenly reversed direction and ran back to the truck as we saw the lion disappear into a thicket. Ronnie and I got out and stalked up until we could barely see the head of the lion lying behind a large bush at about 30 yards. I whispered, "He doesn't have much of a mane." Ronnie said, "The big manes have been shot out of the Kalahari; this is a good lion." I said, "I'm gonna pass." Ronnie said, "You'll be making a mistake if you don't kill this lion." Rick said, "I'm rolling tape." Ronnie said, "He's either going to charge or retreat. You need to shoot him in the chest." I raised my rifle. Ronnie said, "Don't shoot him in the head."

I shot him in the chest twice in one second and his head dropped, so I placed my third shot almost into the dirt and quickly reloaded as the cat ran away. As soon as I had two more in the magazine and one in the chamber, I took shot four and, finally, my fifth shot finished him. When the trackers pulled the lion out of the bush, Ronnie showed me four holes in the chest. Then he opened the lion's mouth and showed me a broken fang. "That was your third shot. If it had been your first, this lion would have been on us in a second."

That night, I mesmerized Capstick with my tale of danger, courage, and grace under pressure. Later, my wife slept soundly, confident that her husband, the great *Bwana* of the desert, would keep the donkeys out of our tent.

L to R: Ronnie, Lorraine, and me with my Kalahari lion.

Sport Hunting on Six Continents

Capstick takes a break in the waterless savannah.

29

CAPSTICK/NAMIBIA AND SOUTH AFRICA

Namibia

Despite all the elephant hunts in which Peter Capstick participated as a professional hunter or as a government cropping officer, he had never shot a jumbo on his own account. So, as we worked our way through the Big Five on video, Peter lined up an elephant hunt in the Bushmanland area of Namibia with Volker Grellmann. I agreed to supply the cameraman and edit the video.

As the time for the safari neared, my first cameraman backed out, so I hired a second one and he had to cancel. Finding a safari-experienced cameraman available to leave home and business on short notice for 28 days was starting to look impossible. I couldn't make the trip, so I decided to hire a studio-experienced cameraman in good enough condition to lug a 25-pound BetaCam in the bush and train him how to shoot a hunt. After a few interviews in Hollywood, I picked a guy (whose name is in the credits for "Capstick: Hunting the African Elephant") and took him to Arizona to video my hunting black bear with the San Carlos Apaches.

The cameraman did okay in Arizona and, shortly thereafter, was on his way to Windhoek via London and Johannesburg. In London, he partied so hard that he barely made the flight to Joburg, but some of my video equipment didn't make it onto his flight and he also lost the shoe that locks the camera onto the tripod. Videotaping the safari was delayed until the equipment was rounded up.

Preceding Capstick to camp by a few days were Jerry and Bam Heiner from California. The cameraman was to video Jerry hunting elephant first and then, starting a few days later, he would video Peter. I had given the cameraman a couple of Capstick's books to read on the plane and they had apparently scared him so much that he didn't want to get near any elephants. When Jerry finally stalked up and shot his elephant, the cameraman must have been 200 yards away so it looked like an ant was shooting a mouse.

To his credit, the cameraman did hang in there the full four weeks, logging a couple hundred miles on foot in hot country, and got close enough to Capstick's kill that, thanks to the zoom lens, he captured both Capstick and the elephant on-camera simultaneously as Peter laid in several heart-lung shots with his .470 Capstick. The tusks, which were of the short Ethiopian-type with big circumferences, each weighed over 70 pounds.

Peter Capstick, left, with Volker Grellmann and Peter's elephant shot on-camera in Bushmanland, Namibia.

South Africa

As with any challenging endeavor, sometimes you have to fight your way through adversity after adversity in order to achieve your goal. For my first hunt in South Africa, my goal was to tell the story of the comeback of the southern white rhino from near extinction and then to produce a documentary of my hunt for a white rhino.

Naturally, I elicited Peter Capstick to help tell the story. He jumped into the project with both feet, booked the safari, and even arranged for the opportunity for me to also produce a video on hunting leopard by baiting; probably his favorite type of big game hunt because he enjoyed the cat and mouse challenge of bringing the cat to the hunter.

On the safari, problems immediately erupted between the "cooperating" professional hunter-outfitters selected by

Capstick and responsible for operating our hunt. On the one hand were professional hunter Dirk Uys and outfitter Stan Szmyrgala. Shortly after our safari ended, both appeared before a magistrate in South Africa and were found guilty of "improper conduct involving a single instance" that took place prior to and unrelated to our safari which resulted in each being fined and Dirk losing his professional hunter's license.

On the other hand was Gordon Cundill, Capstick's good friend from Peter's book titled *Peter Capstick's Africa: A Return to the Long Grass* and the same man who put on such a good show for us in Botswana when he was general manager of Hunters Africa. Gordon had just separated from Hunters Africa under questionable circumstances and had formed his own company named Safari Africa.

Other problems involved tentage, leopard permits, shooting accuracy, and letters of complaint to the Department of Nature Conservation. A month after the safari ended, Johann Grove, the Principal Nature Conservator, contacted me in California and asked me to send him a letter describing what happened on the Capstick-Wilson-Cundill-Uys-Szmyrgala-Martin-Smith safari. Following is my letter of July 23, 1987 to Mr. Grove:

Re: Our May 17-June 1, 1987 safari and video production in South Africa

Dear Mr. Grove:

On May 17, 1987, I departed Los Angeles (in my capacity as a video director and on-camera hunter for Sportsmen on Film) along with Rick Morgan and Dennis Gerber (both video cameramen). In London, we met up with George and Mary Martin for the purpose of their participating in the two videos we were to produce in South Africa. George is the Director of the National Rifle Association Publications and Mary contributes still photography to those publications.

In Johannesburg, we were met by Peter and Fiona Capstick and Campbell Smith, and we all drove to Thabazimbi. Peter Capstick holds the distinction of being the best-selling hunting author in the world. He and his wife reside near Pretoria. Campbell

Dennis Gerber videotaping my 28-inch southern impala shot in Thabazimbi, South Africa. L to R: me, Dirk Uys, Stan Szmyrgala, and Peter Capstick.

L to R: Stan Szmyrgala, Dirk Uys, me, and Capstick. This warthog was a female, but had the biggest tusks any of us had ever seen on a female.

Smith is a licensed professional hunter and outfitter who was along to provide those services for the Martins under the direction of Gordon Cundill, owner of Safari Africa.

At our hunting concession, a traditional tented safari camp awaited us and, as it turned out, provided us with comfortable and beautiful accommodations except for the unusually cold weather that we experienced at night (and for whom we had no one to blame except the Almighty).

In camp, we met Gordon Cundill, Stan Szmyrgala, and

I was required to shoot only this particular rogue rhino. It took us four days to find it!

Dirk Uys as well as the native staff. I first met Gordon Cundill in December 1985 in Pretoria and I then participated in a safari in April-May 1986 in Botswana, with Gordon acting as both a professional hunter and serving in his capacity as the general manager of Hunters Africa. In Botswana, we encountered no difficulties from the standpoint of logistics or comfort.

I met Stan Szmyrgala and Dirk Uys, for the first time, in camp. However, I had traded phone calls and letters with Capstick, Cundill, and Szmyrgala and had a couple brief conversations with Uys prior to our departure so that we would all be straight as to everyone's responsibilities. My understanding was that Capstick was to be the central on-camera personality and expert in the two videos to be produced, and that Cundill-Safari Africa and Szmyrgala-Uys were the co-outfitters and co-professional hunters for the safari. The Martins were to participate for the primary purpose of gathering material to publish in American Hunter magazine (which has a circulation of approximately 1.6 million). The plan was for us to produce two videos, one on hunting white rhino in Thabazimbi and one on leopard hunting on or near Stan's ranch by the Limpopo River near Alldays.

This is the nyala I shot the afternoon after Gordon Cundill packed up his tents and departed.

A few problems arose while on safari which, although inconvenient, were not unusual. To be a successful hunter and video producer, one must be flexible and take a neutral position as far as camp politics are concerned in order to achieve the ultimate goal which is the production of an esthetically viable video. For example, Szmyrgala-Uys did not bring a hunting vehicle and the vehicle they did bring, unfortunately broke down. Therefore they utilized Cundill's hunting vehicle, with his permission, to escort Capstick and me, and this caused the Martins to use a passenger vehicle.

A pattern soon developed whereby we were all very happy while hunting during the day but, in camp at night, the infighting between the two outfitters (Cundill vs. Szmyrgala-Uys) ruined the ambience of the camp and resulted in the possibility of each day being the last day of the safari.

The primary problem seemed to be one of the tentage. Our understanding, before departing from the U.S., was that Gordon Cundill had arranged for a tent company to supply tentage for the duration of the safari in return for being able to take publicity stills of their tents in the field. In camp, Gordon informed me that the tents were merely set-up at Thabazimbi for Stan to see them and purchase them. In camp, Stan said he had no obligation to purchase the tentage and, in fact, did not want to do so. The result was that each night we were faced with the threat of all tentage being removed the very next day. That turned out to be the case on the fifth day when Gordon removed all of the tentage, ostensibly because Stan did not purchase it, and pulled out with his staff.

From a hunting standpoint, I successfully hunted a southern impala, warthog, white rhino, and nyala. Mary Martin harvested an impala and Cape hartebeest, and George Martin shot an impala along with a Burchell's zebra.

Although Mary is a very fine shot, she took four or five shots to drop her impala which became another major incident. The Cundill side claims that the landowner's representative questioned Mary's shooting ability and then asked the Martins not to hunt after the fourth day. Along with a problem with the leopard permits (which I will explain), this caused the Martins to leave on the fifth day when Cundill pulled out. The Szmyrgala-Uys side claims that the owner's rep never asked the Martins to stop hunting and that he only inquired as to the results of

L to R: Stan, me, and Dirk with my Cape eland, shot after we tracked the herd most of the day.

Mary's shots so he could determine if any wounded, but unfound, game remained.

On that fateful fifth day, Capstick stayed with us long enough to shoot the additional video that absolutely required his presence and then he departed with his wife, the Martins, and Cundill-Smith.

The initial plan was for us to all drive to Szmyrgala's ranch after concluding the rhino portion of the safari, but a major point of discussion each evening was that, although Szmyrgala-Uys had permits to shoot two leopards (which permits were to go to George Martin and Peter Capstick), they had not yet received written permission for an exemption to bait leopards. For our leopard video, we wanted to show the traditional hunting method which is baiting. Without the written permission, the leopard portion of the safari would have been discontinued anyway, but the "tentage" and "extra shots" problems expedited that decision.

Our two cameramen and myself stayed with Szmyrgala-Uys until the morning of the sixth day (without tents) in order to shoot additional footage necessary to the rhino video. We then departed for Szmyrgala's ranch only to find that the exemption to bait still had not arrived. Giving up on the leopard hunt, I stayed for six days with my cameramen and obtained footage of my successfully hunting Cape eland, Limpopo bushbuck, and blesbok.

While I have tried to be as candid and comprehensive as possible, I am unsure of the specific details in which you may be interested. My primary handicap is one of bewilderment at the evolution of events, and I feel that the experience was not unlike being a central character in an American soap opera.

Very truly yours,

Ken Wilson

cc: Peter Capstick
    George and Mary Martin
    Gordon Cundill
    Stan Szmyrgala
    Dirk Uys

With Dirk Uys and my blesbok. It was Dirk's last safari as a pro.

CAPSTICK/SMALL SAFARI

Africa. The Dark Continent. The Big Five. Home to over 100 species of game animals. Once you have hunted there, you start planning to return . . . on the plane flight home!

But the Big Five takes time and money. In fact, hunting any game in most African countries takes time and money . . . about $1,400 per day (in 1995) plus trophy fees in Botswana, Tanzania, and Zambia. Cut the rate about in half in Zimbabwe. And half again for South Africa and Namibia. Now we're getting somewhere!

If you have the time and money, there is absolutely nothing in this world the equal of a 21-day dangerous game safari in a tented camp with a top professional hunter and full staff. But let's assume that you're not there yet. Why not go small? But go!

Here's how to do it the small way. Take one week off work. That gives you nine days unless you can sneak off mid-day on Friday. With two days to get there from North America and one day to get back, you can have six to seven hunting days under the Southern Cross.

I really went small on one safari . . . small airfare, small daily rates, small-bodied animals, small trophy fees, and small taxidermy . . . *everything*, including the trophies on my wall, for less than $5,000. Save up your money and enjoy Africa. You can do it!

Peter and Fiona Capstick met me at Jan Smuts Airport in Johannesburg and treated me to frog legs at a quaint French restaurant and a pleasant night in their new home in Waterkloof. The next morning we departed for Messina near the Limpopo River separating Zimbabwe from South Africa. Peter was joining me as an observer in order to get a break and a suntan between books. He couldn't wait to leave his typewriter to re-experience the wildlife, campfires, stars, and characters that are Africa.

Classic Safari, owned by Dierk and Ingeborg Lempertz, were our outfitters and camp was beautifully placed with rock chalets, indoor and outdoor dining areas, and the obligatory campfire and chairs. July is the middle of the South African winter so we were prepared for cold weather. It did drop into the 40s a few nights (8° Celsius) but that's what the campfire was for. Also the rock chalets retained the daytime heat, so sleeping with a single blanket was very comfortable.

As we hunted among the *koppies* (rocky hills and outcroppings), we would generally see a wide variety of game most days including red (Cape) hartebeest, blue wildebeest, Cape eland, gemsbok, Limpopo bushbuck, blesbok, warthog, impala, and nyala, but I had taken good specimens of each of those on previous safaris. This time I was going small for gray duiker, steenbok, and klipspringer. Hey, anyone can shoot the big targets, but those little ones are a real challenge in more ways than one.

Kaiphus on a koppie *pointing out klipspringer habitat for Ken.*

The gray duiker, often called the common duiker, was the most prolific of the small game where we were hunting. They are about 20 inches high at the shoulder and mature males average about 40 pounds. The females are about 25% bigger, but that's not my problem. Also, the males have horns, with four inches considered good and 4 $1/2$ inches excellent.

Peter loaned me his .30-06, the famous .30 caliber first produced in 1906, and a couple handfuls of 180-grain solids . . . definitely enough gun. It only took two pulls of that crisp two-pound trigger to prove the rifle still held zero at 100 meters. With the small bodies I would be hunting in the mopane scrub and thornbush of the northeastern Transvaal, I was expecting 100-meter shots and didn't want my bullet to hit above the crosshairs at that distance. While the solids would be good brushbusters, their main purpose was to make a small exit hole and save the capes.

Here were our challenges. Biltong (meat) hunters had been hammering our area pretty hard so all the big and small game was skittish, but Peter knew I would still see lots of the small stuff because they don't make much biltong. Also, our professional hunters (and we traded off with several) couldn't help us much with spotting and trophy assessment as they drove, so we relied on the trackers who were on top of the Land Rover with us.

Duiker means "diver" in Afrikaans and they are well-named because your first view is invariably of them diving into the bush and disappearing. An effective hunting method is to let them run off and then have the PH drive off while you and your tracker move very slowly for a few hundred meters looking for a shooting opportunity. If we didn't get a glimpse within a few minutes, it was back to the truck.

Amann was my first tracker. When he spotted the first duiker,

The game was small, but the baobab trees were big.

I tapped the cab top and my PH stopped. I turned to Amann and asked, "Male?" He said, "Yes," so off we went, but never found it. This happened twice more before I had my first chance. The duiker was behind a bush at about 60 meters. I put the crosshairs on the chest and, to make sure, I whispered, "Male?" to Amann. He said, "No," so I disappointedly lowered the rifle. Then Amann said, "No male; bull!" Despite the miscommunication, I managed to shoot that duiker as it made its first jump away from the bush. It had respectable four-inch horns which was the luck of the draw because I didn't see the horns until I pulled the trigger.

Steenbok occupied the same turf as the duikers. They are a beautiful little animal about the same height as a duiker, but averaging only about 25 pounds, golden red in color, with large ears that are white with black stripes on the inside. Only the male has horns and they usually run in pairs so, if you see a female, there is usually a male around.

Capstick checks his rifle by a candelabra tree.

If we caught them in the open as we drove along, they would immediately run if they were over about 150 meters away. But if they were closer, especially less than 100 meters, they stood absolutely still so we no doubt drove by a lot more than we saw. The best hunting method seemed to be to drive by them without slowing down until out of sight, and then circle back downwind on foot. I shot an average male this way; a beautiful trophy but I decided that, for a trophy fee of only $250, I would try for another if I had a chance.

Klipspringer are interesting in many ways. They mostly occur in pairs in rocky areas and use their specialized hooves to run the steep rocks to their advantage. The

With Kaiphus, Peter and my steenbok.

bottom of their hooves has a rubbery center that obviously provides great traction.

Dierk set us up to hunt another "farm" for klipspringer (we would call them "ranches"). Virtually all of the farms in the northeastern Transvaal have been converted to fenced game ranches that seem to average about 5,000 hectares (about 12,500 acres which is about 20 square miles or 50 square kilometers) because the cattle and farming schemes just didn't work due to the lack of sustainable graze.

Leaving early in the morning, we ran across a jackal that was returning from an evening of scavenging. Everyone pointed and said, "Shoot," so I did and lucked into a nice, mature black-backed jackal which was much smaller than I thought. Both the male and female stand only about 15 inches at the shoulder with the male averaging a couple more pounds than the female. The one I shot was considered big at about 25 pounds . . . and there was no trophy fee.

The terrain for my klipspringer hunt seemed perfect; a series of *koppies* in the middle of the bushveld. I was assigned Gibson as my tracker and off we went *koppie* climbing. On the second *koppie*, Gibson spotted a klipspringer pair scurrying over the top. We followed them to the third *koppie*. This was fun; like being on a North American sheep hunt only with a 200-foot vertical climb in shorts instead of 2,000 feet in long johns. As we carefully moved along the top, Gibson pointed down and out about 100 meters and said, "Shoot, shoot, shoot!" Now a seasoned veteran, I looked through my scope at the head of the

With Kaiphus and my black-backed jackal.

klipspringer first. Then I disgustedly looked at Gibson and said, "No horns." Gibson was an inveterate meat hunter.

On the fourth *koppie*, Gibson said, "This is the last one; they have nowhere to go." Right. Nowhere except a hundred hiding places, plus the other side of the *koppie*. This pair ran into the bushveld. We tracked them for a few hundred meters before I told Gibson to turn back, because we'd never get a shot in the mopane scrub. As it turned out, the pair had returned to the last *koppie* before us and Gibson spotted them on top and said, "Shoot, shoot, shoot." I whispered, "Which one?" He replied, "Shoot, shoot, shoot!" When they stopped, I spotted the male through my binoculars, looked for a rest but found none, raised my rifle and fired free hand, and missed. We walked back in the growing darkness. When I told Capstick what had happened, he cheered me up with, "It's always darkest just before it's totally black." He was right. The farmer charged me 100 rand for the missed shot!

The next day, Dierk assigned me his best tracker, Kaiphus, who is a true wizard and he got me on a beautiful male klipspringer that I didn't miss. Their coats are truly unique with short, bristly hairs. He weighed about 25 pounds. The females don't have horns and, as with the gray duiker, they average about 25% bigger than the males.

With one hunting day left, I decided to upgrade my steenbok. Late in the afternoon, Kaiphus and I were wandering through the bushveld while Capstick and PH Donnie Botha took an undeserved break by the drink cooler back at the Land Rover. Kaiphus pointed and whispered, "Female." We let it feed out of sight. Then we slowly moved forward and I saw another with the afternoon sun reflecting off horns . . . long horns. Using Kaiphus' shoulder as a rest, I shot it from the right hip through the left shoulder as it fed away. Kaiphus immediately announced that I had missed but soon said, "You got it!" with a big smile. Solids don't put them down like softs, but they sure save the cape on the exit side.

When I walked up, those long horns turned out to be on a duiker, not a steenbok. The late afternoon sun seemed to turn the gray coat of the duiker into golden red like that of a steenbok. Then I had become entranced with the horns which were five inches, a huge difference from my previous duiker of four inches. Oh well, the trophy fee was small and I had upgraded. But I also had to endure Capstick's rather lengthy account of my "steenduiker" hunt

With Kaiphus and my klipspringer shot the day after I got charged for missing one.

SPORT HUNTING ON SIX CONTINENTS

My gray, aka common, aka southern bush duiker.

Capstick by the campfire in his kikoi. I asked him what was under it and he showed me!

around the campfire that night. After he got all the laughs he could at my expense, I asked Peter a serious question ("What advice would you give a hunter going small on his or her very first African Safari?") and received a serious answer.

"Do plenty of research and planning. Just because you may be on safari for just a few days and you may be hunting the smaller animals doesn't mean you should deprive yourself the pleasure of selecting a top area with a top company and PH, and then learning all you can about the species to be hunted. As you know, I'm a believer in solids for the small stuff, because you can still shoot them in the right place and have the exit hole match the entry hole. But my number one tip is to research the animals you will be hunting. How enjoyable can it be to shoot something and then ask what you just shot . . . or worse, shoot something and think you shot something else? Right, Ken?" (Laughter around the campfire.)

PETER CAPSTICK'S LAST SAFARI

Prologue

This story was originally titled "Challenging Africa" because this safari wasn't supposed to be Peter Capstick's last one . . . only the most recent one before the next one and the next after that. The words, written months before Peter's death, have not been changed. The story of his last safari stands as it happened. But his last safari should have been different. He should have been tracking a herd of Cape buffalo, trying to pick out a wounded man-killer, relying on his best trackers, Silent and Invisible, until the old bull broke off from the herd and went into the long grass knowing that Peter would follow him in with a double-barreled rifle loaded 500 grains to the side, step-by-step, waiting for the inevitable charge from close quarters.

Challenging Africa

I can still see the leopard in my mind as I write these words. His head was as big as a soccer ball. His mouth was slightly open and his white teeth glowed in contrast to his evil, yellow eyes. When I first saw him, his head and shoulders were already in my room and his eyes were locked on mine. He took one step and I screamed!

I was sitting upright in my bed. The door to my chalet was closed. I switched on my flashlight and found my room empty. Damn that Capstick! He and his leopard

Peter Capstick on safari in the northern Transvaal nine months before he passed away.

stories around the campfire. They must have gotten to me.

I was in the northeastern Transvaal of South Africa to videotape the safari of a unique man and hunter. Dr. Bruce Melrose is a Doctor of Medicine, Certified by the American Board of Radiology and a Diplomat of the American Board of Nuclear Medicine. He is a certified divemaster and has a Master's License from the United States Coast Guard. And he is an excellent hunter despite having Arthrogryposis Multiplex, a poorly understood congenital condition that effects the muscles and joints.

Peter Hathaway Capstick, the best-selling hunting author in the world, is simply a kick to have on safari. Bruce and I are both friends with Peter and we collaborated to talk him into joining our Transvaal adventure. We caught him at the right time so that Peter took over most of the planning that resulted in my finding myself wide awake and sitting up in bed at 3:00 AM. I listened for a few minutes and, either I didn't scream out loud, or no one heard me. Badly needing to use the bathroom, I cracked open the door to my chalet and shined my flashlight across 30 feet of blackness to the door of the outside bathroom. That's when I decided I really didn't need to go after all, so I returned to bed and read until the 5:00 AM wake-up call because I was still getting used to the seven hour time change from Texas.

Brian Marsh drove down from Zimbabwe to visit Peter in our camp and to assist as a professional hunter. Brian and Peter had recently finished collaborating on *A Man Called Lion,* which is about John "Pondoro" Taylor. Brian has been professionally hunting and a professional hunter for over 40 years starting as a crocodile hunter in what was then Nyasaland in the mid-1950s when the official death rate from crocs was over three humans per day! He was born in Pretoria in 1928 and his family moved to Rhodesia that same year. Eventually, he also hunted in Botswana and Mozambique before moving back to Rhodesia when the game ranching industry was legalized in 1960. Before that time, hunting to profit from wild animals was illegal in Rhodesia. Consequently, the animals had no value so they were decimated in favor of domestic livestock schemes which failed on most lands.

From 1960 to 1967, Brian was the manager of a 500,000-acre spread and in charge

The cast of characters: L to R, Dr. Bruce Melrose, Peter Capstick, Brian Marsh and me.

of meat hunting with a quota of 8,000 pounds of meat a week. Finally, in 1967, sport hunting was allowed and Brian conducted Rhodesia's very first safari. The infusion of dollars from sport hunting has been a huge success in what is now Zimbabwe so that wildlife now proliferates because it has value.

Our outfitter for the safari was Dierk and Ingeborg Lempertz of Classic Safari. Their "farm" would be home base and we would hunt it and four other farms throughout the safari. Their home and our camp was constructed at the base of Klein Bolayi, a huge rock that is probably 200 meters long by 100 meters wide by 50 meters high. "Bolayi" is roughly translated from Zulu as "the place of killing and atonement." In the olden days, bad guys and the smallest baby twin were disposed of by

Klein Bolayi.

dropping them over the side of Bolayi rock. Bad guys were never liked. Neither were twins because they slowed down the mother in the fields.

Bruce had hunted Africa several times before, but this was his first time in the Transvaal. Because of overlapping species in the Cape Province and Botswana, he had already collected gemsbok, Cape eland, blue wildebeest, nyala, and zebra, so he wanted to concentrate on kudu, blesbok, waterbuck, red hartebeest, bushbuck and warthog. But, before we got started, an interesting proposition came up. The northeastern Transvaal was in a severe drought. Water was being pumped into ponds and tanks for the wildlife, but the graze was gone and the browse was getting thin. Many farmers were reducing animal populations by bringing in biltong hunters (meat hunters who dry the meat into strips for the commercial market). One farm in particular had an overpopulation of giraffes and they preferred that a few old specimens be taken by sport hunters because the biltong hunters were not much interested in old, tough giraffe bulls and cows.

Brian and Peter encouraged Bruce to hunt a giraffe because the more that farmers profited from removing a percentage of old giraffes each year on a sustained yield basis, the more they would be encouraged to raise additional giraffes for the enjoyment of both hunters and non-hunters. Bruce agreed and we were off on my first giraffe hunt.

Brian had culled quite a few giraffes in the years before the safari industry was legalized in Rhodesia. "When you have a quota of 8,000 pounds of meat a week, a giraffe looks pretty good about day six." Brian quickly sketched a giraffe and emphasized the triangle formed by the shoulder. "All you have to do is hit the middle of the triangle," he told Bruce.

Bruce had brought a .300 Weatherby for the safari, shooting 180-grain Nosler partition bullets. But, for the giraffe, Peter loaned his .375 H&H Magnum shooting 300-grain A-square monolithic solids. To make sure it was on target, Peter placed a 100-meter shot on the edge of the bullseye at Dierk's rifle range and Bruce put a shot right next to it.

Almost all the farms in the northeastern Transvaal are now game fenced because wildlife is about the only industry that pays since various livestock schemes have proven unsuccessful. The farms seem to average about 20 square miles in size, but this herd of 50-plus giraffes was on a larger farm. In fact, it took us all morning before we even saw the first group of giraffes. I couldn't believe that 15- to 18-foot tall animals could be that difficult to locate, but the trees were taller than the giraffes and, unless you were within 100 meters, the giraffes just weren't visible unless they moved.

None were big enough in the first group but, just as we were ready to break for lunch, Bruce spotted a second group moving away. Out of the Land Rover we piled. Brian led a careful, downwind approach. We wanted to get into the group of four and pick out the biggest, tallest, darkest colored one. Our tracker led the way in and stopped. Three giraffes were looking at us over the intervening thorn and mopane trees. One was big but not "the big one." Bruce and Brian stepped forward. The big one was standing sideways looking at the other three. As it turned its head, Bruce nailed it at the back of the shoulder and once again as it turned to run.

We followed the tracks for about 200 meters when the tracker pointed to his left and yelled, "Shoot, shoot, shoot." Peter was looking through his Swarovskis and yelled, "I don't see blood." Brian had his hand on Bruce's shoulder and said, "That's not the one we want." He walked back to where the big one must have broken away from the group and found it still on its feet but immobile. Bruce gave it a mercy shot and down it went, destroying a big thornbush in the process.

That was one big animal and all three shots could be covered by your palm. By prior arrangement, the farm kept all the meat and Bruce took the entire hide which involved the rest of the day. Since Bruce's trophy room is 30 feet high at the apex, he decided on a half life-sized mount and Peter agreed to make a handful of bracelets from the tail hairs.

All of the other species that Bruce wanted were available on each of the other farms, but we rotated every couple days to reduce the hunting pressure. Late the next evening, Bruce shot a great bushbuck. This was the Limpopo subspecies which has the longest horns, and Bruce's trophy was well into SCI and Rowland Ward

Three days later, Bruce shot two nice trophies. Kudu had been giving us problems. Dierk's head tracker, Kaiphus, is a bush genius and was able to get us onto several groups of kudu, but with no time to pick out a good bull, let alone get a shot.

Bruce by the head of his giraffe. The rest of us are a long way back. L to R: Peter, me, and Brian.

L to R with Bruce's kudu: Kaiphus, Bruce, Dierk, Peter, and Matanga.

On this morning, a group of bulls disappeared from our view, but a good one stepped back into view while looking the other way. Bruce hammered him with his Weatherby and it ran 100 meters and collapsed.

That same afternoon, we located a group of waterbuck including three bulls. This was the Kobus ellipsiprymnus subspecies with the big white circle on their rear ends. Waterbuck bulls weigh 500-plus pounds but they sure can disappear in heavy cover along dry riverbeds. Kaiphus had Bruce perfectly seated overlooking an "opening" that he felt the bulls would pass through. It was an area where the cover was less thick. As the first bull walked by at 80 meters, the assistant PH, Tim Van Eijden, whispered, "Wait." When the head of the next one appeared, Tim whispered, "Now," and the rifle barked. It took some expert tracking to find that bull, but Kaiphus was up to the challenge.

The very next day, Bruce got another double. In the morning, he shot a red hartebeest that qualified for both SCI and Rowland Ward. It was running with a female and really acting stupid. It happens to all of us. The females also have horns, but the male's are longer and heavier.

In the afternoon, our PH for the day, Donnie Botha, found a herd of blesbok; another species in which both sexes have horns. The males were running together at this time of year (late July-early August). Judging 14- to 16-inch horns at 200 meters isn't easy, but Donnie picked out a good one when they stopped to look back and Bruce shot it.

That left Bruce with his nemesis still to collect; the warthog. Since his first safari in 1989, Bruce had longed for a warthog for his wall. After all, they are so ugly they're cute. But something always happened and Bruce still didn't have a warthog. Because of the drought, the warthog population was down and many farmers were reducing populations and selling the meat. It seemed the best chance would be a high seat so Bruce spent several afternoons in one that was situated 160 meters from a waterhole. After lots of action from impala, nyala, guinea fowl and small warthogs, a big one finally came to drink at the far end of the waterhole. We couldn't see the warts from that distance (the males have four protuberances on their faces while the females have two) but the males are considerably bigger and have bigger tusks. This was a big male facing straight toward us which made the target smaller. Bruce squeezed the trigger while trying to control warthog fever, but the shot was off-center, hitting the side and back left leg.

Now came the most masterful job of tracking I have seen. Kaiphus followed the winding spoor and drops of blood for about two miles. At one point, he surmised that the warthog was heading for the fence, so he ran there to thwart a crossing. Even on the largest farms, you eventually hit a fence and no matter how diligent the staff, there are warthog holes under the fence. If a wounded warthog goes under, you need to get permission from the adjacent landowner to continue on the spoor, which is time-prohibitive.

Kaiphus felt he was getting close when he found where the warthog had laid down awhile, so he took off running like a madman and barking like a dog. When we caught up, Kaiphus was standing still and pointing at a hole while still

Kaiphus and Bruce with the warthog that Kaiphus outsmarted.

barking. Apparently, feral dogs, or even farmers' dogs out for a good time, occasionally chase warthogs. Since this one was wounded, it must have felt it couldn't outrun a pack of dogs so it backed its way down a hole with only its head and formidable tusks sticking out. One shot in the back of the head and Bruce finally had his nemesis. He slapped Kaiphus on the back and laughed. Kaiphus laughed back. They had met the challenge.

Around the campfire on that, our last night, Capstick pointed out the team effort required for a successful safari. "Game management conserves the animals. The camp staff conserves the hunter's time. The pro has to run the whole operation without seeming to sweat and, when actually hunting, he has to know enough about the habits of the animals and the abilities and limitations of the client to get the two to meet up on enough occasions to keep things happy around the campfire at night . . . which is where we are . . . and where I just love to be. Is everybody happy?" (Chorus: "Yeeesss!")

Peter Capstick enjoying the conversation around the campfire on his last safari.

32

CAPSTICK RETROSPECTIVE

Peter Hathaway Capstick burst on the African hunting scene in 1977 with the publication of *Death in the Long Grass* which he followed with *Death in the Silent Places, Maneaters, Death in the Dark Continent, Safari: The Last Adventure, Peter Capstick's Africa, The Last Ivory Hunter, Last Horizons, Death in a Lonely Land, Sands of Silence, The African Adventurers* and *A Man Called Lion* as well as serving as series editor of The Peter Capstick Library of reprints of historical books on African hunting and adventure. *Warrior* was published posthumously.

Peter's writing successes caused immense jealousy among a few who questioned whether he really experienced everything he wrote about. I do know, from having produced six videos with him, and having corresponded with him continuously for 11 years, that he was a great observer. He was as interested in the smallest animals as well as the biggest, and in the most common people as well as the most sophisticated. He was also a very fine shot with the big calibers that usually cause big flinches.

Peter died on March 13, 1996 in South Africa from complications following heart surgery. Truthfully, I don't know how he lived as long as he did because he never took care of himself and never went to a doctor unless on a stretcher. I know of at least three stretcher situations. One was a "flare-up" 20 years after a Cape buffalo landed on him and crushed two vertebrae. The doctors wondered how he had been able to walk for those 20 years. Another was when he collapsed in the lobby of a hotel in Colorado Springs, where he was to be a banquet speaker, and underwent emergency surgery for a perforated duodenal ulcer. And third was his last trip to the hospital after he had to be replaced by his wife as a featured speaker at the 1996 SCI Annual Convention in Reno. (Despite the stress, she was brilliant in her recitation about Peter's favorite animal, the hyena.) He had suffered a coronary artery spasm and had to be airlifted back to South Africa where he underwent major cardiac bypass surgery. But it was too late.

Following his death, one of his publishers, Ludo Wurfbain of Safari Press, wrote: "All of us in the safari industry owe Peter Capstick a great debt. He, more than any other person, made safari hunting popular and fashionable again in the 1970s. At that time, Kenya and Tanzania were closed, Zimbabwe in a civil war, and South Africa still a mere shadow of what it is today."

Robert Ruark and Ernest Hemingway were great writers, but as regards the subject of Africana, Peter Capstick was unsurpassed. As I reflect on Peter's last year,

Having fun in Peter Capstick's living room in Waterkloof, South Africa following his last safari.

I believe that he knew he was going to exit early so he pushed me to produce a video on hunting the African leopard which was the only member of the Big 5 without a Capstick/Sportsmen on Film collaboration. As described in the previous chapter, Dr. Bruce Melrose agreed to go along as the primary hunter and, at Peter's insistence, the safari was moved up a year because he wanted to do it NOW. Fortunately, for posterity, it all worked out and I spent many hours behind the camera recording Peter's observations on a variety of subjects in the context of Bruce's leopard hunt. Peter just relaxed and did what he enjoyed the most which was observing. We talked about most of the species indigenous to the northeastern Transvaal, but none more than the animal paramount in our minds . . . the African leopard. Mostly we talked off-camera, but so I don't misquote Africa's master raconteur, following are some of Peter Capstick's on-camera observations regarding the animal that many feel is the most difficult trophy in Africa to hunt.

"A leopard's now wounded let's say, and the professional hunter and his entourage are going in after him . . . because you can't leave dangerous game around; it kills people. A leopard will choose his own ground to defend. Once he realizes he's being pursued, he will pick a spot and he will wait for you and he'll be out just like an anthracite and orange flash. They're unbelievably fast. There was a case in Kenya of a leopard mauling six people before a shot could be fired . . . before he melted back in the bush. Two other professional hunters were sent in to kill that leopard and both of them were mauled by it, so it must have been a very talented leopard and had quite a lot of practice.

"Pound for pound, the African leopard is, I think without question, the strongest of the cats. And he is probably one of the three strongest of the African animals; the other two being the army ant and the honey badger. Leopards have been known to pull $2\frac{1}{2}$ times their weight way up a tree, particularly in an area where you have hyenas.

"Don't let anybody tell you that leopards cannot be maneaters. They certainly can. The two greatest maneaters in history were both Indian leopards. Incidentally, the African leopard and the Indian leopard, or the Asian leopard, are exactly, precisely the same animal although they are normally called a 'panther' in India. They are among the more widely distributed of the world's animals; probably as much as the Norwegian rat, occurring anywhere from Russia all the way south to the Cape. We know, because we have a bunch of newspaper clippings, that they live in places as sophisticated as Johannesburg and Pretoria. Leopard are a tremendously adaptable animal because they are very camouflaged, very quick, and very intelligent, which makes them one of the most difficult things in the world to hunt.

"I suppose there are more dangerous things in the world to confront than a wounded leopard, but I can't think of one offhand. He is probably the most likely African animal to certainly chew a couple of sirloins out of you. He is not as likely to kill you as a lion or an elephant, but he injures far more people every year during the hunting season throughout Africa than any other animal I know.

"This baiting leopard can be most interesting. It's rather like playing chess. I can remember one circumstance some years ago. The big problem, of course, is to get a leopard to come in in daytime because they are nocturnal. And, what they will do when you have the presence of hyenas and jackals and, particularly, vultures, is keep an eye on their food . . . their larder, if you will. They will lie up somewhere. Occasionally you will find them in a tree next to the bait, which is an easy shot if you approach carefully. But not always. They're often on the ground. In this particular instance, there was a big leopard . . . there was a small gully covered with green, riverine vegetation. We found out that he was watching the blind and could see everything that was going on. Whenever we came in, he watched us. Whenever we left, then he came [to feed on the bait]. So we figured that what we would do is blindside him, and it worked quite well. What we did was put two of my men [into the blind] with great noise to get his attention in case he was watching, and we [Peter and his client] just dragged some cover on our left, his right, so we could see down the little gully. And sure as nuts, shortly after my men departed the blind, the leopard came up looking around like that [nose in air, smelling and looking] and, of course, he gave us a perfect shot . . . *bang* . . . so we got him.

"If a leopard does score on you . . . on your sweet body in a charge . . . and it happens a lot more than you read in the newspapers, there are a couple of things, perhaps, that you would like to store in the back of your mind as to what to do. Remember that he is going to try to bite you in the shoulder or face or neck. I used to wear an American football helmet and an old marine [placing both hands to his neck] . . . why they call them

Dr. Bruce Melrose with his leopard.

Capstick Retrospective

'leathernecks' is to protect their jugular against sword strokes. Unfortunately it was stolen . . . my packet . . . my leopard kit. But if a leopard does get hold of you, he'll do it very, very quickly and he will try to anchor his teeth in your face or your shoulder and use that as a pivot point to rake your guts out all over your shoes . . . which I'm sure is very unpleasant.

"The thing about African hunting, and particularly hunting dangerous game, is you never know what's going to happen. So call me a Boy Scout when I say 'Be Prepared.'"

Commenting about warthog: "They're so Africa as to be ubiquitous. They're really the symbol of Africa along with the lion and hyena."

(Author's correction: Peter Capstick is the symbol of Africa, along with the lion and the hyena and the warthog.)

Peter was born in New Jersey in 1940, attended the university of Virginia, served in the Army, became a stockbroker, and then decided to become a professional hunter. But instead of moving to Africa, he spent a year in Central and South America as an apprentice jaguar hunter (which he told me was the most dangerous profession in

Old hunters never die. They just fade into the sunset.

the world; not so much because of jaguars, but because of the Aboriginal tribes that shared their habitat). He then started a travel agency for sportsmen before selling out to become the hunting and fishing director for Winchester Adventures, Inc.

After two years of checking out African safari companies, he moved to Africa and eventually became licensed as a professional hunter in Zambia, Botswana, and Rhodesia. His hunting experiences and his powers of observation, coupled with his brilliant wit, were tested in numerous magazine articles that he authored starting in the late-1960s. In 1977, *Death in the Long Grass* was published and is still the most-read book on African hunting, despite the excellent efforts of Selous, Hemingway, and Ruark, as well as the numerous sequels by the master raconteur himself.

Following his death, Peter Capstick's wife, Fiona, wrote that she would scatter his ashes along the Chobe River of Botswana because it "would be the perfect setting for a man such as he, someone who was an African soul, a true gentleman, whose writings afforded such joy and escape to millions of readers throughout the English-speaking world, bringing alive as they did the African bush as he painted word pictures of the only place in the world that truly mattered to him."

FIRST SAFARI INTO EASTERN ARNHEM LAND

The man had been driving for three days out of Darwin, proud capital of the Northern Territory of Australia (the "Top End"). He was leading a caravan of four trucks and two trailers in mid-November of 1989, trying to beat the first heavy rains of the five-month wet season. After passing south of Kakadu National Park, he turned northeasterly and headed into Arnhem Land, the immense Aboriginal Reserve that constitutes one of the continent's finest wilderness areas. Each member of the caravan carried the required entry-and-traveling permit issued by the Northern Land Council.

The man, Ray McKay, stopped at dark near an unnamed stream and helped his men set up camp. They threw rocks and shined flashlights into the water to keep the crocodiles at bay while they bathed. Then they ate a quick dinner, crawled into their tents, zipped up, sprayed for mosquitoes and fell to sleep.

Before first light on the fourth day, they were back on the dirt track that led them to the Koolatong River and finally to Jalma Bay on the Gulf of Carpentaria, the east coast of Arnhem Land.

At a bush airstrip carved out of the paperbark and eucalyptus forest, the men unloaded tables, chairs, tents, barrels of gasoline, propane tanks, and two refrigerators. They erected a metal shed to store various tools and supplies. After leaving two of the four-wheel-drive trucks at the encampment, they drove the other two trucks and both trailers four days back to Darwin.

Then the rains came.

As a professional hunter with Wimray Safaris, Ray McKay's mission had been to set up a hunting camp so Wimray could fly hunters to the dirt landing strip and hunt water buffalo as soon as the dry season allowed reasonable mobility.

The history of Asian water buffalo in Australia is intertwined with the motivations for McKay's efforts on behalf of Wimray. Water buffalo were formerly distributed throughout Vietnam, Cambodia, Laos, Thailand, and parts of Burma, Bangladesh, Bhutan, Nepal and India. Domestication of the species began several thousand years ago and continues today.

In 1827, Britain established Fort Dundas on Melville Island (just north of present-day Darwin) and Fort Wellington on the Cobourg Peninsula of the mainland. Water buffalo were shipped in to serve as beasts of burden and as a food source. When the forts were abandoned a few years later, the buffalo were released.

In 1838, Britain established Victoria Settlement at Port Essington on the Cobourg Peninsula for the dual purpose of establishing trade and discouraging the French and Dutch from settling northern Australia. New shipments of both water buffalo and banteng (a large ox) were delivered. After many settlers died and all had endured great hardship due to cyclones and disease, Victoria Settlement along with its water buffalo and banteng were abandoned in 1849.

From those initial imports and subsequent releases, the population of wild water buffalo eventually grew to enormous numbers despite market hunting. During a 70-year period starting in 1886, close to 400,000 water buffalo hides were shipped out of Australia. Although not carefully surveyed, the buffalo population certainly exceeded 300,000 by the early 1980s, and it may have exceeded 500,000.

One of the bulls that we passed on. He was in the 105 class.

The first entries in Safari Club International's Record Book of Trophy Animals were from the late 1960s. Trophy hunting for water buffalo became popular in the 1970s. In those days, hunting was conducted right out of Darwin or from nearby camps. As examples, Wimray Safaris established its Wildman Camp only 52 nautical miles east of Darwin. Murray Thomas, author of *South Pacific*

Trophy Hunter, saw 3,000 buffalo in three days when hunting near Darwin in 1982.

Then the government slaughter began in the mid 1980s. Why? According to Noel Bleakley, co-owner of Wimray Safaris with Ray Allwright: "What we are told is the American government said to the Australian government, 'If you don't clean up your feral herds of buffalo by 1992, the Australian beef producers will not be able to export beef to the American market because tuberculosis and brucellosis could spread from the buffalo to domestic cattle.'"

The Brucellosis and Tuberculosis Eradication Campaign (BTEC) was formulated to test specific areas or herds for disease. If just one animal was found to have TB or brucellosis, the entire area was "destocked," first by capturing (with the meat exported primarily to Germany), then by shooting from vehicles and on foot, and finally by shooting from helicopters.

The killing started around Darwin and progressed outward, encompassing hunting camp after hunting camp. So the outfitters kept moving camps further from Darwin, including into Aboriginal Reserves, with permission.

In the early 1980s, fully outfitted water buffalo hunts cost only $2,000 to $2,500, making them one of the best values in the hunting world. But, as the logistics and cost of establishing outlying camps and transporting hunters and staff increased, so did the price of trophy hunting. By 1989, the typical cost of a water buffalo safari had risen to $4,500 while the number of animals seen and the potential for quality trophies had plummeted.

The search for good buffalo hunting led Noel Bleakley to discuss the opening of the previously unhunted eastern Arnhem Land. Arnhem Land is an Aboriginal Reserve much like an American Indian Reservation. It starts about 140 air-miles east of Darwin, extends easterly about 265 more miles, and averages about 190 miles from north to south. As with other Aboriginal Reserves, all visitors must hold an entry permit which takes about two weeks to obtain. Any commercial endeavor, such as sport hunting, requires contractual approval by the Aboriginal clans involved and, in the case of Arnhem Land, approval must also be given by the Northern Land Council which is funded by the Northern Territory government which administrates the reserve.

Several sections of western and central Arnhem Land had been previously sport hunted, but those areas had undergone de-stocking. The eastern portion of the reserve remained a possibility, but presented multiple problems: obtaining the necessary approvals, negative BTEC testing, and the expensive logistics of establishing and servicing hunting camps. Wimray solved the problems.

First, they negotiated hunting concession approvals with several Aboriginal clans in good buffalo habitat. The price of a five-year contract with five-year option was a trophy fee of $1,000 (Australian) per buffalo plus employment for a designated clan member to be present during the hunting. Whereas many Aboriginal clans receive significant royalties from mining concessions (in some cases millions of dollars per year from gold, uranium, and manganese), the income from harvesting the renewable resource of water buffalo is the only income available to many of the Aboriginal landowners in eastern Arnhem land (other than from their own employment or government grants for improvements like clearing the dirt airstrip).

Wimray prepared for hunting in 1990 by sending Ray McKay and his group in 1989, a considerable financial risk considering this was before BTEC testing.

Then in April 1990, BTEC sent in a veterinarian who killed and tested eight buffalo for TB and brucellosis. All eight tested negative. Based on an estimate of 6,000 to 8,000 buffalo in the Wimray concession, BTEC decided to test a total of 800 buffalo. If just one buffalo tested positive, the government would de-stock (although, because of the heavy cover, a percentage of buffalo would almost certainly remain).

My safari was conceived about the same time Ray McKay was driving along the banks of the Koolatong River in November of 1989. Lad Shunneson, attorney, judge, hunter, and roustabout from Boulder, Colorado, gave me a call and said, "This is your lucky day!" Lad had just become the booking agent and quasi-partner of Murray Thomas, the fourth person to successfully hunt the South Pacific 15 (water buffalo, banteng, sambar deer, rusa deer, axis deer, fallow deer, hog deer, red deer, sika deer, tahr, chamois, boar, goat, whitetail and wapiti) and the first to do it with free-ranging game and without the assistance of guides, professional hunters or outfitters. Murray had just arranged to be a booking agent and professional hunter for Wimray's new water buffalo concession. If I was willing, he could guide me on an exploratory hunt into eastern Arnhem Land. I was willing.

The safari details were worked out with Murray, Lad, Noel Bleakley and Ray Allwright at the 1990 SCI convention. I talked about Australia so much in the intervening months that my wife, children, parents, and several in-laws ended up leaving with me in mid-June 1990. They would visit Sydney, Alice Springs and Darwin before meeting me at Wimray's Cobourg Peninsula camp after my buffalo hunt.

Murray met me at Sydney's airport and we immediately flew to Darwin with professional cameraman Rick Morgan who would serve as the lead videographer for Sportsmen on Film's documentary of the hunt.

In Darwin, Ray Allwright met us and put us in a Wimray plane to their Wildman Camp for the first evening. In the meantime, Noel Bleakley flew into the Arnhem Land encampment that had been established seven months earlier. With him were Ray McKay and Terry Powell, a Wildman tour guide, along with food, supplies, and new batteries for the two trucks that had been driven in the year before. While we were at Wildman, Noel radioed Ray that one refrigerator was inoperable, so Ray sent us a second plane carrying a replacement refrigerator while the first plane carried Murray, Rick and me to Jalma Bay with our hunting gear, five cases of video equipment and supplies, and the temporary permit for this first exploratory hunt.

Water buffalo are big, tough animals the size of Cape buffalo. They have impressive head gear with generally wider spreads than Cape buffalo and a different horn configuration. Typically, the horns of a trophy bull grow out from the sides of the head and then back in a curve. But occasionally they grow "sweepers" that grow out extra wide with a shorter curl back. A good sweeper could exceed a spread of four feet and a great one could go five feet. A very few have been wider.

The SCI Record Book system measures the length and base of each horn and then combines the measurements for a final score. In recent years, 90 to 95 points was a reasonable goal (say, 30-inch horns with 17-inch bases). Because our area had only been subjected to aerial surveys, no one really knew the trophy quality including the Aboriginal clans who only concerned themselves with meat quality. Our safari would be one of exploration before pulling the trigger or releasing the bowstring. (I carried both a Weatherby .416 rifle shooting 400-grain soft points and a Spectra 5000 bow, this being eight years before the muskox hunt that ended my bow hunting.)

Tent camp among the paperbark trees.

We started off by viewing the flood plains inland from Jalma Bay, a two-day process that involved driving the mostly dry perimeter and walking for miles and miles in slippery mud and shallow water mixed with green grass and brushy plants. Stalking the perimeter or using the brush for cover were effective methods of getting close enough to score potential trophies on the hoof, but many times we had to walk hunched over and single-file in the open. If the buffalo smelled us, they were gone. If they didn't, and we moved slowly, we could often get within 200 yards and sometimes curious animals would allow us to get closer.

The Australian Aboriginals were estimated to be 20,000 years behind modern man when they were first discovered by European explorers. Until recently, they had nothing more effective for hunting than throwing sticks, so they weren't a threat to the buffalo. In the 20th century, the Aboriginal civilization changed quickly.

Frank Gambali, of the 20-member Balma clan, accompanied us to show us his family's 30-square-mile area, and to make sure we didn't enter any sacred areas ("because our arms and legs would atrophy") and, no doubt, to pass judgment on this thing called a hunting safari. Frank had been educated at Batchelor Aboriginal College and had just married a girl from Alice Springs. When Murray shot a wallaby, as requested by Frank for meat for his family, Frank clapped his hands with joy.

On the second day, we located three big buffalo bulls feeding out on the flood plain. Their black bodies appeared and disappeared as they fed along. Murray and I could see decent horns at one mile through our 10 x 40 binoculars; but for the teacher

Sport Hunting on Six Continents

to score heads for the student, we had to get within a couple hundred yards and see them from the front side. At 500 yards, we ran out of cover. Murray identified the largest one and it was the farthest one, of course. We stooped and then crawled around the wind to within 200 yards. The bull's horns would go at least 100 points, but we couldn't get the front view.

An old male buffalo sports horns with bases that average about 17 inches so it takes 33-inch horns, measured from base to tip along the leading edge, to hit 100 (50 inches of base plus length times two). After having looked at hundreds of trophies, Murray figures he can guess within two points if he can get both views. The biggest buff he had seen in the wild went 105 (the tame one shown in "Crocodile Dundee" was larger).

We crawled to within 100 yards, but the object of our growing affection (it was now at least 105 points) saw us . . . three strange things lying in the grass. (Rick was rolling tape while keeping the camera out of the water.) It was only the second day, so I was carrying my bow and Murray had a rifle. The big bull angled to 75 yards trying to figure out what we were and what to do. Then it turned its head to face us.

Murray whispered, "He'll go 110 plus. Take the rifle." I said, "If we can get him to 40 yards, I'll try the bow."

Murray let out a soft cow-like sound. The buff moved forward trying to smell us, but the wind held. It was big, muddy and mean. It didn't really look at us like we owed it money. It was more like it was going to take our money!

At 50 yards, the buffalo was close to cutting our wind. Then it turned sideways. I drew, put the 40-yard pin at the top of its back and let fly. When shooting a rifle, the instant between trigger break and bullet hit-or-miss is immeasurable. But shooting an arrow at over 20 yards leaves me with a helpless feeling because of the flight time. I suddenly didn't want to lose this great trophy.

The arrow flew true and hit the middle of the lungs on its downward flight. The buff started to turn away just before impact and, as it completed that turn, the arrow stuck to its side and then fell off as the animal hit full speed running straight away.

Murray quickly handed me the .416. I was stunned, but I dropped the bow, grabbed the rifle, jacked a cartridge in the chamber and pushed the safety off. Crosshairs wobbled all over the buffalo's rear end as I jerked the trigger and hit air . . . several times.

Back to the truck we went in silence. It would be up to Murray and Rick to tell Noel (acting as our driver and assistant guide) what happened.

The next day, we explored new territory along the Koolatong River but we couldn't find a bull over 100 points. At dusk, we spotted a good trophy in the forest about three miles from camp. It was too dark for video, but Noel and Murray agreed it would go 105.

I almost shot a different 105 the next morning, but it gave us the slip when we tried an awkward stalk through the paperbark trees trying to get a clear shot between them while using a magnetic termite hill for a rest with the camera rolling

248

behind me. Magnetic termites build their long, narrow mounds north-south to regulate the internal temperature of their home by using the east-west sun. My shot would have been east, but when I raised up to fire, there wasn't any buffalo to shoot.

That afternoon, Noel drove us as far as he safely could near the southern edge of the flood plains so we could have two hours to walk into the wind during prime time. Darkness would fall quickly at 6:30 PM. At 5:30 PM, I spotted a good bull about a half-mile out. The buffalo were plentiful, but that meant seeing 25 to 50 a day, not the thousand a day that Murray viewed near Darwin eight years earlier. But the trophy quality of "our" water buffalo was markedly better and we were seeing more bulls than cows.

Before planning a stalk for a closer look, Murray climbed the last available paperbark tree and glassed the area. He climbed down with a smile. "There's a bigger one out there, but he's way out so we've got to hurry to beat the sun."

The wind was light. Murray checked it with his powder puffer, picked our course, and off we raced. When we closed to 500 yards, I saw the bull for the first time. It was facing away while feeding into the wind and its horns stuck out from either side of its wide body . . . a sweeper!

We moved cross-wind in order to put the setting sun directly behind us and straight into the bull's eyes if it turned. At 300 yards, the buffalo I had first seen was onto us and moving in to check us out. We held tight, but the sweeper moved diagonally to see what his buddy was up to. We lost it in a gully and some bushes. When it emerged, we could see all of the horns for the first time. There was no doubt about my shooting. It was just how and when. Murray said, "113 to 115. Relax." A non sequitur if there ever was one.

The sun was dropping behind us, but I still had a few minutes of shooting light. My problems were with the smaller bull, which was trying to wind us at 75 yards, and the fact that there was no rest for my rifle. The sweeper stopped to ponder its next move at 200 yards.

Murray got on his hands and knees in the mud and whispered, "Use my bum, mate." I don't speak Australian, so I laid my rifle across the small of his back. "Not there, my breathing will stuff your shot." So I laid it across his bum and pushed off the safety with a round already up the spout. I didn't look at the horns through the scope . . . I just put the crosshairs on the heart as the animal angled to the right. The rifle exploded and the bull lurched slightly and then ran right. I jacked in another round and fired, but with too little lead and the bullet slammed into its right flank. At 250 yards, it stopped.

Murray said, "I see blood on his nose. Take your time and let me know when you're going to shoot."

"Now!"

Murray plugged his ears again. I fired again. The buffalo went down and we walked up to it. What an animal! Sixty inches from horn tip to horn tip the short way; over 90 inches along the front edge and across the forehead.

Murray Thomas on the left as Rick Morgan took a quick photo with the sun's last rays.

A minute later, the flash was required for photos.

First Safari Into Eastern Arnhem Land

L to R: Kneeling, Frank Gambali, Noel Bleakley, Ray McKay, and Rick Morgan. Standing: Murray Thomas and me.

FROM COBOURG TO CALEDONIA

Banteng are a wild ox, closely related to the gaur, and native to Java, Borneo, and Indonesia. When the British attempted several settlements in the Northern Territory of Australia during the first half of the 1800s, the settlers brought domesticated banteng, water buffalo, Timor ponies, and Javan boar. Each of those species became feral when the settlements were abandoned.

Today, thousands of banteng are free-ranging on the Cobourg Peninsula which, because of its thick rain forest and grassy glades, has proven to be perfect habitat for the banteng of Australia that have been wild for almost 150 years since Victoria Settlement on Cobourg Peninsula was abandoned in 1849.

The United States Department of the Interior lists all banteng as endangered, but since Australia's banteng are descendants of domesticated Javan banteng from the island of Bali ("Bali cattle"), importation into the United States is allowed and the Cobourg Peninsula is the only place they can be hunted.

Accompanying me to Cobourg were my outfitter, Noel Bleakley of Wimray Safaris, my professional hunter, Murray Thomas, and my cameraman, Rick Morgan. Meeting us, after sightseeing in Sydney, Alice Springs, and Darwin, were my wife, daughter, son, father, mother, mother-in-law, sister-in-law, and niece . . . seriously!

Camp was at the elevated cabins operated by Wimray at Smith Point, the second northernmost point on the Australian mainland. Cobourg Peninsula is over

L to R: Noel Bleakley, Giles and Beverly Wilson, their son, Diane and Maria Serhan, Lorraine and Summer Wilson, and Murray Thomas on the Cobourg Peninsula. The photographer was Margaret Bednar, my mother-in-law.

100 miles long and fenced at its southern perimeter in order to keep the banteng population pure and disease-free. There is no hunting for the first 15 miles south of camp. Naturally, this is the best area for observing and learning about banteng. They are as wild as deer. The females are chestnut red and have small horns. Young males are reddish brown, but slowly change to blackish brown by age three and then to almost black when fully mature. Very old bulls become gray in the face and they exceed one-half ton in weight. If it were not for their large white rump patch and white stockings, banteng would be exceedingly difficult to detect in their rain forest habitat.

Old bulls are usually solitary or with one to three others. They are very agile and have excellent senses. In short, shooting a bull banteng with horns in excess of 17 inches is a very sporting proposition. After returning my extended family to their sightseeing duties, Noel and Murray and I drove south of the 15-mile marker and started hunting. We saw enough banteng of all ages the first day to be able to turn down two 17- to 18-inchers without regret.

During the second day, we had the opportunity to test one of Murray's favorite hunting methods for banteng which is to run at them. We saw four bulls together in the paperbark forest, but could not get a clear enough view to study their horns. So Murray led the way as we ran toward them. Of course, the bulls immediately wheeled and fled, but Murray has found that banteng will only run hard for a short distance and then they'll slow to a trot or fast walk, so you can gain enough ground to sometimes be able to stop, glass, assess trophy quality and, when the horns look good, get a shot either as they walk away or turn to find out if they are still being followed. When we stopped to glass after a 400-yard run, the biggest bull didn't measure up.

That night in camp, Noel decided that we should load a rowboat on top of the hunting vehicle and leave Smith Point an hour before daylight the next morning. These plans always sound great over a beer at dinner and not quite as good when the alarm goes off.

Two hours outside of camp, we reached a stream that Noel said was impassable except by boat . . . something about being 10 feet deep and infested with freshwater crocodiles. Murray poled us across the 50 yards of water, and he and I disembarked with rifle and pack while Noel stayed with the boat in order to increase our chances at still-hunting into the wind.

Periodically, Murray stopped and puffed talcum powder from his windchecker. Then he would adjust our course directly into the light breeze . . . step after slow step . . . stopping . . . glassing . . . and then forward again until we reached a 60-yard wide clearing. Immediately we could see movement 10 yards back in the thicket across the glade. It was a banteng . . . very black, with a graying face, but we couldn't make out its horns. Murray puffed his windchecker and the talcum wafted back in our faces. We were both wearing shorts, tank tops, and sockless shoes in the 90 degree heat of the Top End's winter on July 1. Murray whispered, "Just wait on him and he might come out."

I was in the kneeling position with my .416 resting on my left knee. The bull fed to the edge of the thicket and turned to our left. I slid my safety off but Murray whispered, "Just wait until I tell you to shoot."

"I'm right on his shoulder," I whispered back, but Murray said he wanted me to wait until the bull turned his head and he could see if his right horn was as good as his left. Then the banteng stepped into the clear and walked to my left at 50 yards and then 40. He was huge; at least four feet from brisket to back. And I was within bow range with a 400-grain bullet up the spout and my scope at 1 ½ power.

Suddenly the bull looked at us. Murray saw that the right horn was intact. "Take him," he hissed. *Blam!* Instantly the bull wheeled and sprinted to where he had emerged from the thicket, reaching it in three seconds and

It's best not to wade the waterways on Cobourg.

at the same time that my second shot luckily hit a flying hoof. He stumbled badly and disappeared.

Murray and I ran across the opening and then carefully struggled through 20 yards of thick bush and vines before reaching another opening. Forty yards away the bull turned to face us. Murray and I raised our rifles simultaneously and I fired. The bull dropped . . . dead. We walked up and Murray casually said, "I'd say he's really old, this one. He could be 20 years old."

Thanks to the early success, my entourage and I had time for a sightseeing trip near Kakadu National Park to view Aboriginal rock art in various caves. Many of the paintings were 10,000 to 20,000 years old. Then we all flew from Darwin to Sydney, and my family returned to the U.S. while Rick, Murray, another hunter named Keith Williams, and I flew east about 800 miles to the French island of New Caledonia. We arrived 217 years after Captain James Cook landed and named the island in honor of the Roman name for Scotland (Caledonia). The French annexed the 7,000-square mile island in 1853 after several missionaries and members of a French survey ship were killed and eaten by the islanders. We found the natives friendlier on our visit.

I was there to hunt rusa deer. In 1876, Indonesia sent a gift of 12 rusa from Java to the French governor of New Caledonia. Due to good climate, feed, and lack of predation, the population of rusa reached an estimated 200,000 prior to World War II by which time 40,000 to 60,000 hides per year were being shipped to Australia.

In 1984, Jack Shepherd, the pioneer of foreign trophy hunting in New Caledonia, estimated that the rusa population had been reduced to 25,000 to 30,000, but he noted that the population was growing. Jack was a Canadian geologist who had been sent to the island to explore for nickel and became Director of Mines and Prospecting for the South Pacific Mining Company.

Murray Thomas with my banteng's head, or vice-versa.

Guiding foreign hunters for trophy rusa was his hobby. When Jack retired to Vancouver Island, Canada in 1987, his protege, Murray Cameron, took over guiding hunters and, a few years later, Murray Thomas and others followed.

Murray T. arranged for us to stay with Claude and Yasmina Metzdorf and to hunt their large cattle ranch for rusa. We quickly found that the rusa population was under constant pressure from the ranchers, because they raise cattle to sell but they hunt rusa to eat. In fact, our first job was to head-shoot two spike bucks by spotlight so they could be butchered for the following day's festival at the school where Yasmina was a teacher.

New Caledonia is a mountainous, cigar-shaped island. The hills and valleys and the increasing population of rusa (estimated at over 50,000 at the time of my hunt in 1991) allow for numerous stalks on trophies daily. From the first morning, we heard the groan of rusa in rut even though we had not expected to see rutting behavior that early in July. Rusa stags weigh 200 to 250 pounds, have a coarse reddish-brown coat and grow long, straight main beams with one secondary point and one brow tine per side.

In a flat valley on the afternoon of my first full day of hunting, Murray whispered, "As soon as he lifts his head and I make sure he has both his brow tines, we'll shoot him, mate [Australian for "the client will shoot the deer"]. He's got heaps of length."

I was using Claude Metzdorf's .270 with a set trigger, because it was not possible to import personal rifles. I pulled the first trigger which converted the second one into a hair trigger and then I put my right index finger outside the trigger guard and waited. The rifle barrel was resting on Murray's left shoulder as the stag fed at 125 yards, quartering away. Finally he lifted his head to look around and Murray said, "He's got both brows." *Blam!* A light touch on the trigger and the bullet entered behind the stag's left shoulder but, because of the angle, exited in front of the same shoulder. The stag crashed away into dense cover.

We followed up with a careful and quiet stalk. Murray pointed into the darkness and I could see the rusa laying down with his head up. I shot him through both shoulders and we walked up to claim our prize. After pictures, Murray field dressed the stag, we tied its legs to a wooden pole and, with the deer hanging, carried him a half mile to where Claude could drive his truck.

Later that same day, Murray spotted a monster rusa laying down with his harem. Murray took a good look through his binoculars and advised me that this stag was bigger than the one I had shot and, since I was allowed to shoot two, did I want it. "No," I said. "I would rather spread my entertainment over the full three hunting days instead of shooting two in one day."

So Murray led his Aussie buddy, Keith Williams, on an exciting stalk that eventually led to a kill shot through a narrow opening when the stag finally stood and walked left. Keith's stag measured bigger than any ever shot at that time. So, on the island of New Caledonia, not only did I shoot a respectable Javan rusa stag, but I also got to eat the world record!

I shot this stag in the thicket behind us. We drug it out for photos.

The end of shooting light on New Caledonia.

SOUTH PACIFIC NEW ZEALAND

35

FROM THE NORTH ISLAND TO THE SOUTHERN ALPS

Three million people, 75,000,000 sheep, all green without irrigation, sailboats galore, great rugby teams, fantastic mountains, incredible fishing, so many big game animals that the government launched a 40-year program of extermination, and the birthplace of commercial bungy jumping . . . Harv wrapped my ankles with what looked like a towel and then hooked the bungy cord to the towel. It didn't really look like it would hold. I was on a bridge 143 feet above the Kawauri River at a section where the protective railing had been removed.

"Do you want to touch the water when the cord stretches?'" I was asked when they weighed me in.

"I don't want to get my hair wet," I replied cavalierly.

Then Harv started the countdown . . . 5, 4 . . . a couple hundred people were watching and the camera was rolling . . . 3 . . . my toes were hanging over the edge, my sport coat was still on, but my eyeglasses had been removed . . . 2, 1 . . . I dove straight out for distance and had the immediate impression that "this isn't so bad; kind of like a high dive into a swimming pool." But for the next two seconds, my body suddenly hurtled straight down at 130 kilometers per hour and I thought I was

FROM THE NORTH ISLAND TO THE SOUTHERN ALPS

Before I jumped, I was concerned about the strain to my knees. During my jump, my area of concern changed to my heart.

Lorraine among the thermals of Rotorua.

going to die; if not from impact, then from a heart attack. Quickly, however, the bungy stretched and slowed me so that my hands just missed the water. The rest . . . bouncing up and down, being lowered into a rowboat, and triumphantly rejoining my group with a brave smile and ashen face . . . was anticlimactic. Welcome to New Zealand!

We landed in Auckland at the northern part of the North Island and the largest city in New Zealand; my wife, fellow hunter Lad Shunneson, and cameraman Steve Anderson.

Three hours' drive (on the left side of the road) south of Auckland is the city of Rotorua, which was our home while I hunted sika deer with Murray Cameron . . . the same Murray Cameron who made his name by taking over Jack Shepherd's rusa deer hunts on New Caledonia. Rotorua is situated on a volcanic fault line so the thermal activity abounds. Everywhere you turn the earth is erupting with fascinating natural antics, including spurting geysers and ponds full of champagne bubbles.

In heavily-treed hills near Rotorua, Murray filled me in on how to hunt the secretive sika (pronounced "seeka" down under) . . . "Be quiet, be observant, and have a round in the chamber."

As we still-hunted through the forest, we heard a couple distress barks, so Murray decided we should sit quietly for an hour. Then we resumed our slow walk, step by slow step, until Murray detected movement and sent me ahead. I moved to a tree, rested my rifle on the left side, and waited until I saw movement. Then I pushed the safety off.

A sika stag materialized with good antlers. He was moving away to my left. I followed him in my scope through the trees and, when he passed through an opening large enough to expose his chest, I fired. He kicked up his hind legs and disappeared, but seven seconds later I heard a crash and knew he was mine.

When we walked up, we could see long main beams with four typical points on the right and three on the left. Murray said, "If you get an eight-point sika, you've hit the jackpot because they are such vicious fighters. This stag is seven to eight years old, which means he's dodged a lot of hunters in his time."

From the North Island, we flew to Christchurch, the largest city on the South Island and about midway down on the east coast. Christchurch is a garden city called "the most English city outside of England." From there, we flew 220 air miles south-

From the North Island to the Southern Alps

west to the resort city of Queenstown located next to 48-mile-long Lake Wakatipu and facing the craggy mountains of the Remarkables Range.

Mike and Julie Hodder of Reel Hunting (so named because they conduct fishing as well as hunting excursions) met us in Queenstown and drove us to their home on beautiful Lake Wanaka for an overnight. The following morning, Lad, Mike, and I were helicoptered into the Southern Alps, the famous mountain range that looms some 7,000 to 9,000 feet above the nearby Tasman Sea and forms the backbone of the South Island.

Pilot James Scott dropped us off with our supplies near one of the almost 200 huts maintained by the Department of Conservation for the benefit of hikers and hunters. Mike had reserved Whymper Hut for us in the middle of tahr and chamois country. The hut was constructed with sleeping bunks, a woodburning stove, and a rainwater collection system.

Himalayan tahr were first introduced to the South Island

L to R: Murray Cameron, Lad Shunneson, and me with my seven-point sika.

in 1904 and are ideally suited for the most difficult terrain of the Southern Alps. Mike eventually spotted a good bull at the bottom edge of the sub-alpine bush in a huge basin one mile distant. We hiked close and dropped our packs. Mike and I split at that point with him climbing higher to act as a blocker in case the tahr spotted me and ran uphill. While Mike climbed up, I climbed horizontally, to my left, through two to four foot high bush and grass.

Suddenly, below me was the bull tahr, facing away and looking down. I raised my rifle and shot him between the shoulders and then watched as he rolled through the bush for a couple hundred feet. When we found him, he had beautiful long, golden

Our hut was near the top of treeline in the Southern Alps. L to R: me, Lad Shunneson, and Mike Hodder.

Lad tries to warm the coffee and the hut while Mike watches.

hair (at the end of fall in May) and a nice pair of characteristically short, heavy, curving horns.

Next on my list was chamois, the goat-antelope introduced from Austria in 1907. It was the middle of the rut, so the males were acting a little crazy.

"We're looking for horns at least to the top of the ears, which will give us $7\,^1/_2$ inches plus about two more inches for the hooks," Mike told me.

When we saw a candidate that we liked, we slipped and stumbled across a rocky, snow-covered slope. When the chamois saw us, I dropped my pack to use as a rest. The buck was climbing up a long, open face. I shot and hit him too far back. He ran 50 yards and laid down, so I shot again and he slid half the 200 yards down toward us.

At the chamois, Mike said, "Now's the best time to get them, mainly because of the condition of the snow. If you hunted in the middle of winter, two months from now, there would be a lot more snow which makes for hard climbing."

Lad shot his chamois that same day, but he was continuing to have trouble getting a tahr. The following morning, he and Mike spotted a bull at 400 yards as it ran into a cave. "Bounce a shot off the rocks and above the cave," Mike advised. When Lad shot, two tahr came charging out and ran across the steepest pos-

FROM THE NORTH ISLAND TO THE SOUTHERN ALPS

Lad on the left and Mike on the right with my tahr.

Chamois were easy to spot, but hard to reach

sible rock face with ice thrown in for good measure. Lad's next shot stopped the tahr and the shot after that killed him before he crashed down in a couple big, tenderizing bounces. Hours later, Mike and Lad reached the tahr and determined that the horns were, miraculously, unbroken.

Next stop was Southland. On the way there, I made the aforementioned bungy jump from the bridge where A.J. Hackett started the "sport" commercially in October 1988. About 70,000 crazies had preceded me off that bridge.

Lorraine, standing on the porch of our Southland cabin.

Southland is the southernmost area of the South Island. We traveled to the hills southwest of Denedin. Home was a picturesque cabin located in a big valley. It was here that Lad shot a spotted fallow and we each shot an Arapawa ram which is a type of shep first released on Arapawa Island, between the North and South Islands, by Captain Cook in the late 1700s. We climbed above a small herd of rams and waited for them to feed closer at which time Lad and I reduced their numbers by two.

Later that afternoon, we caught a glimpse of a great red stag. The next morning Lad and I flipped a coin and I won the right to take the first shot. Our strategy was for Lad to climb to the top of the large basin in which we had seen the stag the afternoon before. Mike and I hid near the bottom. Over the next few hours, we saw several smaller stags, and a good one with one antler broken completely off at the base, but not "The Big One." Then Lad signaled and Mike and I strained to see what he had seen.

Suddenly, Mike tapped my shoulder and pointed to antler tips floating above the bushes. I moved my pack forward and prepared my rifle as the antlers continued downhill. The stag must have seen Lad and was unknowingly picking his way down toward me. I followed the antlers through my scope until the stag took a step into an opening and stopped to look for danger. Nevertheless, danger arrived in the form of a 180-grain Federal Nosler partition bullet in the center of the left shoulder. "The Big One" ran 75 yards downhill and fell on his side.

Mike and I climbed down to admire the 18 points. Then Lad joined us a few minutes later for handshakes. Since there was no way to get a vehicle closer than a half mile, we caped and quartered the stag and made two trips to the truck with the cape, antlers, and all the meat. Then we drove to our cabin after dark.

For a joke, we took pictures of Lorraine sleeping alone that night and me sleeping with those antlers. To this day, Lorraine claims that I wasn't kidding.

With Lad and Mike and the red stag that was the result of a coin flip.

Sport Hunting on Six Continents

36

RACING THROUGH SPAIN

Hemingway made the Running of the Bulls famous in his first novel, *The Sun Also Rises*. When I decided to produce a video on hunting in Spain in conjunction with Wayne Pocius, I planned my portion of the hunt around being in Pamplona in early July for the Running of the Bulls. Of course, July is not the best hunting month in Spain. The antlered game is only half-grown and the horned stuff is several months away from the rut. In fact, I had to receive special permission to be able to hunt ibex in July.

Lorraine and I flew into Madrid on Iberia Airlines and were met by our outfitter and guide, the always laughing Eduardo Fernando de Araoz who had just purchased Ricardo Medem's hunting operation, Cazatur. The year was 1989.

In Madrid, a reception was held for us at the home of Spain's Consul General to the United States, Miguel de Aldasoro and his wife, Judith, both avid hunters. They introduced us to Valentin de Madariaga, Spain's most famous hunter (well, maybe the second most famous after Don Juan Carlos I, the King of Spain). Valentin has shot more species of big game than any other hunter in history.

From Madrid, we flew north to San Sebastian, a lovely town on the Cantabrian Sea. First on the agenda was for me to run with the bulls in Pamplona, 1 ½ hours distant by van if you're a fast driver. And Eduardo is a fast driver. Apparently staying in Pamplona would have been too easy. Eduardo needed the challenge of racing,

SPORT HUNTING ON SIX CONTINENTS

L to R: Cameraman Rick Morgan with Lorraine and me. I'm wearing the traditional costume for running with the bulls.

The Fiesta de San Fermin is a two-week party with continuous dancing in the streets.

tailgating, passing on curves, and swearing in Spanish while laughing in English.

Our first reckless race from San Sebastian to Pamplona did not thrill my wife or Eduardo's girlfriend, Paloma (but she must have recognized other qualities in Señor de Araoz because she married him the following year). When the heavy traffic around Pamplona caused me to miss getting to the staging area for the runners, I was not thrilled either. But I was thrilled with the city of Pamplona. The Fiesta de San Fermin is the world's biggest party and it lasts two weeks. There was literally dancing in the streets and on the balconies day and night. Food, booze, music, and people everywhere . . . all the time. I could have stayed for days. My wife had her fill in an hour.

While in Pamplona, we lucked out and rented a room, for video purposes, with a balcony overlooking the route the bulls would run the following morning. Then we returned to our hotel in tranquil San Sebastian. The next morning we departed an hour earlier in order to be sure to make the Running of the Bulls.

As it turned out, despite a good race, we barely made it into Pamplona before the release of the bulls, and I mean barely. I didn't have time to reach the staging area so Eduardo dropped me off by a barricade midway in the route. I was wearing the traditional costume for the running, white pants and a red bandana around my waist, as I climbed the barricade, jumped down, and ran back toward the start.

The shops were barricaded, the crossroads were barricaded, the narrow streets

RACING THROUGH SPAIN

were empty, and all the balconies were crowded with people. Suddenly, a crowd came down the street toward me, running, packed close together. I knew to let the first few hundred runners pass so I could at least be in proximity to the six bulls and six steers running behind; otherwise I would not really be running with the bulls.

When I first saw those black bulls galloping, tossing their heads up and down, I started running the remaining 600 yards to the bullring. In the next two minutes, I became an expert, an

The view from the balcony of the room we rented, so Rick Morgan could video the Running of the Bulls the next day.

If you go down when running with the bulls, lay flat and still, cover your head, and pray.

269

aficionado of running with the bulls, and, therefore, can pass on a few tips.

• Once you start, you have to run all the way to the arena. I saw several runners try to climb the barricades only to be pushed back down by the crowds on the other side who were looking for a good show.

• The bulls are very fast. I was shocked to see them run by me after only a couple hundred yards.

• The steers aren't very dangerous and are primarily included to encourage the bulls into the arena in case there is a pile-up or other problems. So, if you're going to be brave, be brave with the steers.

• Carry a rolled newspaper. If a bull runs close behind you, you won't be able to outrun him, so divert his attention by waving the newspaper in front of his nose and away from you.

• The greatest danger is from pile-ups in front of you. If your head is turned when the guy in front of you goes down, you'll go with him and that is when most gorings occur.

Lorraine, enjoying the view of the harbor in beautiful Marbella.

- The most dangerous place in the running is the entrance to the narrow tunnel into the arena. This is where the most deaths occur.
- Once in the arena, unless you really know what you are doing or you just want to entertain the crowd, stay out of the way of the bulls until the pop of the rocket signaling that all of the bulls have gotten through the people in the ring and into the corrals.

From Pamplona, we returned to San Sebastian on the north coast, then raced to the airport and barely made our flight to Malaga on the south coast; the transportation hub of the Costa del Sol. Then we drove westerly, at an unrelaxed pace, along the coast to the beautiful resort city of Marbella which, it has been said, will relieve you of your money quickly, efficiently, painlessly, and in five languages.

From Marbella, we quickly traveled inland, 40 miles up a winding road to the old fortress city of Ronda which is perched high above the surrounding countryside. Fernando's troops conquered the city in 1485, as did Napoleonic troops in 1808. Ernest Hemingway was a frequent visitor to Ronda and Orson Welles' ashes are buried on a bull farm outside of town.

Lorraine still complains that, on the video, it looks like the trip from San Sebastian to Ronda was a leisurely journey when, in fact, it had been a typical Eduardo race. "But sweetheart, we had ibex to hunt," is always my reply.

Because of feed or weather or genetics, the ibex of Ronda have developed the smallest bodies and horns of all four categories of Spanish ibex. They also have the lightest colored coats.

Isadoro was both the gamekeeper and our guide. Eduardo and I followed him up the steep, rocky trails. When we passed a bed of dried grass, I asked Eduardo if that was an ibex bed. "No," he answered. "It's a game warden's bed. That's where Isadoro spent last night."

Eduardo speaks perfect English, but the gamekeepers generally speak none, so I had already been schooled in the language of the hunt. Female ibex are called *embras* or *capras*. Older males are called *macho montes* which means "male of the mountain."

Late in the afternoon, we made a stalk on some *macho* ibex. We reached some rocks where I could see them feeding in and out of low bushes in the shadows near the top of the mountain. Eduardo took a long look through his binoculars and pointed in the direction he wanted me to shoot. "His horns are shining in the sun."

I picked out the same animal and shot, hitting him a little too far back. Several ibex ran passed him and then I shot again. "Don't shoot anymore," Eduardo advised. "He just laid down."

For the video, Wayne had already hunted a Gredos ibex (as well as chamois, red stag, and mouflon). At my Ronda ibex, Eduardo pointed out that the horns on the Ronda are straighter and narrower than the typical horns on the ibex from the Gredos Mountains. He said mine was a good trophy of 10 years of age.

Back in Ronda, we actually had time for some sightseeing before racing off to hunt the Sierra Nevada ibex. First we "traveled" east to Granada where one of the more interesting sights was the Alhambra or "red castle" which overlooks the city and is the foremost tribute to the turbulent 8th century Moorish occupation of Spain. In Granada, there is a monument commemorating the location where Christopher Columbus obtained, from King Fernando and Queen Isabella, the charter to explore the route to Asia by sailing west.

From Granada, Eduardo drove *muy rapido* into the Sierra Nevada Mountains where we stayed in a Parador Nacional by one of the ski resorts. Being July, there were no skiers, but there were still patches of snow in the higher elevations where the *macho montes* tend to locate in the summer. We were within hiking distance of Mulathin, the highest mountain on the mainland of Spain and, in fact, we climbed it during my hunt. Mulathin rises about 11,000 feet above the Mediterranean Sea which is only 30 miles south, but was invisible because of the smoke from all the harvested crops that were being burned at the time.

With Eduardo Fernando de Araoz and my Ronda ibex.

Lorraine, sightseeing in the old fortress city of Ronda.

Our gamekeeper in the Sierra Nevada was Felipe, who led us up, up, and away from three anti-hunters who yelled that we better not kill an ibex. We eventually climbed to an old rock cabin and met Antonio, another gamekeeper who was living among and observing the ibex. Antonio led us to the slopes of Mulathin where we spotted a herd of 60 to 70 ibex. We climbed to a jumble of big, broken rocks and tried to pick out a trophy. One of my favorite video scenes was shot at this location when Rick made a slow pan of eight big, male ibex on the edge of a cliff and then pulled back to Eduardo, Lorraine, Felipe, Antonio and me. Eduardo picked out the biggest ibex and, as I got ready to shoot, the game wardens conferred and then told Eduardo that it was a good specimen with 70 centimeters of horn but they had seen a few bigger ones, so I decided to pass.

The next day, we spotted an old ibex feeding in a grassy basin accompanied by three other males, two of whom were repeatedly bashing heads. Following a brief conference, I was given the okay to shoot. This ibex had the over 70 centimeters of horn that I was looking for. We climbed down several hundred yards to a rocky outcropping that angled down at 45 degrees. I slid forward on my belly as Felipe held my ankles. Then I raised my rifle.

The big ibex was walking away at about 250 yards. Then he turned right and started feeding again. I hit him high on his hindquarters so that his back legs collapsed. He turned directly away from me as I placed my second shot between his shoulder blades so that both ends of him were down and out.

At the ibex, Eduardo informed me that the Sierra Nevada ibex, also known as the southeastern ibex, is the only Spanish ibex whose horns cut the extension of the line from the tip of the nose through the eye. Its coat was much darker than that of the Ronda ibex and its horns longer. I asked Felipe how many centimeters long the horns were. "The same here as up there [pointing to where I shot from] . . . 73."

The next day, the horns were officially measured at 28.75 inches, so Felipe was low by .02 inches, but I didn't have time to kid him about his error in judgment, because we had to race to the airport for the flight back to the United States!

L to R with my Sierra Nevada ibex: me, Felipe, Eduardo, Antonio, and Lorraine.

EUROPE　　　CZECH REPUBLIC

37

THE EASTERN EUROPEAN 6

The African Big 5 conjures images of big tusks, massive horns and sharp claws. The Grand Slam of North American Sheep brings thoughts of lung-searing climbs in high places. The South Pacific 15 and North American 29 represent years of hunting achieved by few. Now, with the lifting of the Iron Curtain, the Eastern European 6 is available to international hunters, and is achievable in one or two trips.

In Eastern Europe . . . Bulgaria, the Czech Republic, Hungary, Poland, Romania, Slovakia and the former Yugoslavia . . . commonly hunted animals are red deer, fallow deer, roe deer, mouflon, wild boar and chamois: the Eastern Europe 6. Hunters can spread the travel and adventure over several trips and countries or, with careful planning and good luck, complete the Big 6 in one expedition.

My opportunity came at the 1994 convention of Safari Club International. I was considering a red deer hunt in Eastern Europe, but became intrigued with hunting all six of Eastern Europe's commonly hunted big game animals. My friend and Colorado character, Lad Shunneson, is married to Lenka, a Czech. In Lad's booth, I met Carl Stelzer, one of the two principals of Stelko Hunting along with Milan Kostka. Stelzer and Kostka played for the Czech national basketball team until Carl defected in 1968 when the Russians invaded Czechoslovakia. He then spent 20 years in Austria, New York, New Mexico and Germany before moving back to the Czech Republic after the "Velvet Revolution" of 1989. He reunited with his long time friend, Milan, to form an import and export business along with his true love — Stelko Hunting.

Because I wanted to complete a video on hunting the Eastern European 6 for Sportsmen on Film before the 1995 SCI convention, I booked to hunt during the last half of September and the first week of October. In the Czech Republic, the roe deer season ends September 30 and the alpine chamois season starts October 1. Lenka Shunneson knew a chance to return to her homeland when she saw it, so she insisted that Lad and she join the expedition and that I bring my wife, Lorraine. Lad rationalized that he needed to hunt the Big 6 in order to properly advise his clients.

With two hunters going for six species each on video, plus sightseeing, Carl wanted us to allocate three hunting days per animal, but we settled on a total trip of 17 days. These would include travel, and our wives would be with us for the first 11 and without us the last six . . . in case we had to go to the limit to achieve our goals.

Our point of arrival was the capital city of Prague, which is considered one of the most beautiful cities in Europe. When we arrived, a project to refurbish the old buildings to their former splendor was in full swing and the unemployment rate

Prague! Still beautiful after World War II and 40 years of decay during communist rule.

was one-half of one percent! Prague is located in the center of the western part of the Czech Republic known as Bohemia and was built on both sides of the Vltava River. We would be hunting throughout the eastern part of the country, which is known as Moravia.

The Czech Republic is bordered by Germany to the west, Poland to the north, Slovakia to the east and Austria to the south. The language is Czech, but a large percentage of the people speak German and/or Russian. Only a small percentage spoke English, but their numbers are growing as the Russian influence diminishes.

With my wife on the bridge over the Vltava River that connects Old Town with New Town. Construction in New Town started over 500 years ago!

Some of the highlights of the long and interesting history of the Czech Republic are that from the 10th century until 1918, Slovakia was a province of Hungary. Prague University was founded in 1348, and Wolfgang Mozart conducted the world premiere of his opera, *Don Giovanni,* at Prague Estates Theater. Gregor Mendel, the founder of modern genetics, was from the Czech Republic, as was Sigmund Freud. As Austria-Hungary collapsed in 1918, the World War I allies recognized the Czechoslovak Republic as the will of Czechs and Slovaks to co-exist in a common state. In 1939, Hitler transformed the Czech lands to a German protectorate and established the Slovak state as a satellite of the Third Reich. Czechoslovakia was liberated in 1945, but in 1948 a communist coup put an end to democracy. The Iron Curtain was drawn.

In 1968, when Czechoslovakia moved toward "socialism with a human face," the Soviet Union and its allies invaded and returned it to a totalitarian state. Gorbachev's *perestroika* led to the peaceful Velvet Revolution starting in 1989. By mutual agreement, on January 1, 1993, the Czech Republic and the Slovak Republic became mutually independent.

From Prague, we drove about two and a half hours northeast to the Jeseniky Mountains in northern Moravia to hunt red stag and roe deer. As in most of Europe, the outfitter is paid a daily rate plus a trophy fee depending on the animal's CIC score. Generally, a CIC silver medal animal is equivalent to SCI gold. A CIC gold becomes progressively more expensive until trophies close to the world record test the check-writing ability of the wealthiest.

On the other hand, representative trophies are reasonably priced, the game animals have been well-managed for centuries and the chance for success is generally

With Carl Stelzer and a beautiful roe buck.

high. The trophy fees can be likened to the salary cap in football — you can allocate your money to all bronze or all silver or mostly bronze plus one or two gold, and so on.

Carl Stelzer believes that the easiest hunting is for the biggest animal available . . . although achieving that goal can be time-consuming . . . and the most difficult is to hunt for an animal within a certain point range (i.e., price range) because both small and large trophies need to be passed over and the gamekeeper

L to R, displaying the results of our mid-day mushroom picking between the morning and afternoon hunts: Lad and Lenka Shunneson, me and my wife, and Carl Stelzer.

requires extra time for trophy judgment to make sure that the client won't be unhappy with the trophy for the price. Then the hunter must shoot the correct animal before it disappears.

With just a few days before roe deer season would end, Lad and I concentrated on Europe's most commonly hunted deer. We hunted near the Polish border from both high seats and by still-hunting the perimeter of forests and fields. We both took good, typical six-point bucks. In fact, we each shot two roe bucks because the lease owner hadn't filled his quota and gave us a good price on the second deer.

The meat from all of the game in the Czech Republic is owned by the landowner or leaseholder, and is sold to restaurants and butcher shops. Throughout the hunt we discussed which species tasted the best and my vote was for roe deer as prepared in one of the little country restaurants that we visited during the traditional break between the morning and afternoon hunts.

With my old, and small, red stag. L to R, standing: the gamekeeper, Lad, and Carl.

Typically, we would hear the awful sound of the alarm at 4:30 AM and be on our way at 5:00 AM, hunt from 6:00 AM to 11:00 AM, and then hunt again from 2:30 PM until dusk at about 6:15 PM. After we got used to the seven-hour time change, we spent the middle of the day with our wives lunching, touring, and engaging in such activities as mushroom picking, which seemed to be the national pastime. In the evening, the food and camaraderie were both of the highest level. I particularly enjoyed maintaining my svelte waistline while Lad let out his belt three notches, because he couldn't lay off the desserts after soup, salad, entrée, beer and coffee.

Lad is a roe deer connoisseur with over 20 to his credit — which would make him a rookie among eastern European hunters. He was selective while I was less so and luckier. My early success gave me $1 \frac{1}{2}$ days to hunt red deer before a change of venue.

On the evening of the second day, my gamekeeper and Carl and I hiked into the middle of three roaring stags, and we waited them out until I got a shot at an old monarch that was an incredible 14 years old. It didn't quite make CIC bronze, which was okay with me because I was saving my money for mouflon — the Czech Republic has the best rams in the world.

We loaded the Stelko motor home with enough gear to make an Alaskan bush pilot weep and headed south past Stelko's headquarters in Ostrava to the Beskydy Mountains where we stayed in the lodge on a game preserve that was over 400 years old. The first wing of the castle in the preserve was completed in the year 1240. From one of the ponds, trout were netted one afternoon, cooked for us in the adjacent cottage and served on china set out on white tablecloths. Outside, a few fallow stags roared and mouflon rams cracked heads.

It was here that Lad shot his CIC bronze mouflon (he was saving his money for a red stag) and we both shot good fallow deer. Interestingly, the CIC scoring method for fallow rewards length of palm, which SCI does not, and gives no credit for length-of-points. (An SCI record book hunter can look for fallow deer with wide but short palms and lots of long points, pay CIC bronze and end up with SCI gold.)

The fallow stags that we saw on two different preserves were huge by Texas standards and hunting a large, reproducing population with the wallet in mind proved to be excellent sport. As an additional bonus, the rut was just starting and we witnessed the phenomenon of the females coming to the males, which is unique to fallow deer.

Our next stop was southern Moravia, near the Austria and Slovakia borders, where the steep mountains of the northern forests give way to the rolling hills of wine country.

Wine making is a hobby for many families, and they have

With Carl Stelzer and my fallow stag. All of the fallow in the Czech Republic are brown-spotted. If not, they are culled.

their own wine cellars that are 50 to 100 feet long and burrowed into hillsides so the interior temperature remains constant. It was in one such cellar that I was cajoled into drinking several glasses of "fresh" wine between the morning and evening hunts for mouflon. Before I could feel any adverse effects, I was told that fresh wine is just a few days old and has virtually no alcohol content. My sobriety helped neither the evening hunt nor both hunts the next day. Leaves and nuts were falling from the trees and our crunching steps warned any mouflon of our presence before we arrived at the top of each hill to glass for them. Nevertheless, I had several chances. But to translate Czech to English, pick out a CIC gold ram — my goal — and get both the crosshairs and the cameraman on the correct ram simultaneously was proving too difficult. On the third day we changed our strategy and waited in the forest for mouflon to feed into one of the meadows.

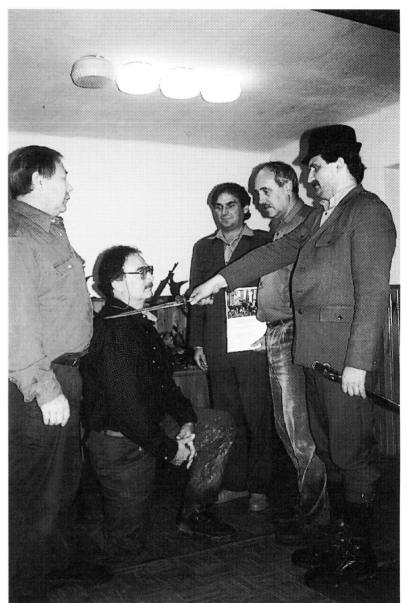

After our hunt in the Beskydy Mountains, Lad and I were inducted into the local hunting organization. Lad figured this meant our checks had cleared.

The rut was approaching, but most of the rams still were hanging in groups. On the third afternoon, I was rewarded when a group of huge rams moved into the meadow and we were able to stalk down a drainage for a 150-yard shot. The gamekeeper was aware I wanted a low CIC gold trophy and he quickly told Carl to have me shoot the third ram from the end, which became the second and then the last. I swept my crosshairs past the ram's horns, settled on its shoulder and squeezed off the 180-grain bullet from the Sako .300 rifle I used throughout the safari. The 90-pound animal bolted to the left and somersaulted. I felt like doing the same thing!

When we walked up to the fallen ram, the gamekeeper performed the traditional European ceremony that Lad and I experienced with each animal we shot. Two small branches were removed from a nearby tree, one placed in the animal's mouth as its last bite, and one brushed in the blood of the animal and handed to me to place in the band of my hat. Then the gamekeeper excused himself and returned a half hour later with two horn-blowers shortly before dark.

Most of my Czech trophies were shot near sunset. My mouflon was shot earlier, but it took awhile for the horn-blowers to reach us. L to R, kneeling: the gamekeeper, me, Carl, and Lad.

Carl explained that I had shot a high CIC gold ram and would experience a ceremony available for all species harvested in the Czech Republic, but usually reserved for the most special. In my ram's case, the horn weight was so heavy (11 inches at the bases and 10 inches at the second quarters) that they made the 38-inch by 37-inch horns look much smaller from the ravine in which the gamekeeper gave me the final approval to shoot.

To see those horns on a 90-pound animal was awesome. And of course, I kept asking Lad why they never played two horns after he shot an animal.

The Eastern European 6

Maybe I asked too soon. Two days later, near the southern Moravian town of Brno, where the rifle of the same name is manufactured, Lad and I got into a couple bunches of wild boar in the rolling hills after a rain. The potato chip-crisp leaves turned soft as wet lettuce and our footsteps were unheard. It was there, among the trees, that I shot a 400-pound boar only to learn that Lad had already shot a larger one and that his guide had immediately pulled out a bottle of Russian vodka and two glasses from his immense overcoat and toasted the great pig hunter from Colorado.

I will never forget skinning those two carcasses until midnight in a light rain. It reminded me of the bison carcass scene in "Dances With Wolves," only in damp moonlight.

With four days left, I needed only the chamois to complete the Big 6, but Lad needed both the little goat-antelope and a red stag. The stags had just stopped roaring in southern Moravia, so we returned to the north where the chamois population is good and the stags were still in full rut. It was on the next afternoon that Lad shot his 13-point stag when it tried to keep its harem intact. Its long, white tines swirled

Don't call them "Russian wild boar!" L to R: the gamekeeper, Carl, me, and Lad with my Czech wild boar.

through the thick cover when a 140-grain bullet in the lungs from the classic Rigby .275 fired by Arlad William Shunneson put it down.

That took the pressure off and we relaxed so much that we were both unsuccessful with chamois the next day. The following morning we continued our search for the 75- to 100-pound animals. We made several sightings but no shots. Lad and I were holding out for bigger trophies, but that evening, we both connected on good males although we were prepared to take long-horned females if we saw them.

Around the dinner table, and after some good-natured kidding about who achieved the Eastern European 6 first, both guides agreed I had been first. My bribes to each before dinner had paid off.

My alpine chamois was shot at last light, and rolled into the long grass.

38

ARGENTINE SAFARI

I was on a big game safari in Argentina, hunting with a .300 Winchester Magnum but, at that instant, I longed for a 12 gauge shotgun to knock down the huge pigeon that loudly flapped from the tree in front of us. My guide, Mario, was even louder than the pigeon as he yelled derogatory comments about the bird's mother. In between the pigeon's flapping and Mario's yelling, we could hear the hoofbeats of the stag and his harem as they quickly moved deeper into the forest. Our evening hunt was over and all we could do was trudge back four kilometers to the rendezvous point with the other hunters.

Our group had arrived in Buenos Aires three days before. The city is huge, cosmopolitan, and very clean; more European than South American, and very crowded with a population of 11,500,000, about one-third of the population of the entire country. Dave Harshbarger and Tom Grimes had flown in from California, Lad Shunneson from Colorado, and my flight originated in Texas. Dave and Tom would hunt 1 x 1 while Lad and I would be hunting 2 x 1 since we were videotaping each other for Sportsmen on Film's video production to be titled "Argentine Safari."

We were able to spend March 17 seeing some of the sights in B.A., such as the world's widest street, before flying to Bahia Blanca early the next morning. There, our outfitter's wife, Stella Wirsky of Argentina Safari, met us and we were driven westerly 300 kilometers to their southern camp which is home to a large population of free-ranging red deer that descended from deer originally imported from Europe at the turn of the century. Coincidentally, Hugo Wirsky's family emigrated to Argentina from Germany about the same time.

SPORT HUNTING ON SIX CONTINENTS

Downtown Buenos Aires . . . clean, orderly, and crowded.

Argentina is known for its beef and restaurants. L to R: Lad Shunneson, Dave Harshbarger, Tom Grimes, and me.

Camp was comfortable with a kitchen, indoor and outdoor dining areas, two-man cabins, and a combination shower-bathroom building. La Pampa Province was different than I expected. It is virtually flat, whereas I had expected rolling hills, and wherever the land was uncleared, it was covered with a thick growth of 10- to 20-foot trees, 5- to 10-foot bushes, and 1- to 2-foot grass. Even though we were just a few days from the start of fall in the southern hemisphere, it was warm . . . very warm . . . much too warm for the wool pants and shirts we all brought in preparation for weather similar to fall in North America.

The red deer rut in La Pampa generally lasts from mid-March to early April so, despite the wrong clothes, our timing was good and the stags were roaring. I was wearing black Levis that were intended as my traveling pants and a green T-shirt that was to have been my undershirt. I had no alternative to my heavy hiking boots. Our jackets and gloves were never unpacked, day or night.

But complaining about flat terrain and limited visibility and warm weather was short-lived because the stags were roaring . . . lots of stags were roaring.

Red deer are about two-thirds the size of Rocky Mountain elk; similar in appearance, but with a reddish tinge to their hair and with crowns of three or more points at the top of each antler for most mature males. A typical mature stag will have 12 points (three or more on each side plus three-point crowns) with some having 14 points (four-point crowns) and a very few having more.

Our stag hunt was scheduled for five days which allowed for 10 hunts, five each morning and five each evening. A typical day was to arise at 5:00 AM, leave camp by vehicle at 5:30, arrive at a hunting area by 6:00, and walk into the bush so as to be in position at first light at 6:30. Then we would wait for the roaring to start. A stag's roar is unlike an elk's bugle. In fact, it's similar to the rasping grunt of an African lion. While the roar says, "Here I am," it's not quite that easy, as we found out.

Typically, the roaring would end by 8:30 AM and Hugo wanted us out by 9:30 because tramping around trying to jump deer just doesn't work when there are lots of hinds with each mature stag. At 8:30 each morning, we would reluctantly start walking out and we'd usually reach camp by 10:00 AM. Then we'd eat light, shower, sleep, eat heavy, prepare, and head out at 5:00 PM so we could again be in position by 6:00 and hunt until dark at 8:00 when we would start walking out.

Our guide, Mario, was an expert at determining the age of a stag by the deepness of its roar. His favorite strategy, though only occasionally possible, was to listen for two older stags roaring and then move between them and wait for the stags to seek each other and hopefully step into lanes of visibility. To try to directly approach a lone stag continually proved ineffective because the satellite hinds would usually see us first; although, on one stalk, we saw a single hind first which allowed us to drop into the tall grass undetected. Fifteen tense minutes later, the 12-point stag appeared for about two seconds before disappearing in the heavy growth. By the time I raised my loaded rifle and pushed off the safety, my crosshairs only reached his hindquarters before he was gone.

My chance came when we found a heavy-antlered 14-pointer roaring in a manmade clearing as he tried to keep a harem of about 10 hinds together. When the trees and brush are knocked down and plowed, grass is easily grown without irrigation, which makes La Pampa such fine cattle country. Cattle roam by the thousands between four-foot-high slick-wire fencing. There were even some cattle in the hunting areas, which was not unwelcome because their noise and movement tended to mask our hunting efforts.

"My stag" was at the edge of a clearing. We moved downwind to within 250 meters where I found a convenient tree limb to rest my rifle with a view of part of the clearing. But Lad couldn't video over the intervening brush, so we carefully closed to 200 meters. At that point, Lad could see, but I had no rest. When the stag abruptly turned and trotted away, I moved left, dropped to my right knee, and fired. The stag reared up and bolted left across the clearing surrounded by his hinds. I should have gotten off two more shots, but I had trouble ejecting my spent cartridge. By Argentine law, whenever we were traveling in any vehicle, such as to and from hunting, there can be no cartridges in the magazine and the bolt must be removed from the rifle. Since the dirt roads were very dusty, my rifle was dirty from riding in the open Jeep. After this episode, I always carried my rifle, bolt out, in a closed case when traveling.

To get on with this painful recollection, I managed to jack in a second round while thinking the same words that Mario had uttered the day before about that pigeon's mother. I swung on the stag as it ran to my left at about 150 meters, but there were hinds on both sides of him. By the time he cleared the hinds, I had swung my crosshairs all the way by him and, with the brush about to engulf him, I stopped my rifle swing and fired.

Mario immediately pointed to the side of his stomach saying, as best as we could interpret, that I had made a wonderful gut shot. Lad didn't think I connected with either shot. Two kilometers away, Tom's guide, Paco, said I missed the first shot but that he heard the second shot hit. Apparently Paco could hear like Superman.

We searched for blood and found none. Tracking one animal out of a herd, even though the stag's hooves were considerably bigger than the hinds', proved fruitless. Later, two afternoons of searching on horseback yielded no clues. Since Lad had captured the action on video, those few seconds of tape were played over and over for everyone at camp and the big debate was on.

On first viewing, Hugo said I definitely hit him with the first shot because the stag clearly jumped, turned, and ran, but I missed the second shot. Mario said he didn't care what the video showed, I missed the first, and hit the second. Unfortunately, because the camera was so close to the muzzle of my rifle for the second shot, there was a one second video dropout at that point. When I unpacked the headphones and plugged them into the camera for playback, everyone agreed that I missed the first shot because the stag's jump occurred about a second after the shot in reaction to the noise; not in reaction to a hit. Hugo decided to go with Mario's eyes and Superman's ears so my stag hunt was over. Wounded and lost counts the same as a kill.

ARGENTINE SAFARI

Actually, the most embarrassing part of reviewing the video was that it appeared that "my stag" was not running away when I first shot, but was chasing a hind and, if I had waited, he probably would have circled back for a better shot. That was the bad news. The good news was that the vultures eventually found my stag and, even though they were quite hungry, they did not eat the antlers. Hugo later obtained a replacement cape for me from a European hunter.

Two days later, after a tedious afternoon stalk, Mario got a quick look at "Lad's stag" while its head was down feeding but, as we tried to position ourselves for a shot, one of the hinds saw or heard something she didn't like and the whole group ran off. Mario signaled that the stag was a 14-pointer. Lad turned to me and said, "They're all 14-pointers when the hunter doesn't see them." Then we heard a deep-throated roar. Everyone quickly perked up as we immediately crossed an opening and moved into the brush again, risking moving quickly to get close before we lost shooting light. This time we saw the stag undetected. Lad later said that the sunset reflecting off the wide antlers made his stag look like an Irish elk as it faced away from us. When the animal quartered left, Lad fired twice. The first shot hit the spine

Lad's stag lay where he shot it at sunset.

The vultures tracked my stag down for me, but the cape was ruined.

just in front of the hindquarters and the quick second shot from Lad's .300 semi-auto took out both shoulders. The first shot became known as the "high gut shot" and ended Lad's kidding about my gut shot. The primary difference was that Lad had a magnificent 14-pointer on the ground with long tines, heavy main beams, and symmetrical four point crowns.

On the last day in the southern camp, Tom shot a 12-pointer and Lad and I each shot a rhea (the south American version of the ostrich) which we ate for dinner. Dave had still not taken a shot, although he had passed several legal but thin-antlered stags. Lad and I left that night for Argentina Safari's northern camp; a 1,250-kilometer drive in a chauffeured van to Entre Rios Province ("between rivers"). We later learned that Hugo let Dave hunt the next morning before Dave and Tom left for a fishing excursion near Bariloche and that Dave shot a stag on that hunt.

Lad and I arrived at the estancia of Jose Manuel de Anchorena bleary-eyed but raring to go for the afternoon hunt. Entre Rios is northwest of Buenos Aires and is quite tropical; warm, humid and with lots of water. The hunting here would be difficult, unique, and most enjoyable. There are no roads on the estancia, but there were the inevitable cattle and low cattle fencing. In addition to lots of grass and brushy trees with thorns, there are numerous palm trees and yucca-type bushes.

"Camp" was Jose's 5,000-square-foot home in the middle of nowhere: a true oasis and a welcome sight at the end of each long hunting day. On the veranda, we would consume gallons of juice to rehydrate and then discuss hunting with Jose before dining and retiring early.

The game available was brown brocket deer, Indian buffalo, and the possibility of capybara; each species uniquely interesting. Lad and I both considered the brown brocket to be the prize of the safari. It is a small deer, indigenous to northern Argentina and much of western South America, about 35 to 40 pounds, and with mature males having slender, spike horns of three to five inches. It comes into rut twice a year. Some would be in velvet as we hunted in late March and most would be in hard antler.

The Indian buffalo is a sub-species of water buffalo introduced to northern Argentina around 1900 and different from the sub-species introduced to Marajo Island, Brazil and to northern Australia. The horn tips of mature males grow up and in, like the horn tips on Cape buffalo. Jose told us that he preferred using a pistol to place a bullet between the eyes and nose when a wounded Indian buffalo charges from short range in heavy cover. That, I would like to see . . . at a safe distance.

Finally, the capybara is truly unique. It is the world's largest rodent with mature males weighing up to 150 pounds. They live in and around waterways, graze on grass, have feet similar to a hippo's and can submerge for an hour and walk on the bottom of waterways.

We entered the tropical jungle led by our Gaucho guide, Ico Rivarola. I would be the first hunter, so I followed closely behind Ico, with Lad closely behind me with the camera. At first Ico didn't like the idea of a third person reducing our chances for success, but he soon figured out what the camera was about and he got to hamming it up pretty good. The hunting method was the same no matter what the species . . . LSD . . . long, slow distance. We would walk hour after hour very slowly . . . very, very slowly; and very quietly. Great care would be taken to step around the noisy yuccas and under the thorny brush. If a limb were too low, we would crawl under it or lift it up to pass through. Speed did not matter; only quietness and Ico's ability to spot game mattered.

The first afternoon, we spotted two female brockets. In each case, Ico pointed and then made a circular motion indicating no horns. The first female was walking away and quickly disappeared. Jose had said any shots would be 10-40 meters, which was the limit of our visibility. The second female was in the open for several seconds and moving cautiously and alertly. We turned slowly as she moved and she didn't spook.

Jose has hunted brocket all his life; the last 15 years on this estancia. He had cautioned us to make slow movements, such as when raising a rifle, in which case the brocket would then usually not run unless they winded us. I slowly raised my rifle. Ico again signaled "female." I nodded my understanding, but I couldn't help putting my crosshairs on her shoulder for several seconds until she disappeared.

At sunset, we turned and walked back with a crosswind. The mosquitoes were now eating us up and we had no repellent. Two hundred bites each was lesson enough to coat up twice a day from then on. In the dwindling light, Ico stopped and pointed. I strained to see the brocket, but could see nothing. Ico whispered, *"Bufalo de agua."* Then I saw the horns of a huge, black buffalo standing motionless and staring in our direction. Jose had said the buffalo would run instantly upon seeing us, but it was now difficult to see and we had been moving slowly and quietly. This was the first Indian buffalo I had seen in Argentina, although tracks and droppings were everywhere. It was also my first day of hunting out of the northern camp but, from the photos I had seen, only the big, old bulls had horns that grew that far up and in. Jose had said it took 20 years for a bull to attain such horn length, so I decided to shoot. Above the bull I could see my crosshairs but, when I dropped them down, the crosshairs disappeared. Also, I couldn't tell which way his body was facing, so I stood up and the bull immediately ran to his left at about 75 meters. I swung my crosshairs above him so I could see them, dropped the crosshairs down, and fired. He ran on!

It was only about 15 minutes after sunset, but darkness settles quickly in northern Argentina and we found ourselves tracking an 1,800-pound animal by starlight. Ico, who hunted as much by smell and hearing as by sight, had been in on too many buffalo charges to continue this lunacy (and Gauchos only carry a knife and sharpener) so we headed back to *la casa grande*.

The next morning, with three dogs, two rifles, and Jose's handgun, we returned

I was into my "shoot now, find later" phase. L to R: Jose Manuel de Anchorena, me, and Ico Rivarola, with my Indian water buffalo.

ARGENTINE SAFARI

to the scene of the action. Ico went directly to a hack mark he had made in one of the palm trees the night before. Then he surmised the route that the buffalo had taken when hit. If the bull charged in that thick jungle, it would be from a matter of feet. Ico sniffed the air, and then bent down to look into the darkness of the low canopy of a large tree. He pointed. I eased off my safety and moved around the tree with him. Suddenly I saw the buffalo lying there, but before I could raise my rifle, Ico smiled. The buffalo was lying on his left side . . . dead. He had died from a liver shot; just where I had aimed . . . I said.

We couldn't roll the bull onto his stomach for photos so Ico field dressed him where he lay and then we pulled him out from under the canopy of trees for picture taking. Jose lit a couple of short palm trees on fire to mark our location so a crew of Gauchos could ride in on horseback to cut up and carry out the meat (the burning eliminated the dead fronds but did not kill the trees) and Corcho caped the trophy, so Lad and Ico and I could keep hunting.

Between the morning and evening hunt (with a two-hour lunch and rest break), we walked 11 hours of LSD that day and sighted only one more female brocket. In

Ico gives the signal for horns, which means he sees a male brocket deer.

the heat and humidity, it was too much. The next morning we were exhausted, but we wanted to continue to hunt the far end of the estancia so, for the next two days, Jose arranged horses for us to ride several kilometers each morning before dismounting and hunting on foot. This made the hunting day quite enjoyable; especially the ride back in darkness each evening.

When I was starting to think it might never happen, Ico slowly raised two fingers; the signal for a mature male brocket. Surprisingly, I could see the buck exactly where Ico was looking. It was facing away from me and standing still at 40 meters. By previous arrangement, Ico was to signal "small" if we saw a male with under 10 centimeters of horn, but he made no such signal. I slowly raised my rifle as the brocket looked over his shoulder, and shot him end-to-end with a 180-grain bullet. Elmer Keith preached using enough gun, and I followed his instructions. If I hadn't decided on a one rifle safari, I would have brought a .243 for the brocket, a .300 for red deer, and a .375 for buffalo.

The little buck lay where he had been shot; as beautiful dead as alive. His muzzle, just above his nose, had turned white with age. When we opened his mouth, we found he did not have a single tooth above his gums. Jose later said it was the oldest deer shot there in 20 years. I don't know how it gummed enough to stay alive.

It was Lad's turn to hunt that afternoon. As we carefully walked by an area of tall, green grass, Jose pointed to what looked like a huge brocket, but it was far too big. Maybe baby buffalo were reddish before turning black. Or maybe it was a baby cow. When it moved, we could see that it was a capybara out feeding. Lad quickly made his patented high gut shot at 100 meters offhand and the capybara dropped. Then Lad moved up and finished him off. And it was a "him" . . . a big male estimated at 125 pounds with two huge beaver teeth uppers and matching lowers and with the characteristic three toes in back and four toes in front on what Ico called *manos* ("hands") instead of feet. A very interesting creature. A very unusual creature. And legal to hunt in Argentina for meat, but not exportable to the U.S.

Ico field dressed the capybara. Then he and Lad lifted the rodent onto one of the horses which promptly bucked it off, so Ico covered the big "rat" with branches and later sent a Gaucho to pick it up with a less particular horse. The next night we ate breaded capybara and it was absolutely delicious; like fine veal. Lad said it was "the best rat I ever ate."

We still had a couple hours of daylight left and Lad wanted a brocket badly. As we continued our LSD, we heard a couple capybaras plunge into a nearby waterway. Ico quickly handed me my rifle, I handed Lad my camera, Lad handed Ico his rifle, and I was hunting again. We moved into the wind and along the water's edge. Ico pointed, Lad videotaped, and I saw nothing. Then another capybara plunged into the water and we could see the current as it walked the bottom to a hole in the bank which it entered underwater. Ico pointed again and I saw nothing except an eye at 50 meters. When I looked through my scope, set at three power, I could see the head and neck of a capybara surrounding the big eye. My blast shattered the soli-

With Ico and my gray, aka brown brocket buck.

Ico and Lad with the "big rat."

Ico knew what the camera was all about. When Hollywood wants to do a movie on the Gauchos, Ico should get the lead.

tude and the capybara lay dead... a big female that weighed over 100 pounds... not as big as Lad's, but much prettier.

The next day was our last and Lad was getting nervous. He had great respect for the difficulty of brocket hunting which made him want one all the more. Ico and his horses arrived at the ranch house before first light so we would be in position to start our LSD an hour earlier than usual. And it paid off. Not 10 minutes after dismounting, Lad had his trophy on the ground. It happens like that sometimes when hunting brown brocket deer in Argentina.

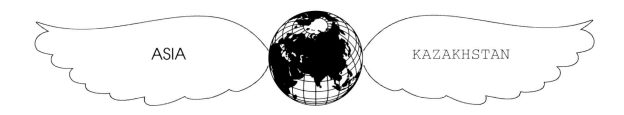

ASIA KAZAKHSTAN

39

SAIGA SAGA

"This hunt was your idea, so I hold you personally responsible for how I feel," spoke my hunting partner and co-cameraman for Sportsmen on Film, Lad Shunneson. Where we were was in a Polish biplane, sitting on one of the two bench seats, surrounded by supplies stacked high and loose, and skimming over the undulations of an Asian desert while our heads throbbed and our stomachs churned. I held my head in both hands and tried to remember how I got here and why.

We had flown through Frankfurt to Almaty, Kazakhstan where we were met by representatives of The Hunting Consortium. Kazakhstan is one of the CIS countries formed during the break-up of the former Soviet Union. It is about one-third the size of the continental United States and is surrounded by Russia to the west and north, China to the east, and all the "stans" to the south (Uzbekistan, Khrgystan, Turkmenistan, Tajikistan, Afghanistan, and Pakistan).

The human population of Kazakhstan in 1995 was estimated at 17 million with about 1.5 million residing in the City of Almaty (spelled "Alma Ata" on some maps which is the Russian spelling).

But the population in which Lad and I were interested was that of the saiga antelope, the nomads of the steppes of the Kazak desert and one of the most unique animals in the world with their great bulbous noses. Like most caribou, saiga migrate in their search for food. They are very prolific breeders, with females able to conceive before their first birthdays and with mature females able to produce a set of twins per year. The saiga population was estimated at two million by local wildlife authorities, but is subject to wide fluctuations with breeding on the positive side and

Sport Hunting on Six Continents

A recently renovated Russian Orthodox church that had been closed for 75 years following the Russian Revolution of 1919.

poaching for the Oriental horn market on the negative side. Naturally, sport hunting is a positive influence on the population, since the infrastructure and value of sport hunting discourages poaching.

When we arrived in Almaty in late September, scouts for The Hunting Consortium reported that the saiga herds were near their greatest distance away, so we were immediately booked to fly northwesterly about 1,500 kilometers to Aktyubinsk near the Russian border. However, our Kazakhstan Air jet experienced a problem as we were rolling for takeoff, so the flight was canceled and we were rebooked for the next morning. This gave us the day to sightsee in Almaty and it also points out the vagaries of Asian travel which is why The Hunting Consortium allows for a six-day itinerary for saiga to insure ample hunting time, despite occasional problems.

The next morning, Kazakhstan Air lifted off the Almaty runway and landed in Aktyubinsk 2½ hours later. We were met by Dr. Yuri Paul, the CIS Operations Coordinator for The Hunting Consortium, and its President, Robert P. "Bob" Kern. Plans had already been made to fly south from Aktyubinsk about 400 K and catch up with part of the southerly saiga migration in the middle of the Kazak steppes. Our mode of transportation was the aforementioned ANZ Polish biplane which uncomfortably seated 11 of us, including part of our camp staff, and all of our gear. Flying low and slow, we got a monotonous view of the desert for a little over two hours until landing in the middle of nowhere.

The Polish biplane used to transport us in and out of the Kazak steppes. L to R: Dr. Doug Yajko, Bob Kern, me, and Lad.

SAIGA SAGA

The third hunter in our group was Doug Yajko, M.D., past president of Safari Club International. Dr. Yajko was full of enthusiasm because he had just collected a maral stag, Siberian roe deer, and mid-Asian ibex on a multi-species hunt with The Hunting Consortium. I was a little worried, however, because I had seen less than 50 saiga out the windows of our biplane before we landed. "You were not exactly maintaining a constant vigil," Lad pointed out while mimicking my head-holding position.

Camp consisted of two tents for staff and an army transport truck equipped with beds for the hunters. Water was not a problem because we were situated next to a large waterhole, complete with flocks of ducks and a pair of swans. Since the sparse grasslands of the Kazak steppes are home to herds of domestic sheep, goats, and cattle plus the much wilder horses and camels used by the herders, waterholes were seemingly scattered every 10 to 30 K. Bore holes easily reach the high water table and the water pressure then pushes water into the ponds.

In some areas of the migration, the terrain is rolling and allows spotting from the hilltops and stalking over great distances to reach the scattered herds. But we were surrounded by virtually flat land with no cover whatsoever, so our hunting

L to R, 400 miles from nowhere: Dr. Doug Yajko, our camp cook, Lad, Mischa, a staff member, Bob Kern, four staff members, and me. A Russian Army "sleeping truck" and the staff's tents are in the background.

method would be to wait for herds passing to or by the water. Having landed in the middle of the day, we immediately set out for the afternoon hunt. Lad and I walked a kilometer to the widest point of the waterhole (which was about 30 acres) and, with the help of our guide, Mischa, we cut and planted several clumps of reeds on a small embankment in order to break up our outlines. While we were involved in this project, Dr. Yajko was driven about 15 K to the next closest waterhole. Then we waited.

Mischa was a member of the local hunting club in Aktyubinsk that does the scouting and provides the cooks and guides and camp staff for The Hunting Consortium. He appeared to be in his 20s and, like most of the camp staff, was European in appearance, whereas a couple herdsmen that we met in camp were right out of a Genghis Khan movie, except for their motorcycle with sidecar!

Two herds of about 50 saiga came to water about 150 meters from us that afternoon so we were able to learn more about the animal that we were hunting. The herds approached the water very cautiously and as far away from the reeds as possible. Wolves follow the herds and no doubt enjoy ambushing the saiga at waterholes. In fact, we saw a lone wolf at about 1,000 meters looking our way. He departed as soon as we moved to glass him.

In each herd, a few brave saiga would walk or pronk toward the water and then quickly retreat at the slightest gust of wind or upon seeing their own shadows. Eventually they see-sawed back and forth until safely reaching the waterhole at which time the rest of the herd would trot to the water; some animals wading in up to their shoulders to drink. Then, as each animal drank its fill, it would quickly retreat. We realized that this did not allow us much time to pick out a trophy, wait until he separated for a clear shot, and then make the shot at the waterhole or while he was retreating.

Two herdsmen drove into camp on their motorcycle with sidecar. Our biplane is tied down in the background.

The males in each herd seemed to have either two-inch horns or 10- to 12-inch horns with nothing in between. Between the ages of one and two, the males' horns must grow to virtually their full length. As yearlings, the small horns of the males are dark colored but, as mature specimens, the horns grow a translucent, yellow-wax color. As they get older, the males sometimes rub off their dark tips so that older males can have shorter horns than younger, mature males. This phenomenon of limited horn growth results in a greatly compressed record book wherein almost all entries are 10 to 12 inches with basal circumferences that don't vary appreciably from five inches. The first afternoon, we didn't see the length we were looking for so neither Lad nor I took a shot. At the other waterhole, Dr. Yajko had a similar experience.

By the next morning, the wind was creating scattered dust clouds and the saiga were not moving early. A lone horse stopped by. And then, out of a cloud of dust that covered the horizon, slowly moved a herd of 12 camels; 10 with two humps (Bactrian camels) and two with one hump (Arabian camels, also known as dromedaries), led by a huge cream-colored male . . . a magnificent sight befitting a Hollywood movie. The camels watered at their leisure. In fact, they watered so leisurely that Mischa decided to walk down and scare them off . . . which he succeeded in doing but, after he returned to our position, the camels calmly returned to finish drinking. Eventually they moved off and a herd of 30 saiga moved in, but they were all females (the breeding season is December-January with calves born April-May). Then another herd of about 50 arrived. With my video camera on 28 power, I whispered to Lad, "It looks like there are several good males in this group." Lad adjusted my Nikon 16-47 spotting scope and said, "I already see the one I want. Its horns look dark compared to the others, but I believe they are the longest."

When the herd reached the water, the dark-horned saiga rushed in with several females on each side. When they walked back out, the male separated just enough for a clear shot and Lad hit it with a 165-grain Barnes X-Bullet from his 1964 Winchester Model 100 semi-auto in .308 caliber. The buck ran about 75 meters and dropped as the herd scattered. Then we circled the pond and walked up for our first hands-on look at the great bulbous, convex proboscis of this unique species. It is believed that the saiga developed its nose to warm and moisten inhaled air. The horns were a little over 11 inches with slightly worn tips. We estimated his body weight at 110 pounds compared to about 70 pounds for the females.

Now it was my turn and, after about an hour, a huge herd, later counted at 175, appeared on the horizon and slowly worked its way toward us. But this herd must already have watered elsewhere, because it stayed away from the waterhole and eventually moved about 500 meters past us and bedded down; presumably to wait out the windstorm and then continue its migration. We were still on the small embankment with our transplanted reeds, but now our backsides were exposed to the herd. We slowly turned and glassed and determined that there were several good males in this herd. Through my spotting scope, three seemed to have that extra inch of horn I was looking for.

The herd stayed bedded, with a few animals taking turns standing and wandering, for about an hour. During that time, three other much smaller herds came to water and left, but none contained bucks with that elusive extra inch. As the third herd moved off, the big herd stood and started walking cross-ways behind us. "Decision time," Lad said.

Lad poses with saiga antelope number one.

We belly-crawled to the other side of the embankment without being seen. The herd was strung out, mostly one to three abreast, and angling a little closer to us as they walked by our position. When they reached 300 meters, I cranked a 180-grain Federal Nosler partition bullet into my Sako .300 WM and then looked to Mischa for input by hand signals and body language, which was our only method of communication, and not a bad method when you have 175 high-strung animals walking close by.

Mischa signaled "one" or "three" with his fingers and a shrug. I gave a quick look through my binoculars and felt that the first buck had the taller horns so I tracked him with my crosshairs as he closed to 200 meters. Then, when I was comfortable, I finished my trigger squeeze and heard the bullet hit. As the herd sprinted right, my buck ran left and dropped. He was a beautiful specimen of over 12 inches with un-rubbed black tips that turned inward.

Since Dr. Yajko had not yet returned, we decided to skip lunch and stay out hunting. After having traveled 9,000 miles from Colorado, Lad decided to hunt for a second saiga if he found one to his liking. Eventually he did as a herd came through a cloud of dust, inexplicably bolted off, and then ran back just as quickly. Lad dropped a waxy-horned male in his tracks. It measured the same as his first one; virtually

With Mischa and my saiga antelope.

twins except for the difference in horn coloration. When we walked up to his second saiga, Lad turned to me with a big smile and said, "This hunt was your idea, so I hold you personally responsible for how I feel."

Back at camp, we discovered that Dr. Yajko had already returned with a nice 12-incher. With everyone filled out, we were offered the choice of staying another night for game viewing or biplaning back to Aktyubinsk for a sauna, shower, and camaraderie with one of the local hunting clubs. Having seen about 1,000 saiga, we decided to head 'em out. We just couldn't wait to get back in that biplane!

ASIA　　MONGOLIA

40

HUNTING THE LAND OF GENGHIS KHAN

Brief History

In the year 1162 A.D., a boy named Temujin was born in Mongolia. He was orphaned in his teens, but became a great warrior and an even greater politician who was most adept at creating alliances and allegiances. By 1206, his success in tribal warfare caused him to be proclaimed ruler of All the Mongols with the rank of Khan (monarch) and the title of Genghis (roughly translated "the ocean").

After Genghis Khan gained control of all of his potential nomadic rivals, he probed deep into north China for eight years culminating in the sacking of Beijing in 1215. Leaving a general in charge, he withdrew to Mongolia and then campaigned westward, conquering the lands all the way to northern Iran. This accomplished, he turned back toward China where he died in 1227 on a successful campaign against the wealthy Hsi Hsia of northwest China, leaving further campaigning into Russia and the edges of eastern Europe to his generals and his sons.

Genghis Khan's grandson, Mongke, became Great Khan in 1248 and continued an expansionist policy. His successor, Kubla Khan, conquered China and moved the Mongol capital to Beijing where he utilized Marco Polo and his family to help administer his empire. The Mongols eventually lost China to the native Mings in 1367 and, by 1380, the empire was reduced to the Mongol homeland.

Hunting the Land of Genghis Khan

The Adventure

"Are you tired?" Ankhbayar asked me. I had just flown from San Antonio, Texas to Los Angeles, California to Tokyo, Japan to Beijing, China to Ulaanbataar, Mongolia and had then been driven 12 ½ hours in a Russian jeep to our camp in the middle of the Gobi Desert. I smiled the smile of the weary traveler and replied, "I'm ready to go hunting." Ankhaa (as his friends call him and, after 12 ½ hours together in a jeep, I qualified) said, "Good. We'll awaken you with hot tea at daylight in five hours."

My accommodation was a traditional ger (which rhymes with "air" and is known as a "yurt" in Russian) of which I was familiar after having passed hundreds enroute southeast from the capital of Ulaanbataar, and after having been invited into one for *airag* (fermented mare's milk) some hours earlier.

My companions were Bob Kern of The Hunting Consortium, who arranged my safari and was along to open a new hunting area, Lad Shunneson, a fellow hunter and co-cameraman for Sportsmen on Film, and Gary Goodgame, who would serve as a cameraman for the first leg of our hunt before traveling to Tibet for sightseeing. Ankhaa is the Manager of Hunting Operations for Juulchin which is the Mongolian tourism

The statue of Genghis Khan in the central square of Ulaanbataar.

Ulaanbataar was a town of gers until after World War II.

305

Our camp in the Gobi Desert. L to R: me, Bob Kern, Lad Shunneson, and Gary Goodgame.

agency that has been accommodating foreign tourists (hunters and non-hunters alike) for the past 40 years. We were in the mid-Gobi Desert to hunt both white-tailed and black-tailed gazelle. Our camp of felt-lined gers was well-located, because we were soon to discover herds of 50 to 200 white-tailed gazelle (also known as Mongolian gazelle) on the flats and groups of five to 15 black-tailed gazelle (aka Hillier goitered gazelle) in the hills.

Gers are quite comfortable and can accommodate four or more people. L to R: Bob, Gary, me, and Lad.

From a distance, the gazelles look similar, but the herd size is a good indicator of the species and the way black-tailed gazelle hold their tails erect when running is a giveaway. Primary hunting methods are to stalk from the hills or to wait in ambush as a couple drivers show themselves to a herd from long distance. The median horn length in the SCI Record Book is about 10 inches for the white-tailed gazelle and 12 inches for the black-tailed gazelle which are about the sizes that Lad and I each shot in two days.

With Zoright and my white-tailed gazelle.

Back to Ulaanbataar we drove and overnighted prior to our departure to Siberian ibex camp. The next morning, we were told to spend the day sightseeing in Ulaanbataar, because the national airline was low on fuel and our flight to Khovd, the gateway to the western Altai Mountains, would be delayed a day. The hunting museum, temple of the 80-foot Buddha, central square, and marketplace were all worth seeing.

The following day we flew four hours to Khovd and then rode by a now-familiar Russian jeep on bone-crushing dirt paths eight hours northerly to ibex camp, where we arrived at 1:00 AM. At daylight, we drove into the mountains for an hour and then set off on foot. Whereas the altitude had been 5,000 feet in our gazelle camp, it was 7,000 feet at ibex camp with climbs to 8,000 feet.

Like most mountain hunting, you climb high and glass and then move to the next peak and glass. We were hunting in September when the males and females herd separately. My guide, Togtokh, spotted several herds of ibex and, with the aid of my spotting scope, selected one to stalk. Our circuitous route brought us within 278 meters of

Zoright shows the tail of my black-tailed gazelle.

the herd according to Ankhaa's Bushnell laser rangefinder. Sliding forward on his belly, Togtokh placed my sweater on the rocky ridge top. I quietly chambered a round and slid my rifle forward so that Togtokh could place it on top of my sweater. Then I slid forward and looked at the herd for the first time. There were about 30 ibex resting with one standing guard.

"Shoot the one standing," Ankhaa whispered. I pushed the safety forward, placed the crosshairs on the shoulder, and missed low! The herd arose as one and sprinted uphill as I just missed with my second shot and then they were gone. The disappointment was palpable. Togtokh and Ankhaa tried to cheer me up by informing me that I had missed a very good ibex in the 42-inch range. Hours later I slept on that thought.

After a couple aborted stalks the next day, Togtokh and I decided to climb several steep peaks without the rest of the entourage. Late in the afternoon, Togtokh spotted a lone male ibex feeding in a rocky cut about a mile distant. We waited until he bedded down. Between us and the ibex were no less than five peaks and 20 ridges. In rudimentary English, Togtokh asked me if I could make the same shot that I missed the day before. "Yes," I said. "I can make it."

Togtokh looked at all those peaks and ridges for over a minute in order to burn each into his brain, and then we took off . . . down, up, down, over, and up. Very slowly Togtokh looked over the last ridge. Then he backed off and motioned me to follow him up the ridgeline. He looked over the ridge again and then placed my sweater and rifle on top of a rock. "Slow," he mouthed. I carefully peered through my scope, set at nine power, but could not see the lone ibex. So I slowly moved my Swarovski binoculars to my eyes and searched the rocky cut between two ridges for the resting ibex. Still I could not find him. So Togtokh took my binoculars and placed them under the butt of my rifle so that, without moving my scope, I could finally make out the horns and chest of the ibex resting with his head up, facing me, his horns curling over his back, and his brown, black, and white pelage blending perfectly with the surrounding rocks. I guess you could say I couldn't have found him without my Swarovskis.

My view of this magnificent animal through the rifle scope was a jolt. I shook slightly. Togtokh moved near my ear and whispered "I good shot. I shoot for you." With that bit of encouragement, I steadied the crosshairs and carefully killed the ibex so that he stayed on the ledge on which he was resting. The shot had been 290 meters across a very deep canyon so that it required 45 minutes to climb down and back up to reach my trophy. He was not the monster we had thought when we first saw his perfect horn configuration and his black shoulders and white back (a sure sign of old age), but his horns did have 11 annual growth rings and measured about a meter in length.

Returning to camp long after dark, I learned that Lad had run into an amazing herd of almost 100 males and had shot a good one only to watch as several great ones followed. Watching the playback of the video, I could understand why Lad was too

Togtokh liked my ibex and loved my camera.

distraught to eat dinner and he doesn't miss too many meals!

Next were four days of torture for the sake of trying to help Bob Kern open a new maral stag camp in the military area along the Chinese border where no foreign hunters had ever hunted according to Ankhaa. From ibex camp, we drove back to Khovd only to encounter gas rationing of 15 liters per vehicle per week. It took Ankhaa past dark to solve that problem for our two jeeps, so he arranged for us to stay in a room above the airport lobby until the next morning.

Near ibex camp, a woman milks a yak while a calf drinks from the other side.

In the western Altai, where there are no trees, yak dung is collected, dried, and stacked for use as fuel.

Khovd, like most cities built during Soviet domination, is on a central hot water system. The problem is that, when the system breaks down, the entire town is without hot water or heat. The system in Khovd had been broken down for over two years! Electricity was available one hour each morning and three hours each night. There was no shower or tub. But Bob, Lad, and I loved our accommodations because we had an actual sit-down toilet instead of the traditional Asian hole in the floor.

The next day we drove 12 hours to base camp; the last 45 kilometers taking three hours on the roughest path imaginable. In the morning we rode horses up, up, and up for five hours and set up fly camp.

Maral are virtually identical to North American elk and are called Altai wapiti by SCI. The western Altai is reported to have the biggest maral in Mongolia, but we were not to see them. Instead, we saw team after team of woodcutters and their strings of camels dragging cut timber out of the valleys. I was disappointed, but Bob Kern was doubly so.

Inside a ger near the Chinese border.

After a long discussion, Bob and Ankhaa decided that we should abandon the exploration and transfer to one of the "sure as sure can get" maral camps north of Ulaanbataar. So the next morning we rode by horseback and jeep back to Khovd and collapsed in our familiar beds at the airport at 2:00AM. The following day we flew to Ulaanbataar, reorganized for an hour, and then drove north through the night for 280 kilometers on a roughly paved road and then another 70K over a dirt path, arriving at our hotel in Dulaankhaan just before sunrise.

Most maral camps consist of gers but, with only two days of hunting left, Bob and Ankhaa didn't have time to organize a proper camp. Our no star hotel had no hot water, no heat, and no indoor bathrooms. At the time, this hardly mattered. Lad and I dropped our bags, grabbed our rifles, got in separate jeeps, and headed for the mountains where we arrived tired but ready to go.

In his two days of hunting, Lad reported seeing almost 100 stags of which five were trophies, but he never fired a shot. He passed on a very heavy 5 x 5 and a lighter 5 x 6 and 6 x 6, but couldn't get within range of the heavy 6 x 6 that he glimpsed. The bulls were bugling like crazy, but it was a few days before the rut and they were hanging in the timber instead of physically challenging each other. The five gray wolves Lad encountered were part of the problem, but the main problem was the lack of time since most maral hunts last four days.

The head man sat in the middle of his ger and was the center of attention.

I was more fortunate. On the first morning, Ankhaa spotted a herd of maral about a mile up a steep, grassy mountain. There was a 6 x 6 bull feeding 100 meters from a scattered herd of cows. We figured we could climb an adjacent cut, then cross above the stag, and hopefully get a shot before he laid up in the trees. So up we climbed accompanied by our driver, Sherif. Upon reaching the top, we glassed to make sure we wouldn't scare anything toward "my" bull. At that point, Sherif pointed out a yellow spot on a hill in the middle of the valley below us. Ankhaa took a look through his binoculars and whispered, "That's a better bull than

The woodcutters relied on their camels to find the way out of the mountains on their own.

the one we're after. He has heavier horns and he's probably by himself because he's older and resting for the rut."

Before we started down, Ankhaa said something to Sherif in Mongolian like, "You have good eyes for a driver. The guy with the rifle will no doubt increase your net worth if he shoots this stag. Stay here and only show yourself if the stag moves. We'll climb down to the valley floor and then up the left side of the hill and, if the wind holds and the stag holds and my heavy-footed hunter can keep up without breathing like a steam engine, we'll see if he can kill a maral at 20 meters."

Thirty minutes later, we were 20 meters from where the stag should have been, but he had picked his resting place in a depression so we still could not see any part of him. Ankhaa looked up for Sherif, but he was not showing himself so the stag must not have moved. We took one more step and I heard the bull crashing away and then I saw him at 60 meters as he emerged from the depression running straight away. At 70 meters my safety was off, at 90 meters my crosshairs found his left shoulder as he angled uphill, and at 100 meters I killed him with a spine shot.

After pictures and before caring for the meat and trophy, Ankhaa and I ate our lunch of bread, water, cucumber, tomato, and ox tongue while Sherif climbed back down the grassy side of the mountain to bring the jeep closer. In the distance, a goat herder moved his goats to that day's feeding area, a young girl milked a mare, and her brother captured a horse with a long pole and noose for his morning ride to water the camels and yaks. Except for my rifle, it could have been the 12th century.

HUNTING THE LAND OF GENGHIS KHAN

With Ankhaa and my maral stag that dropped next to a cliff, one jump from either freedom or suicide.

EPILOGUE #1

THE EVOLUTIONARY TROPHY ROOM

In *Great Hunters: Their Trophy Rooms & Collections*, Safari Press publisher Ludo Wurfbain wrote, "Trophy rooms and collections have curiously short lives. When we investigated collections for [*Great Hunters*], we heard about dozens of once-famous trophy rooms that no longer exist. Late in their owners' lives, or after their deaths, collections are sold, donated, or sometimes even destroyed. It is quite possible that twenty years from now, the beauty and art featured in *Great Hunters* will be gone forever...."

I believe that trophy rooms are evolutionary. First of all, they have to start somewhere . . . usually with that first mount that you bring back from the taxidermist. My trophy room started "innocently enough" (as my wife would say) with three mounts from my first big game hunt. Even my wife admitted that the moose looked good over our fireplace and the Dall sheep shoulder mount looked good on the oak wall and the grizzly bear rug looked good in front of the fireplace.

About one year after my first African safari, I picked up my trophies from the taxidermist, including a full-mount lion and a shoulder-mount Cape buffalo. With the wisdom of hindsight, I should have introduced only the lion to start (which my wife agreed looked good in our living room) and then occasionally added an impala here and a hartebeest there. But, of course, I hung the whole shebang and when my wife saw that big, black Cape buffalo staring down at her . . . "the very essence of

The Evolutionary Trophy Room

LEFT: The trophy and fireplace that started it all.

ABOVE: The "very essence of evil" that almost ended it all.

evil" . . . we had to have a "little talk." As in all good marriages, a compromise was negotiated . . . . "The buffalo must come down and nothing, and I mean nothing, can be added in our house from this day to forevermore."

This was a serious problem. I eventually solved it by moving my offices from an office condominium in Tarzana, California to a former cabinet building shop in Calabasas, California which I remodeled into offices for myself and for lease. The cabinet shop was rather unique because it had a 30-foot by 60-foot opening in the roof over a 20-foot by 40-foot swimming pool. My personal office, located next to the pool, was 2,000 square feet so as to accommodate my new trophy room.

I have a lot of good memories of this second step in the evolutionary process of my trophy room. My office was very functional, I was surrounded by great sights and memories, and there were sliding glass doors that opened on the pool and surrounding deck so that, even at only 2,000 square feet of interior space, some rather large and raucous parties were possible.

One such party involved Peter Capstick as my guest of honor. Somehow, word of Capstick being in Calabasas on such and such date reached a few celebrities of the big and little screen and they called and asked for permission to attend. Permission granted. Not to name drop, but Frank Stallone was so thrilled about meeting Capstick that, shortly thereafter, he booked his first African safari. After Frank returned from Africa, I asked him how he liked the experience and, swear to God, he said, "After reading Capstick and watching your videos, I thought there would be non-stop action, but there were days that we went hours at a time without even seeing an animal." I told Frank that I found my videos to be more saleable if edited to about 60 minutes of action as opposed to being produced in real time.

SPORT HUNTING ON SIX CONTINENTS

Two views of my second trophy room in my Calabasas office.

THE EVOLUTIONARY TROPHY ROOM

My Calabasas trophy room was great for parties and had an adjacent outdoor pool area.

My son, Ryan, four years before his first hunt.

This is where my Alaska moose was moved when it left our fireplace. The bartender seems thrilled.

For "the Capstick party," a lot of people showed up with his books to be autographed. L to R, seated: Peter Capstick, Bruce Boxleitner, and Donna Lozano. Standing: Frank Stallone, my wife, and me.

Evolutionary change number three involved my move to Kerrville, Texas in 1992. Step one of trophy room three was to pack up trophy room two and put it in storage in Kerrville. Step two was finding the location for trophy room number three. Criteria one was that I wanted to locate my office in the trophy room and have it double for a meeting and party room, since that concept had worked so well for me in California. Criteria two was that it needed to be large enough to display the 100 species that I had hunted at that time and with enough blank wall space for another 50 that I hoped to hunt during the balance of the millennium. Criteria three was that there needed to be room to expand.

After about a year of inspecting my mounts under plastic in storage, Lorraine and I bought a building in the historic downtown area of Kerrville. The ground floor was leased for retail, but the second floor had not been occupied, except for storage,

THE EVOLUTIONARY TROPHY ROOM

for 15 years. Among the drawbacks of the second floor were no heat and air conditioning. The building had been constructed in 1907 with a 5,500-square-foot basement, same for the ground floor, and same for the second floor, which had been an eight-room boarding house in back and two offices in front.

After putting the offspring of my electrician, plumber, and air conditioning salesman through college, my current office-trophy room was completed and includes two bathrooms plus a shower, laundry, and kitchen (so if it has to double as a doghouse, it will at least be comfortable). I knocked down enough walls to create four rooms: one large one for African mounts, another large one for North American mounts (with corners for South America and exotics), and smaller rooms for the South Pacific and for Europe/Asia. The eight-foot-wide hallway is being filled with

Trophies on the back wall of the North American Room of my Kerrville office. A projection television hangs from the ceiling.

mounts from all continents.

As this is being written, there is still wall space available and that is a comfortable feeling and allows me to continue to put pressure on my taxidermists to deliver my trophies on time. When my current allocation of 3,500 square feet is full, I can always give notice to one or both of our second floor tenants and take over another 1,000 to 2,000 square feet. If you happen to be one of those tenants, I want to assure you that I will honor your lease and that it currently looks like my wall space vs. hunts-probable graph won't cross for about seven years, so please keep paying that rent!

My cougar from Utah, whitetail from east Texas, and western Canada moose from British Columbia.

THE EVOLUTIONARY TROPHY ROOM

The kitchen portion of the North American Room, which has a "South American Corner" at the upper right.

I call this the "Exotic Corner," since most of these trophies were introduced to North America (all except the javelina, Rio Grande turkey, and whitetail).

The eight-foot-wide hallway allows for several displays, including this Texas Sheep Slam. Clockwise from upper left: Hawaiian black, corsican, mouflon, and Texas Dall.

321

Sport Hunting on Six Continents

Half of the African Room.

My desk is located in the African Room (no, not the pool table!). The photo behind my desk is of my favorite, best, and number one trophy . . . but the trophy fee never stops!

322

The Evolutionary Trophy Room

LEFT: The hyena is from Zambia, the red lechwe, gemsbok and blue wildebeest are from Botswana, and the blesbok and genet are from South Africa.

ABOVE: Every trophy in my trophy room is accompanied by a plaque with an 8-inch x 10-inch photo of me with my trophy in the field, and usually includes my guide and any observers along at the time. Each plaque notes the species hunted, where, and when. Murray Thomas was my PH on this hunt.

BELOW: As the sign says, this is the South Pacific Room, with trophies from Australia, both islands of New Zealand, and New Caledonia.

SPORT HUNTING ON SIX CONTINENTS

The European/Asian Room displays trophies from Spain, the Czech Republic, Kazakhstan, and Mongolia.

From L to R, the "small safari" animals along the hallway wall are: steenbok, klipspringer, black-backed jackal, gray duiker, Cape grysbok, blue duiker, and Natal red duiker.

EPILOGUE #2

SPORTSMEN ON FILM: THE FIRST 15 YEARS

I would like to thank the producers, directors, cameramen, and editors who trained me and helped me the first three years to the point that, ever since, I've been the writer, director, editor and, in many cases, the cameraman for Sportsmen on Film.

Special thanks to:

Dave Goldson, my first editor, who looked at all the footage of talking heads when I returned from Tanzania and asked, "Where are the cutaways?"

Dave Arnold of Cahuenga West Video in good, old Hollywood (actually it was Studio City) and all his offline and online editors.

The sarcastically witty **Harry Wiland** who, after a hunt, would ask if I "brought home the bacon" (enough good footage to produce a good video) and who taught me the art of ruthless editing with the goal of "don't put the poor viewer to sleep."

All of my cameramen, most of whom had to lug 25-pound BetaCams wherever I went; especially **Rick Morgan, Dennis Gerber, Steve Anderson, Lad Shunneson, Brian Hawkins,** and **Ryan Wilson.**

And to all of my professional hunters, guides, outfitters, and staff. You are the experts and you put up with the shenanigans that a video requires.

For those of you who have purchased Sportsmen on Film videos, thank you for your support and your kind comments. You have encouraged me to keep doing it. In fact, the finished video has become as much a trophy of my hunts as the animals that I've hunted. And it's a good thing because, with the extra time required in the field and the blown opportunities caused by the need to capture events on-camera, I have collected fewer species than if I had been purely hunting. But how else could you see what it's really like?

Very truly yours,

Ken Wilson
P.O. Box 1818
Kerrville, Texas 78029